Louis C.K. and Philosophy

Popular Culture and Philosophy® Series Editor: George A. Reisch

VOLUME 1 *Seinfeld and Philosophy: A Book about Everything and Nothing* (2000)

VOLUME 2 *The Simpsons and Philosophy: The D'oh! of Homer* (2001)

VOLUME 3 *The Matrix and Philosophy: Welcome to the Desert of the Real* (2002)

VOLUME 4 *Buffy the Vampire Slayer and Philosophy: Fear and Trembling in Sunnydale* (2003)

VOLUME 9 *Harry Potter and Philosophy: If Aristotle Ran Hogwarts* (2004)

VOLUME 12 *Star Wars and Philosophy: More Powerful than You Can Possibly Imagine* (2005)

VOLUME 13 *Superheroes and Philosophy: Truth, Justice, and the Socratic Way* (2005)

VOLUME 19 *Monty Python and Philosophy: Nudge Nudge, Think Think!* (2006)

VOLUME 25 *The Beatles and Philosophy: Nothing You Can Think that Can't Be Thunk* (2006)

VOLUME 30 *Pink Floyd and Philosophy: Careful with that Axiom, Eugene!* (2007)

VOLUME 35 *Star Trek and Philosophy: The Wrath of Kant* (2008)

VOLUME 36 *The Legend of Zelda and Philosophy: I Link Therefore I Am* (2008)

VOLUME 39 *Jimmy Buffett and Philosophy: The Porpoise Driven Life* (2009) Edited by Erin McKenna and Scott L. Pratt

VOLUME 42 *Supervillains and Philosophy: Sometimes Evil Is Its Own Reward* (2009)

VOLUME 45 *World of Warcraft and Philosophy: Wrath of the Philosopher King* (2009) Edited by Luke Cuddy and John Nordlinger

Volume 46 *Mr. Monk and Philosophy: The Curious Case of the Defective Detective* (2010) Edited by D.E. Wittkower

Volume 47 *Anime and Philosophy: Wide Eyed Wonder* (2010) Edited by Josef Steiff and Tristan D. Tamplin

VOLUME 48 *The Red Sox and Philosophy: Green Monster Meditations* (2010) Edited by Michael Macomber

VOLUME 49 *Zombies, Vampires, and Philosophy: New Life for the Undead* (2010) Edited by Richard Greene and K. Silem Mohammad

VOLUME 51 *Soccer and Philosophy: Beautiful Thoughts on the Beautiful Game* (2010) Edited by Ted Richards

VOLUME 52 *Manga and Philosophy: Fullmetal Metaphysician* (2010) Edited by Josef Steiff and Adam Barkman

VOLUME 53 *Martial Arts and Philosophy: Beating and Nothingness* (2010) Edited by Graham Priest and Damon Young

VOLUME 54 *The Onion and Philosophy: Fake News Story True, Alleges Indignant Area Professor* (2010) Edited by Sharon M. Kaye

VOLUME 55 *Doctor Who and Philosophy: Bigger on the Inside* (2010) Edited by Courtland Lewis and Paula Smithka

VOLUME 57 *Rush and Philosophy: Heart and Mind United* (2011) Edited by Jim Berti and Durrell Bowman

VOLUME 58 *Dexter and Philosophy: Mind over Spatter* (2011) Edited by Richard Greene, George A. Reisch, and Rachel Robison-Greene

VOLUME 60 *SpongeBob SquarePants and Philosophy: Soaking Up Secrets Under the Sea!* (2011) Edited by Joseph J. Foy

VOLUME 61 *Sherlock Holmes and Philosophy: The Footprints of a Gigantic Mind* (2011) Edited by Josef Steiff

VOLUME 62 *Inception and Philosophy: Ideas to Die For* (2011) Edited by Thorsten Botz-Bornstein

VOLUME 63 *Philip K. Dick and Philosophy: Do Androids Have Kindred Spirits?* (2011) Edited by D.E. Wittkower

VOLUME 64 *The Rolling Stones and Philosophy: It's Just a Thought Away* (2012) Edited by Luke Dick and George A. Reisch

VOLUME 67 *Breaking Bad and Philosophy: Badder Living through Chemistry* (2012) Edited by David R. Koepsell and Robert Arp

VOLUME 68 *The Walking Dead and Philosophy: Zombie Apocalypse Now* (2012) Edited by Wayne Yuen

VOLUME 69 *Curb Your Enthusiasm and Philosophy: Awaken the Social Assassin Within* (2012) Edited by Mark Ralkowski

VOLUME 71 *The Catcher in the Rye and Philosophy: A Book for Bastards, Morons, and Madmen* (2012) Edited by Keith Dromm and Heather Salter

VOLUME 72 *Jeopardy! and Philosophy: What Is Knowledge in the Form of a Question?* (2012) Edited by Shaun P. Young

VOLUME 73 *The Wire and Philosophy: This America, Man* (2013) Edited by David Bzdak, Joanna Crosby, and Seth Vannatta

VOLUME 74 *Planet of the Apes and Philosophy: Great Apes Think Alike* (2013) Edited by John Huss

VOLUME 75 *Psych and Philosophy: Some Dark Juju-Magumbo* (2013) Edited by Robert Arp

VOLUME 79 *Frankenstein and Philosophy: The Shocking Truth* (2013) Edited by Nicolas Michaud

VOLUME 80 *Ender's Game and Philosophy: Genocide Is Child's Play* (2013) Edited by D.E. Wittkower and Lucinda Rush

VOLUME 81 *How I Met Your Mother and Philosophy: Being and Awesomeness* (2014) Edited by Lorenzo von Matterhorn

VOLUME 82 *Jurassic Park and Philosophy: The Truth Is Terrifying* (2014) Edited by Nicolas Michaud and Jessica Watkins

VOLUME 83 *The Devil and Philosophy: The Nature of His Game* (2014) Edited by Robert Arp

VOLUME 85 *Homeland and Philosophy: For Your Minds Only* (2014) Edited by Robert Arp

VOLUME 86 *Girls and Philosophy: This Book Isn't a Metaphor for Anything* (2015) Edited by Richard Greene and Rachel Robison-Greene

VOLUME 87 *Adventure Time and Philosophy: The Handbook for Heroes* (2015) Edited by Nicolas Michaud

VOLUME 88 *Justified and Philosophy: Shoot First, Think Later* (2015) Edited by Rod Carveth and Robert Arp

VOLUME 89 *Steve Jobs and Philosophy: For Those Who Think Different* (2015) Edited by Shawn E. Klein

VOLUME 90 *Dracula and Philosophy: Dying to Know* (2015) Edited by Nicolas Michaud and Janelle Pötzsch

VOLUME 91 *Its Always Sunny and Philosophy: The Gang Gets Analyzed* (2015) Edited by Roger Hunt and Robert Arp

VOLUME 92 *Orange Is the New Black and Philosophy: Last Exit from Litchfield* (2015) Edited by Richard Greene and Rachel Robison-Greene

VOLUME 93 *More Doctor Who and Philosophy: Regeneration Time* (2015) Edited by Courtland Lewis and Paula Smithka

VOLUME 94 *Divergent and Philosophy: The Factions of Life* (2016) Edited by Courtland Lewis

VOLUME 95 *Downton Abbey and Philosophy: Thinking in That Manor* (2016) Edited by Adam Barkman and Robert Arp

VOLUME 96 *Hannibal Lecter and Philosophy: The Heart of the Matter* (2016) Edited by Joseph Westfall

VOLUME 97 *The Ultimate Walking Dead and Philosophy: Hungry for More* (2016) Edited by Wayne Yuen

VOLUME 98 *The Princess Bride and Philosophy: Inconceivable!* (2016) Edited by Richard Greene and Rachel Robison-Greene

VOLUME 99 *Louis C.K. and Philosophy: You Don't Get to Be Bored* (2016) Edited by Mark Ralkowski

IN PREPARATION:

Batman, Superman, and Philosophy (2016) Edited by Nicolas Michaud

Discworld and Philosophy (2016) Edited by Nicolas Michaud

Orphan Black and Philosophy (2016) Edited by Richard Greene and Rachel Robison-Greene

David Bowie and Philosophy (2016) Edited by Theodore G. Ammon

The Ultimate Game of Thrones and Philosophy (2016) Edited by Eric J. Silverman and Robert Arp

Deadpool and Philosophy (2016) Edited by Nicolas Michaud and Jacob Thomas May

Peanuts and Philosophy (2016) Edited by Richard Greene and Rachel Robison-Greene

Red Rising and Philosophy (2016) Edited by Courtland Lewis and Kevin McCain

Jimi Hendrix and Philosophy (2017) Edited by Theodore G. Ammon

For full details of all Popular Culture and Philosophy® books, visit www.opencourtbooks.com.

Popular Culture and Philosophy®

Louis C.K. and Philosophy

You Don't Get to Be Bored

Edited by
MARK RALKOWSKI

OPEN COURT
Chicago

Volume 99 in the series, Popular Culture and Philosophy®, edited by George A. Reisch

To find out more about Open Court books, call toll-free 1-800-815-2280, or visit our website at www.opencourtbooks.com.

Open Court Publishing Company is a division of Carus Publishing Company, dba Cricket Media.

Copyright © 2016 by Carus Publishing Company, dba Cricket Media

First printing 2016

Printed and bound in the United States of America.

ISBN: 978-0-8126-9906-7

This book is also available as an e-book.

Library of Congress Control Number: 2015959265

For Dianna

Perhaps I know best why man alone laughs: he alone suffers so deeply that he had to invent laughter. The unhappiest and most melancholy animal is, as is fitting, the most cheerful.

—FRIEDRICH NIETZSCHE, *The Will to Power*

The bitter, the hollow and—haw! haw!—the mirthless. The bitter laugh laughs at that which is not good, it is the ethical laugh. The hollow laugh laughs at that which is not true, it is the intellectual laugh. Not good! Not true! Well, well. But the mirthless laugh is the dianoetic laugh, down the snout—haw!— so it is the laugh of laughs, the risus purus, *the laugh at the laugh, the beholding, the saluting of the highest joke, in a word the laugh that laughs—silence please—at that which is unhappy.*

—SAMUEL BECKETT, *Watt*

Contents

A Note on "Louis" and "Louie"   xi

The "Other Shit" that Louis C.K. Wanted to Talk About
    MARK RALKOWSKI   xiii

I Everybody Has a Competition in Their Brain   1

1. Everything's Amazing and Nobody's Happy
    MAX ELDER   3

2. Sex Has Something Behind It
    JOHN HEANEY   11

3. When to Hate and When to Be Irate
    DANIEL MALLOY   23

II Misery Is Wasted on the Miserable   37

4. On Being a Dead Person Who Hasn't Died Yet
    MARK RALKOWSKI   39

5. Just *Want* a Shitty Body
    BEKKA WILLIAMS   59

6. You're Gonna Die
    ETHAN MILLS   69

III Raising the Grown Up They're Going to Be   79

7. Because Nothing Can't Be!
    JOSEPH R. KIRKLAND   81

8. Should Jane Get to Be Bored?
    DANIEL ADDISON   93

9. What Fuckin' Chance Does a Kid Have?
    JOSEPH WESTFALL   107

**IV That Knowledge that It's All for Nothing
     and You're Alone**   119

10. On "Crying Like a Bitch"
    ROBERTO SIRVENT AND JOEL AVERY   121

11. Louis C.K.'s No-Bullshit Philosophy
    MARIE SNYDER   131

12. Confronting the "Forever Empty"
    BRANDON POLITE   143

V Did You Look in the Downstairs Bathroom?   155

13. Why? Why? Why?
    JOEL WALMSLEY   157

14. Louis C.K.'s God
    SILAS MORGAN AND ROBERTO SIRVENT   167

15. God Started in 1983
    MATT DESTEFANO   177

**VI Having a Lot of Beliefs and Living by None
     of Them**   187

16. You're Not Starving
    PHIL SMOLENSKI   189

17. Louis's Little Believies
    RYAN JAWETZ   199

18. Believies are Not Motivaties
    JASON DOCKSTADER   211

**VII Take Some Responsibility for the Shitty
      Words You Want to Say**   223

19. The Playful Thought Experiments of Louis C.K.
    CHRIS A. KRAMER   225

20. Feminists *Can* Take a Joke
    JENNIFER MARRA   237

21. If You're Not White, You're Missing Out
    MYISHA CHERRY   247

VIII Of Course but Maybe . . .

255

22. Sometimes Cartesian
ERIC SCHOLL   257

23. Louis C.K. Meets the Unconscious
DUNCAN REYBURN   267

24. An Hour
JAMES BLISS   277

References   287

Some Dead People Who Haven't Died Yet   291

Index   297

A Note on "Louis" and "Louie"

I mean it's me—it's autobiographical fiction, I call it sometimes, because it's the way I would act in those situations. But I'm being myself mostly, although I let myself make huge, terrible mistakes that I wouldn't make in real life. And I let myself have worse judgment than I have in real life because it's more entertaining.

—LOUIS C.K. in an interview with James Poniewozik, 2010

In the interest of clarity and consistency, the writers of this book call Louis C.K. "Louie" when they refer to the character he plays in his FX series *Louie*, and they call him "Louis" or "Louis C.K." when they refer to the stand-up comic or the man who appears in interviews.

The "Other Shit" that Louis C.K. Wanted to Talk About

MARK RALKOWSKI

> We have the choice. We can say something or we can say nothing.
> Not everything true is funny, and not everything funny is true. Most
> comics *feed* prejudice and fear and blinkered vision, but the best
> ones, the best ones . . . illuminate them, make them clearer to see,
> easier to deal with. We've got to make people laugh till they cry. Cry.
> Till they find their pain and their beauty. Comedy is medicine.
>
> —TREVOR GRIFFITHS, *Comedians*

Louis C.K. says it takes twenty years to make a good comedian. "For the first ten years you're just trying to learn how to be funny." You're developing stage presence and learning how to generate jokes that you know are going to work. "So you learn to come up with, 'Hey, maybe a joke about rocks would be good', and you apply your comedy knowledge to rocks." After rocks, you might turn to current events. But "those come and go, and you're also sort of joining a chorus of hate when you do that." Eventually, through trial and error, you write material that works, jokes that make people laugh. But then you repeat those ideas for five years, without knowing why. And in time, "you end up hating it."

These aren't lost years, Louis says. They are the necessary first steps in the development of a young comedian. It's like learning piano by playing "really shitty pieces, but you *are* getting the skill." After about ten years of this—"of learning how to be funny and how to just do the work of a comedian"—you realize that it's time for a change. The transition is slow and painful. "You go through five years or so of realizing that you've wasted ten years talking about *nothing* to drunks in bars and it's too late to go back and do anything else with your life. It's a bad time." In fact, it's a time when you bottom out or you go write for a better comedian, "or you give up or kill yourself . . . *Or* something else comes in and gives you something else that you want to talk about."

For Louis, something else came along. "Other shit came to me that I wanted to talk about." According to his friend Marc Maron, this was the moment when Louis changed as a comedian and writer. He transitioned from being a "uniquely poetic absurdist comic" to a master of "personal revelation comedy." He transitioned from talking about rocks to what *Time* magazine once called "reflections on what it means to be human."

Our hope with this book, *Louis C.K. and Philosophy*, is that we've managed to say a few interesting things about this "other shit" that Louis wanted to talk about.

Samurai Swords and Breaking Pitches

If you're a fan of Louis C.K.'s comedy specials and his television show *Louie*, you probably already think of Louis as a hilarious comedian. But maybe you didn't know that he spent so many years "in the trenches," honing his craft. His "voice" as a comedian and writer is a product of at least two decades of relentless work and persistent failure. As he told Charlie Rose, "failure is the road to being a great comic." Even now that he's become extremely successful, his bits take a long time to develop and the writing process involves months of trial and error. Louis compares writing an hour-long comedy special, a show like *Hilarious* or *Live at the Comedy Store*, to making a samurai sword.

> I used to describe it like the way they make samurai swords, or I used to. They bang it and then fold it, and then they bang it and fold it and keep banging it. So they pound on it and they fold it so they're squeezing out all of the oxygen—you know what I mean? They just keep making it perfect. So every time you think, ok, I've got an hour, 'No, you don't.' Write another hour and then fold it into that one, and then get rid of all the impurities and all the bad stuff, and keep doing that. (Interview with Charlie Rose, May 6th, 2014)

Louis develops a new show every year. Once he has filmed a complete show and released it on his website, that's it for that material. He forces himself to move on. He refuses to repeat his old bits, and so his creative process starts all over again. When he's at this point in his work cycle, he won't be ready to film another comedy special until he has spent a full year working on new material in small comedy clubs, like the Comedy Cellar in New York City. These little clubs are his workshop, the place where he does his "banging and folding," purging the new bits of their "impurities and all the bad stuff." It's in front of these small audiences that he discovers what works and what doesn't, what needs adjusting and what's ready to go. On HBO's *Talking Funny*, Louis told Chris Rock, Jerry Seinfeld, and Ricky Gervais that he likes to be really hard on himself during this developmental phase. He feels he owes it to his audiences to make his specials as good as they can possibly be.

> **Louis:** There's a huge amount of pressure. People are coming; they paid a lot of money; they had to park and they got in a fight with their date or whatever it is. So, there's a huge challenge in not having your old act. But I think you rise to the occasion. You don't rise to the occasion if you don't put the void there. If you take away your old material from yourself—like one thing I started doing when I was developing hours is I would take my closing bit and I would open with it, just to fuck myself, because then I have to follow my strongest bit.
>
> **Jerry Seinfeld:** That's how he got good. You see this attitude?
>
> **Louis:** Because then the end of your act cauterizes it. It gets stronger because you don't have a choice. You know what I mean? That's why I started doing it. You get rid of all of your best weapons, and you have to or else you're dead. It brings something out of you.

Louis "got good," as Seinfeld says, by constantly pushing himself to be better than his last best bit, by taking away his easiest paths forward. He could continue to perform his most popular material—such as his reflection on why he won't buy cell phones for his daughters, or his "Why?" bit from HBO's *One Night Stand*, both of which have been watched over 10 million times on YouTube—but he wants to give his audiences more. "I have an ongoing relationship with my audience," he says. "A lot of people come back to see me" (*Talking Funny*), and so he feels an obligation to replenish his act every year.

Louis takes the same approach to writing for his television series, *Louie*. He combines this spirit of tireless self-overcoming with a mixture of experimentalism and perfectionism that pulls his audiences out of their comfort zones. Everything he does is deliberate, and sometimes it's carefully designed to be provocative and even uncomfortable.

> Not just each episode, but each piece inside each episode has its own goal. I like to keep trying different things. I think in terms of baseball and boxing a lot . . . There was a pitcher for the Yankees once called Orlando Hernandez. They called him "El Duque." And what made him hard to hit was that he had many arm angles, like sometimes the ball would come from here, sometimes—you just didn't know what the hell. And I sometimes think of my relationship with the audience as an adversarial one . . . I want to keep them off their—I don't want them crowding the plate, you know? You have a fastball. Those are jokes. But then you have weird sliders and breaking pitches that make people nuts. They don't know when they're going to see what. I like putting audiences in that place where they're not sure what the fuck you're doing because when you have them off balance then you hit them with something simple and funny. Then they go, "Oh my God, I can't believe I laughed, because I was starting to go, like, I'm not into this anymore." (Interview with James Poniewozik, November 3rd, 2010)

Louie is often very strange; sometimes it's depressing and uncomfortable, and sometimes it isn't funny at all. This is all calculated. It's essential to the stories that Louis wants to tell and the ideas he wants to express or evoke with his show. He isn't interested in writing a series that is merely entertaining. He has larger ambitions than that. In fact, every year he gives up hundreds of thousands of dollars—the money he could make at a different network if he agreed to write the show differently—in exchange for absolute creative control.

> **LOUIS:** It's the greatest deal I ever made in my life.
>
> **HOWARD STERN:** Why?

Louis: They don't even know what the show is going to be until they see it. FX doesn't even read the scripts. They don't know what the show is about until they watch it.

Cohost: So you have complete control?

Louis: More than anyone on television.

Howard Stern: So in other words, because you accept so little money, what you get in exchange is complete freedom.

Louis: That's right. (*Howard 100 & 101*, May 5th, 2014)

The "greatest deal" Louis ever made in his life is one in which he gets paid considerably less than he could be paid! And he accepts this "pay cut" because it allows him to maintain creative control over *Louie*. He doesn't need to get scripts preapproved by FX. He doesn't even need to tell them what an episode or a season is about. They simply wire him cash to make episodes, and in time he sends them his work.

Truth or Entertainment?

Trevor Griffiths, a British dramatist, wrote a play about forty years ago called *Comedians* in which he suggested that every comedian has a choice: he can write about the truth and turn comedy into a kind of "medicine" that helps us find "our pain and our beauty," or he can write for entertainment and laughter, and turn comedy into "coloured sweeties" that "rot the teeth." Griffiths describes the entertainment option when a talent scout in his play gives young comedians the following advice.

Don't try to be deep. Keep it simple. I'm not looking for philosophers, I'm looking for comics . . . Any good comedian can lead an audience by the nose. But only in the direction they're going. And that direction is, quite simply . . . escape. We're not missionaries, we're suppliers of laughter.

According to this industry representative, comedy is about entertainment and distraction, not philosophy! Its aim is to make people laugh and provide them with an "escape," to supply laughter, not to be a missionary.

A comedy teacher in the play, a character named Eddie Waters, has a very different idea about the purpose and possibilities of comedy. He sees it as a revelatory art. It's about something more than mere entertainment. It's about the truth. The *real* comedian is a kind of philosopher. He certainly isn't just a teller of jokes.

> It's not the jokes. It's not the jokes. It's what lies behind 'em. It's the attitude. A real comedian—that's a daring man. He *dares* to see what his listeners shy away from, fear to express. And what he sees is a sort of truth, about people, about their situations, about what hurts or terrifies them, about what's hard, above all, about what they *want*. A joke releases the tension, says the unsayable, any joke pretty well. But a true joke, a comedian's joke, has to do more than release tension, it has to *liberate* the will and the desire, it has to *change the situation*.

Waters teaches comedy by inviting his students to look inside themselves. He wants them to find real things, painful and hidden things, to talk about in their acts. For him, comedy is a profound art. When it's *daring*; when it sees what others are afraid to confront; when it sees a truth about things that terrifies and hurts people; when it faces up to what is hard and what people *want*—that's when comedy liberates people and changes them.

> Think about yourselves. What you've been, what you've done, what you are, what you want. All right? Keep thinking. Now, take one incident, anything, any little thing, that means something to you, maybe something that embarrasses you or haunts you or still makes you frightened, something you still can't deal with maybe, all right? Now think about it. It may be something very gentle, very tender, something you said, something you did, wanted to do . . . All right. Open up. (*Comedians*)

For Waters, the choice is between truth and entertainment, medicine and candy. When you write merely for laughter and an audience's desire for escape, you've "moved away from a comic art and into the world of 'entertainment' and slick success." But "you're better than that, damn you. And even if you're not, you should bloody well want to be." Writing the revelatory, medicinal kind of comedy requires deep, challenging introspection. But when it's done well, it changes the people who hear it; it helps them see themselves and the world differently. It helps them find "their pain and their beauty."

Louis says he reached a point years ago when he needed to give up writing jokes about rocks and peaches and lots of other meaningless things, the ideas he repeated for years without knowing why. Those jokes were entertaining. They made people laugh. But they weren't about anything that mattered, to Louis or to his audiences. This is how Louis describes the subjects he most enjoys writing about now.

> The areas I'm going into are touchy . . . You feel a little sweat on the back of your neck when you get there, but if you stay there for a second, you can find something joyful and funny in it. And it's such a great thing to go to a scary place and laugh. I mean, what's better than that? I just couldn't help straying into these areas. It's a little [mischievous]. I just want to go over there and see if there's anything there. That's just always been my nature. . . . I'm also not afraid of it. I'm not afraid if I go somewhere and I upset everybody. I've been there. I guess I was in trouble a lot when I was a kid, so I got used to it. When you're never in trouble, you can never go to places like that. . . . I know I can survive everybody being pissed off at me. So when I started going onstage, I realized if I talk about this stuff I might upset people in the room, but it's worth it because maybe there's something there. (NPR interview, May 19th, 2014)

If Trevor Griffiths's character Eddie Waters is right, every comedian has a choice: to entertain or to tell the truth. For a comedian, that is *the* question. And it's a question that Louis seems to have reflected on and answered for himself.

Louis doesn't see himself as a philosopher, and he doesn't like to call himself anything other than a comic. But he has admitted that his life's work is about something more than entertainment and popularity. It's about some "other shit" that came to him years ago, which he now puts at the center of his comedy specials and his show *Louie*, at a huge annual cost to himself. What exactly is this other material all about? What is this "other shit" that is so important to Louis? We hope this book can help show that it's nothing other than what Waters refers to as the "truth" in comedy. What else could it be?

Before anyone objects, let's happily concede that *of course* we should trust Louis when he says he isn't a philosopher. Of course. But maybe there's more going on in some of his "jokes" than we tend to realize. When he writes about certain subjects that "reflect on what it means to be human"—things like love and death, marriage and divorce, having beliefs and living according to none of them, raising kids as a single parent and dating after forty, aging and gaining weight, boredom and technology, language and race, gender and sex, religion and wonder—maybe his ideas are worth thinking about a little more. We thought so, and so we wrote this book. We hope you'll read it and see whether you agree.[1]

---

[1] I would like to thank Nicole DiSarno, Emma Grundhauser, and Daniel Grover for their help in putting this book together. They worked as research assistants and were particularly helpful in gathering ideas and examples from Louis's large body of work.

I

Everybody Has a Competition in Their Brain

1
Everything's Amazing and Nobody's Happy

MAX ELDER

> Now we live in an amazing, amazing world, and it's wasted on the
> crappiest generation of just spoiled idiots that don't care.
>
> —LOUIS C.K.

Like other great comics, Louis finds a way to criticize everyone. No one's safe, not even his own children. He finds a way to
captivate the hearts of millions, and he's hilarious. How does
such a human being—a bald, divorced, overweight man in his
late forties—do this so successfully? How does he captivate us
in a way that he gets nominated for over thirty Emmys and is
considered by many to be the "undisputed king of comedy"?

Friedrich Nietzsche, the famous nineteenth-century German
philosopher, probably thought equally self-deprecating things.
He also may have found Louis to be as hilarious as we do today.
Nietzsche can operate for us as a King Midas of sorts, turning
the "other shit" Louis wanted to talk about into gold.

Like Louis, Nietzsche takes a very critical stance toward
almost everything and everyone, including himself. In the pref-
ace to his book *The Gay Science*, he makes a claim about
philosophers, about those who claim to "teach the object of existence," which will help us understand the psychology of Louis
C.K. The argument is simple: All philosophy is a personal confession, an unconscious memoir, as opposed to an objective
description. Philosophers do not describe how the world *is*, but
instead describe how *they wish the world was*.

Riffing on Genesis, when God made the world in His own image, Nietzsche believes that we all create the world in *our* own image (and thus all have a spark of divinity). Such an understanding of how people see the world is extremely helpful for appreciating Louis and his comedy. The worldview that Louis describes, with its humility and healthy perspective on our place in the cosmos, is a sort of revelation in the modern confessional that is a comedy club. He poignantly uncovers dark truths in our lives, truths that we're often too uncomfortable to confront, and tells us that we don't need to run away from them. Instead we can embrace them, laugh at them, and ultimately be redeemed by them.

Duality

In the tale of King Midas, Midas is granted a wish, and he chooses for whatever he touches to turn to gold. Initially, this sounds like a great deal. What riches! However, Midas quickly realizes that the blessing is also a curse; he goes to feast and all the delicious food he craves turns to gold. According to one version of the story, Midas even turns his daughter into gold. What poverty.

Louis shows us that what we often think of as gold might actually be shit, and that shit sometimes can glitter just as gold does. For example, Louis helps us appreciate the modern marvels in life that we so often complain about: "People say 'my phone sucks.' No it doesn't! The shittiest cellphone in the world is a miracle. Your life sucks. Around the phone" (*Hilarious*). Here Louis humbles us, in a deprecating manner, in order to show us how amazing our world really is. The joke lies in a reversal: Louis also shows just how shitty our lives are when we can only see the bad.

Such reversals and dualities have comedic value. They also are instrumental in helping us see the world for what it truly is.

The Duality of Laughter

It's easy to overlook the importance of laughter in life; job interviewers never ask how often you laugh; doctors don't check laughter off their list during your annoying annual checkup, and your loved ones never call and tell you they're worried that you don't laugh enough anymore. However, if you ask someone what they love most about their spouse, one of the first responses is often that they have a great sense of humor. We love people who make us laugh.

Laughter has some surprising characteristics that we don't often realize. It's a double-edged sword: it can produce a feeling of unity and joy, such as the communal laughter at a comedy show, but it can also provoke horrible feelings of embarrassment and mortification, such as when you are the butt of a joke at that comedy show. Just as a smile can quickly turn from a kind gesture to a signal of vile enjoyment, laughter too can be heart-felt or malicious. Louis tells us that laughter is "like a black hole in a good way, everything starts to fall into it" (Poniewozik interview).

The so-called 'black hole' of laughter is pretty unique to humans. There is some evidence that primates exhibit signs of laughter and play similar to humans, but it's clear that laughter is grounded in mammalian evolution. Why do only mammals laugh, and more specifically, why do humans seem to laugh on such an intensified level compared to other mammals? Why do we pay good money to have someone tell us that he has started to recreationally hate people, just so we can laugh?

Nietzsche thinks he might have an answer to these questions: "Perhaps I know best why man alone laughs: he alone suffers so deeply that he *had* to invent laughter. The unhappiest and most melancholy animal is, as is fitting, the most cheerful" (*Will to Power*, p. 56). Nietzsche here highlights the weird duality to laughter discussed above; positivity is often found in pain. He also views laughter as an invention, a tool that we've built in order to live. It's no surprise that people like Louis find themselves naturally drawn to comedy.

Nietzsche and Louis both know *best* what it's like to be a melancholy animal. Nietzsche's life story is one famously filled with alienation, loneliness, loss, disappointment, and eventually insanity. Louis grows up as an immigrant, an outsider, estranged from his father. In high school, he falls into drugs and debauchery. In his mid-life, he falls out of a marriage and into depression. It's fitting, then, that both are so interested in laughter and comedy. Nietzsche and Louis are companions in their ability to feel and laugh at pain.

The Duality of Beauty

In the second season of *Louie* (Episode 8), Louie frantically argues with a Christian woman for his right to masturbate in peace. "That's what's so sad," she says. "That you don't know the darkness that you live in." "Oh no," Louie assures her, "*I know the darkness.*" Louis is a comic Virgil guiding us through the Dantean hellscape of our darkest, most disgusting thoughts, only to tell us that it's okay to think them; to believe anything else is to rob oneself of all the beauty in being human. Louis lights up the dark, and in doing so highlights the fundamental duality of laughter and, ultimately, of life.

Louis beautifully depicts this duality—between darkness and light, melancholia and cheerfulness—in Season Two of his TV series. He opens the episode "Subway/Pamela" by entering the Grand Central subway station to find an immaculately dressed and devilishly handsome violinist playing the Italian composer Vittorio Monti's most famous work, *Csárdás*. By any measure, this is a beautiful man and a beautiful composition—so moving that Louie takes a folded up bill out of his pocket and tosses it to the violinist. Irrespective of Louie's donation, it is evident from the emotion on his face that this violinist is playing for beauty, not money.

As Louie digests this emotionally arresting scene, a homeless man dressed in an ensemble of giant plastic bags descends the subway staircase, stops just behind the violinist, crudely pulls his shirt off, and bathes his filthy body in water. This juxtaposition of the prim and polished against the background of the unabashedly disgusting produces a duet which Nietzsche himself would appreciate.

It's said that many people report feeling a renewed sense of life after a near-death experience; we almost need to get closer to death in order to get closer to life. In a similar sense, we can only *truly* appreciate a heightened sense of beauty when it's contrasted with its opposite. In this case, Louie can only *truly* hear the beauty of *Csárdás* when it's presented in the context of the ugly. If this is true, it means we should not run away from the shit in life. We should not run away from the jokes that Louis so poignantly makes. We should not run away from "the darkness that we live in." Nietzsche might view this opening scene in "Subway/Pamela" as a sort of baptism; after the homeless man is showered in water, we emerge with a new and deeper understanding of both the ravishing and the repulsive, and how they are interlinked.

To really live, to really be human, we must appreciate both the joy and the sorrow in our lives. Louis unapologetically unearths all the sorrow, grief, and disappointment in life and in doing so allows us to see something inspiring, joyful, and, in a strange sense, something divine.

Divinity

Nietzsche loved history. He studied philology, or how language has been written down in the past and evolved over time. A lot of his work is on historical topics, such as a genealogy of morals and a historical analysis of concepts such as good and evil. In the beginning of *The Gay Science*, Nietzsche provides a poignant historical comment on our modern lives when he says that "The comedy of existence has not yet 'become conscious' of itself," and thus we "still live in the age of tragedy, the age of moralities and religions" (*The Gay Science*, p. 28). Nietzsche is arguing that we live in the age of religions because we are incapable of recognizing the comedy so inherent in our existence—if only we could recognize the comedic and all of its implications, we might be able to live in a world without religion. This idea has vast implications for the role religious institutions play in our lives, what divinity means, and how we might surpass the trapping of religious vanity in a future where the comedy of existence "becomes conscious" of itself.

Nietzsche believes that religious institutions come into existence to fulfill a uniquely human need. They provide life with a purpose. Classical economics can tell us this story very straightforwardly: humans, by our very nature, have a demand for something (meaning), and the market responds with a supply to meet that demand (currently, moralities and religions). We need a purpose for living, and history is full of people more than happy to teach us what that purpose may be—especially for a price. In other words, religion is a great pacifier; it provides momentary relief from the tears, loneliness, and shit in life.

Nietzsche exposes a tension between what religion offers (meaning) and laughter. He says that the "teacher of the purpose of existence . . . wants to make sure that we do not laugh at existence, or at ourselves—or at him . . . again and again the human race will decree from time to time: 'There is something at which it is absolutely forbidden henceforth to laugh'" (p. 29). If you look, you'll find with a cursory review of the *Bible* that God laughs only a handful of times in the entire text, and in each case God's laughter occurs from derision rather than joy. God often only laughs as an expression of arrogant mockery.

Why might some religious leaders wish to prohibit laughter? Nietzsche's answer is that they hope to corner the market on supplying salvation; religions want a monopoly on redemption. We turn towards religion in order to cope with the horror or absurdity of existence. However, inevitably "every one of these great teachers always gave way again and returned into the eternal comedy of existence." The comedic and the religious are drawn in parallel for Nietzsche, both offering us meaning in life.

Pushing this argument further, laughter and the comedic has a redemptive quality for Nietzsche. Laugher can provide meaning and, in doing so, redeem us from all that's bad in life. This Nietzschean notion of redemption involves a gestalt switch—or a new framework through which we can see the whole of the world as something more than the sum of its individual parts. Take the scene in Grand Central from the "Subway/Pamela" episode again. A 'religious' lens might see the good and beautiful (the violinist playing *Csárdás*) juxtaposed with the bad and ugly (the homeless man bathing in his own filth). Louis approaches this situation differently. He purposefully puts this scene together so he can unearth laughter in us. The violinist playing his beautiful music himself is not funny, nor is the homeless man bathing on the subway platform. Instead, Louis shows us the comedy in life by playing on the tension between the ugly and the beautiful, and in doing so changes the way we look at both. In a very real sense, we've found redemption from the vulgar through recognition of the comedic.

Not only laughter, but also art can transform "these nauseous thoughts about the horror or absurdity of existence into notions with which one can live: these are the *sublime* as the artistic taming of the horrible, and the *comic* as the artistic discharge of the nausea of absurdity" (*The Birth of Tragedy*, p. 60). The comedic artform offers us a quasi-religious form of redemption through which the bad and ugly in life becomes so intimately tied to the beautiful that it's no longer viewed in isolation. Nietzsche ties these ideas back to religion when he proclaims, "This laughter's crown, this rose-wreath crown: to you, my brothers, I throw this crown! Laughter I have pronounced holy; you superior humans, *learn* from me—to laugh!" (*Thus Spoke Zarathustra*, p. 259). The Romans affix the head of Jesus with a crown of thorns in an attempt to mock him before his death. Remember, God's laughter in the Bible is overwhelmingly a mocking laughter. Nietzsche shows us that there is a way to laugh that does not crucify but instead redeems. Instead of tempting us with the dangerous crown of thorns, Nietzsche throws us a crown of roses, of laughter, through which we see the world differently. This gestalt shift offers redemption from evil through a new view of the world that manifests as laughter.

Louis is a modern day embodiment of Nietzsche's philosophy; he is someone who shows us that there is lightness and "height" in the deep darkness in life. Nietzsche and Louis might offer a unique twist on the famous Oscar Wilde quote, "We are all in the gutter, but some of us are looking at the stars." Instead, they both might say, "it is only from the gutter that some of us truly see the stars."

Louis wears Nietzsche's crown of roses; he is a contemporary savior of sorts, teaching us how to laugh, and thus how to cope with the darkness of life. Louis has a cult-like following in the comedy world. His following is evidence that redemption is no longer found in the pews of churches but instead in the seats of comedy venues.

Everything's Amazing

Nietzsche offers a lens through which we can better understand the genius of Louis C.K. We can better recognize the way he plays off of the duality inherent in life, the duality of laughter, and the duality of beauty. We can see how Louis offers, in a very real way, redemption through comedy. This redemption knocks on our door only when we appreciate that life is both full of suffering and full of meaning, and how meaning and suffering are connected.

Louis understands that laughter is healthy. He sees how it can be redeeming. Thus the comedy of Louis, like the philosophy of Nietzsche, is at its core a coronation: we are invited to place atop our heads this crown of roses and, in doing so, learn to laugh. We can see all the ugly in the world, all of the shit, *as gold*.

Louis has a famous bit on the Conan O'Brien show where he laments the disenchantment of the world. He complains that people don't fully appreciate all the incredible things that we are able to do (like sitting in a chair in the sky and flying across the entire United States in five hours). The most arresting thing he says during the entire interview is that, "everything's amazing and nobody's happy." This deeply upsets Louis. Too many people simply don't see the beauty in the world. We're blind to what is awesome, literally awe-inspiring, about existence. Such blindness is a sign of child-like ignorance, which is creatively depicted in the following dialogue from the episode, "Country Drive" in the second season of *Louie*:

> JANE: I am bored. I am bored! I'm boooored. Why don't you answer me?
>
> LOUIE: Because 'I'm bored' is a useless thing to say. I mean, you live in a great, big, vast world that you've seen none percent of. Even the inside of your own mind is endless; it goes on forever, inwardly, do you understand? *The fact that you're alive is amazing*. So you don't get to be bored.

Louis so clearly echoes Nietzsche here: take up this rose-wreath crown, and learn to laugh! Life is too amazing to do anything else. Through laughter, we can see the world in a different light. We can see the duality of the good and the bad, the beautiful and the ugly. When it offers a source of meaning—an awe-inspiring view of the world—laughter becomes divine.

2
Sex Has Something Behind It

JOHN HEANEY

Louis surely ranks among the most pessimistic comedians. When asked "what's new" by his doctor on *Louie*, his character admits to feeling "boilerplate misery—alone in the world, might as well be a maggot sucking on a dead cat's face, what's the point?—but nothing *new*" (Season Three, Episode 8). The first idea he pitches to a Hollywood bigwig is "a movie where a guy's life is really bad, and then something happens and it makes it worse . . . so his life just gets worse and worse, and darker" (*Louie*, Season Two, Episode 10).

In this respect, he shares much in common with Arthur Schopenhauer, a famous nineteenth-century German philosopher and perhaps the greatest pessimist in the history of philosophy—a pessimist's pessimist, you might say. Schopenhauer concluded that "human existence must be a kind of error," and suggested the best that might be said of life is that 'it is bad today and every day it will get worse, until the worst happens" (*Parerga and Paralipomena,* Volume 2, pp. 287–299).

Looking at *Louie* in the light of Schopenhauer would reveal this startling similarity in their worldviews; however, there is actually a much deeper parallel that connects their work, and this one has to do with sex. Schopenhauer's caricature as the philosopher of gloom means that his most radical contribution to philosophy—his focus on sexual love—is often overlooked. Long before Freud was born and began his famous speculations about human sexuality, Schopenhauer had highlighted "the important role played by the sex-relation in the world of mankind, where it is really the invisible central point of all

11

action and conduct, and peeps up everywhere, in spite of all the veils thrown over it" (*The World as Will and Representation*, Volume 2, p. 513).

Yet it is not Schopenhauer's unflinching focus on sex alone that illuminates Louis's work, nor even its unrelentingly bleak worldview. Rather, it is its constant oscillation between these viewpoints. Sexual arousal and suicidal despair are the poles of the Schopenhauerian universe, as they are for the universe of *Louie*, whose inhabitants are caught and torn between them. Many of these characters regularly comment on the worthlessness of existence. So why do they go on? Schopenhauer's philosophy offers some compelling answers.

The Desire of Desires

Schopenhauer's one big idea was that the entire cosmos is the expression of a primordial 'will-to-live'. Everything in this world—gravity, matter, plants, animals, humans—is a manifestation of this "endless striving," which exists outside time and goes on devouring itself eternally. Humans may appear higher in the hierarchy of beings, but we are fundamentally identical to animals, plants—even Cinnabons—in being expressions of this will-to-live.

We find it hard to recognize our identity with these things because of our overdeveloped minds, which Schopenhauer was ahead of the curve in describing in evolutionary terms. He viewed the brain much as Louie's doctor sees the spinal column, as a survival aid that has exceeded its original remit: "It's an engineering design problem; it's a misallocation. We were given a clothes line, and we're using it as a flagpole" (Season Four, Episode 1). Schopenhauer was just as unsurprised that this misuse results in unbearable pain, as our enhanced consciousness brings with it an increased capacity for suffering, and he therefore recommended a stoic attitude, and negative understanding of happiness, which is remarkably similar to that espoused by Dr. Bigelow: "Every second spent without back pain is a lucky second."

If a clear-sighted, rational view of the world reveals it to be a horrific place, why do we go on? We keep going because we're not wholly intellectual beings. In fact, in the alliance of conscious and unconscious elements that Schopenhauer believed formed the human self—the intellect and the will—the former is very much the junior partner. The intellect was brought into existence to serve the will, and while it has some freedom, it remains ultimately subservient.

Sex was vitally important to Schopenhauer because it provided irrefutable evidence of this skewed power dynamic. The intensity of the sexual urge—"the most vehement of cravings, the desire of desires, the concentration of all our willing"—reveals the startling degree to which our thoughts and conscious selves can be commandeered by our physical drives. This is because "what ultimately draws two individuals of different sex exclusively to each other with such power is the will-to-live which manifests itself in the whole species, and here anticipates, in the individual that these two can produce, an objectification of its true nature corresponding to its aims" (p. 536).

What interests Schopenhauer especially is the way in which the will tricks the intellect into continuing the miserable drama of existence. As any *Louie* fan will tell you, finding a sexual partner and then taking care of children is no skip in the park. Schopenhauer therefore suggested that the intellect had to be "hoodwinked", mischievously, by way of instinct:

> Nature can attain her end only by implanting in the individual a certain delusion, and by virtue of this, that which in truth is merely a good thing for the species seems to him to be a good thing for himself, so that he serves the species, whereas he is under the delusion that he is serving himself. In this process a mere chimera, which vanishes immediately afterwards, floats before him, and, as motive, takes the place of a reality. (*The World as Will and Representation*, p. 538)

Schopenhauer believed that the intoxication of sexual attraction offers us a unique insight into instinctual behavior generally, even suggesting that an insect searching for a spot to lay its eggs may do so with the untiring joy of a love-struck teenager! Humans are aware of the final aim of these instinctual actions in a way that animals are not (we know where babies come from), but we are not guided by this knowledge when we have sex:

> Let us for a moment imagine that the act of procreation were not a necessity or accompanied by intense pleasure, but a matter of ratio-

nal deliberation; could then the human race continue to exist? Would not everyone rather feel so much sympathy for the coming generation that he would prefer to spare it the burden of existence, or at any rate would not like to assume in cold blood the responsibility of imposing on it such a burden? (*Parerga and Paralipomena*, p. 300)

Sex Has Something Behind It

The "delusive ecstasy" of sexual desire takes center-stage in Louis's comedy. Like Schopenhauer, he takes great pleasure in tracking high-flown feelings of romantic love to their base origins. The stand-up set from "Come on, God" (Season Two, Episode 8) is based on the idea that men

can't have a beautiful thought about a woman that isn't followed by a disgusting thought about that same woman. We're not capable of it. We can't do one without the other. If you're a woman and a guy has ever said anything romantic to you, he just left off the second part that would have made you sick if you could've heard it.

Louis doesn't suggest that this is a trait peculiar to him, but maintains it is something common to all men, and inevitable, because it is biological: "That's how our brains work." Louis returns to this dichotomy in his comedy repeatedly, emphasizing the dirt and filth from which the flowery and romantic must necessarily grow.

Schopenhauer's discussion of sex, while shockingly frank in its day, appears tame by the standards of the Comedy Cellar (particularly if you happen to be a heckler). Furthermore, the notion that our actions are governed by unconscious sexual desires doesn't sound quite so radical to an audience weaned on the discoveries of Darwin and Freud. Nevertheless, in "So Old/Playdate" (Season One, Episode 8), Louis is able to get big laughs from what sounds remarkably like a condensed summary of Schopenhauer's 'Metaphysics of Love' essay:

Sex *drive* has to come from somewhere, and it's not just about sex. Sex has something behind it, and it's weird because we ignore it. Sex is really trying to get somewhere: it's trying to have a family. You don't really wanna know that, because we've separated those things, but the entire reason sex exists is to have babies. That's the only reason

it exists at all, but we're such a narcissistic species that we've separated those things. . . . Because that urge is the urge to procreate. A
horny teenage boy is thinking "I wanna baby, oh yeah! I wanna precious baby of my very own to take care of, oh dude! Look at her tits,
I want her to feed my little baby with her big tits." That's what that is,
but we make it this separate thing.

What Louis is saying here, in slightly racier language, is that
"what appears in consciousness as sexual impulse, directed to
a definite individual, is in itself the will-to-live as a precisely
determined individual" (*World as Will and Representation*, p.
535). Given that we've had two centuries to digest these discoveries, how is it that this still sounds jarring enough to raise
a laugh? This is in fact Louis's main point: there is a part of us
that refuses to accept this seemingly obvious fact. We *"don't
really wanna know that* . . . the entire reason sex exists is to
have babies." But why this reluctance?

When Louis claims that "we've separated those two things"
because "we're such a narcissistic species," he is effectively highlighting the same blind-spot in our consciousnesses that
Schopenhauer highlighted two centuries ago, when he pointed
out that "egoism is so deep-rooted a quality of all individuality in
general that, in order to rouse the activity of an individual being,
egotistical ends are the only ones on which we can count with certainty" (p. 538). Like Schopenhauer, Louis revels in highlighting
the degree to which our supposedly personal desires have been
implanted in our minds by our biological needs. Louie may feel he
has fallen for Pamela because, as he tells her, "you're so beautiful
to me . . . and you're just fun and you shit all over me and you
make fun of me and you're real" (*Louie*, Season Two, Episode 6),
but in actual fact his unconscious self has merely intuited that
their offspring would stand a good chance of survival.

The reason we're so resistant to this notion is because it
directly contradicts the image we have of ourselves as rational,
self-determining beings, and reveals us to be blind puppets on
the strings of instinct. Sex offers us a frightening view of ourselves as entirely instinctually driven creatures, chasing after
ends that have no rational worth. In the alternately hilarious
and heart-breaking episode, "Eddie" (Season Two, Episode 9),
the character Eddie confronts a startled open-mic audience
with the ultimately delusory nature of sexual gratification:

Do you how much stupid stuff we do just to get pussy? Sex is so absolutely boring, it's such a one-note thing and it drives so many people to do so many ridiculous . . . so many problems . . . sex is, it's not even like, it's gross! You know, just break it down to what it is. If you're not in the mood for it, it's disgusting. Do you ever watch porno after you come? Yuck! I get a boner, it springs up on me randomly, I treat it like the medical condition that it is, and I drain it like a cyst quickly.

What is particularly unnerving about this insight we are offered in sexual intoxication is that it inevitably suggests a more general delusion chaining us to existence. For if our thoughts and desires can be manipulated in this way during sexual attraction, what is to say this is not true of all our thoughts? This is precisely what Schopenhauer believed. He claimed that the "trick" the will-to-live performs in sexual arousal is only a more intense form of the ruse whereby it fools us into thinking that life is bearable. This is due to the fact that we *are* the will-to-live, which reveals itself most nakedly (pun intended) in sexual desire. That's why Schopenhauer went so far as to claim that we *are* sex, saying that "man is concrete sexual impulse, for his origin is an act of copulation, and the desire of his desires is an act of copulation, and this impulse alone perpetuates and holds together the whole of his phenomenal appearance" (p. 514).

It is perhaps no accident then that Louis has a speech about the un-desirability of the sexual act delivered by a character who has awoken from the more general delusion of the will-to-live: "I'm forty-shit years old. I got nothing, I got nobody. And I don't *want* anything, I don't *want* anybody; and that's the worst part—when the want goes. . . . I've gone soft in the last three pussies I've been in." Louis appears to be saying something very similar to Schopenhauer about the relationship between our sexual appetites and our lust for life in general. Eddie has quite literally lost the will-to-live, but what's interesting from a Schopenhauerian angle is that Louis relates this directly to his having lost the will-to-*love*.

Losing the Will-to-Love

The conflict between a clear-sighted view of the suffering world and our subjugation to sexual instincts is portrayed repeatedly throughout *Louie*. Think of the final scene in "Come on, God" (Season Two, Episode 8), where Louie's attempts at self-pleasure are disrupted by news reports of horrific atrocities from around the world. The comic potential of this interior struggle is most perfectly captured in "Bummer/Blueberries" (Season Two). Louie spends the first part of the episode preparing to ask out a young, attractive woman, and is ecstatic when she agrees. He is awoken from his sexual intoxication by a sudden encounter with death, witnessing a decapitation at disturbingly close quarters. In keeping with Schopenhauer's claim that "death is the real inspiring genius . . . of philosophy" (p. 463), this encounter causes Louie to assume a decidedly philosophical viewpoint:

> It's just so arrogant the way we live our lives. You know, we're constantly right on the edge of existence and *nothing*, and we live in total disrespect of that. . . . and it's just, it's bullshit! It's meaningless. I mean, I started this day obsessed with how this would go, this 'non-date' with you. You don't want to date me, I know that! But I was: 'Oh, please God, could this woman want to go out with me?' And maybe if I could upgrade us to a date with bullshit conversation by seeing some crappy movie. And it doesn't mean anything! I mean, you could get hit by a truck or shot in the chest by a gun guy. I could get thrown out of a helicopter. You know, Janice, you're gorgeous, and I find you very attractive and you're very nice—you're not even nice, honestly—and I just . . . I'm just sick of living this bullshit life.

Louie's feelings about the insignificance of human existence recall existentialist thinkers, like Jean-Paul Sartre and Albert Camus. What is particularly Schopenhauerian about the scene is the way these thoughts are placed in direct opposition with the urge for sexual gratification. The worries rendered 'meaningless' by Louie's brush with mortality are specifically sexual: his 'obsession' with how the date would go. Louie suddenly realizes that he has been almost openly deluding himself in his attempts to begin a sexual relationship with her: "You don't want to date me, I know that!" The final irony is that Janice finds Louie's nonchalant indifference to everyday concerns hugely attractive, and she kisses him passionately. Yet when she discovers the reasons for his studied cool—he witnessed/caused a decapitation minutes before—her ardor cools. The episode closes on an image of the old Louie, cleansed of all existential perspective by the small interest shown in him by Janice, traipsing after her: "Do you want to . . . I didn't mean to upset you . . . I just . . . I thought it was kind of going well."

Louie is filled with moments like this, when our biological drives reveal the pretentiousness of our individual hopes and desires. A striking example is "Elevator Part 4" (Season Four, Episode 7). After a short opening scene in which Louie and his ex-wife bicker through a meeting with their child's psychologist, the episode flashes back to their younger selves, holed up in a hotel room. The distance between the couple is palpable, as is the relief when they mutually decide to divorce "out of kindness" (taking advantage of the fact that "we don't have any kids"). Louis's script underscores the intellectual hubris of his younger self, who sees their separation as a kind of victory over the constraints binding normal couples: "Are we being crazy, or are we geniuses? Because we can do whatever we want now."

The comic comeuppance to this inflated pride suggests that, like Schopenhauer, Louis believes that the chains that bind us are internal (that in fact they lie below the belt). With this newfound feeling of freedom having set relations between the couple on a noticeably more relaxed footing, their natural sexual magnetism is reignited and Louie suggests they have sex. Louis even seems to deliberately emphasize his younger self's desire to 'separate those two things', in his suggesting that they not even remove their clothes, and insisting pointedly, when Janet asks if he wants to 'make love', that this is *not* what he means. The final joke, as ever, belongs to the will-to-live, although it is Louie who gets to cue it up: "What if, just now, you got pregnant?"

The Dupe of the Species

Schopenhauer would say this scene demonstrates the will-to-life's disregard for our insignificant lives, which it casts aside to fulfill its own primary objective of creating a child with "*this* individually and precisely determined nature, a nature that it can obtain simply and solely from *him* as father and from his beloved as mother" (p. 554). That this does not fit in with the couple's newly hatched plans to go to Africa or become a comedian is irrelevant: "the will-to-live expressly demands this existence."

Schopenhauer argued that this was indeed only fit and proper, since the petty worries that concern us individually are irrelevant when compared with the future composition of the human race. The small price to pay for this is personal happiness:

> In fact, love is often in contradiction not only with external circumstances, but even with the lover's own individuality, since it casts itself on persons who, apart from the sexual relation, would be hateful, contemptible, and even abhorrent to the lover. But the will of the species is so much more powerful than that of the individual, that the lover shuts his eyes to all the qualities repugnant to him, overlooks everything, misjudges everything, and binds himself forever to the object of his passion. He is so infatuated by that delusion, which vanishes as soon as the will of the species is satisfied, and leaves behind a detested partner for life. (p. 555)

If it is a bit of a stretch to describe Janet as a "detested partner for life," this is due to the fact that they were able to end the marriage. The volatile argument between the couple at the beginning of the episode certainly indicates that their personalities were not ideally matched, and the frequency with which Louis returns in his comedy to the difficulties of long-term relationships implies that, like Schopenhauer, he believes that "satisfied passion leads more often to unhappiness than happiness."

So much of Louis's work speaks to the particular kind of entrapment and disillusionment described in the above passage. In a stand-up segment from "Subway/Pamela" (Season Two, Episode 6), he takes the peculiarly antagonistic relationships between old couples as his theme, suggesting that this kicked in "as soon as they figured out they're not getting out." This is how he explains one of his married friend's love of going for long walks: "He's running out the clock on the rest of his life. He's trying to stay as far as possible from the person he's going to spend the rest of his life with. And it's like your grandparents, when your grandmother talks about your grandfather: 'He just stands in the back yard for hours, he's crazy!' That's 'cause he hates you a lot! He hates you a lot. He hates you more than he loves you, Grandma."

Yet if Louis is the poet laureate of a certain brand of middle-aged angst, these darker aspects are lightened considerably by his obvious devotion to his children. In this, he is again completely in line with Schopenhauer: "Connected with procreation is the maintenance of the offspring, and with the sexual impulse parental love; thus in these the life of the species is carried on" (p. 514). Schopenhauer believed that, in cases of successful reproduction, the delusion that grips us in sexual arousal does not disappear completely, but is often transferred to the resultant offspring. Louis describes this process directly in his stand-up:

> When you first get married, you have a relationship that's so important to you, and you're working on it together. But then you have a kid. And you look at your kid and you go, "Holy shit, this is my child. She has my DNA. She has my name. I would die for her." And you look at your spouse and go, "Who the fuck are you? You're a stranger."

Although Schopenhauer was unaware of DNA, this is essentially the very point he makes: once the female has been impregnated, there is no longer any need for the delusion that had made the sexual object so alluring, and this same delusion is now transferred to the child. He even attempts to illustrate the strength of this love (or the intensity of the delusion) in exactly the same way, noting that parental love "has, like the sexual impulse, a strength far surpassing that of the efforts which are directed merely towards itself as an individual," and that "in particular cases we see it entirely overcome self-love, and even go so far as a man's sacrificing his own life" (p. 515).

Schopenhauer believed that parental love was intimately related to the delusory intoxication that clouds our minds in sexual arousal, since in the love of a parent for their child, "as well as in the sexual impulse, the will-to-live becomes to a certain extent transcendent, since its consciousness extends beyond the individual, in which it is inherent, to the species." Louis implies repeatedly that this particular "delusion" is the only thing that keeps him struggling in the world. In "So Old/Playdate" (Season One, Episode 4), he confides to Pamela that "on Jane's eighteenth birthday—that's the day I stop being a dad, of *children*, officially; like the day I just become a guy, not 'Daddy', I just become some dude—I think that on that day I might kill myself."

Again, however, it is in "Eddie" (Season Two, Episode 9) that the battle between suicidal despair and enslavement to desire becomes most painfully apparent. When Eddie interprets Louie's inability to name "one good reason I've got to live" as evidence that none exists, Louie is indignant: "I got my reasons to live, I worked hard to figure out what they are, I'm not just handing them to you." The implication that those "reasons" are two blonde-haired little girls is confirmed by Louie's parting shot: "I hope you don't kill yourself. I really do. But I gotta go home. I gotta pick up my kids in the morning." In its way, this line encapsulates the Schopenhauerian elements of the *Louie* universe: the world is a miserable place, filled with cruelty and suffering. Although there are no rational reasons to persist in this existence, we are chained to this life by our most primal instincts: to eat Cinnabons, bed young ladies and care for our children. In the absence of such 'delusions', we might as well book our tickets to Maine.

3
When to Hate and When to Be Irate

DANIEL MALLOY

> Someone who is angered at things and at people one ought to be angered at, and also as and when and for as long as one ought to be, is praised.
>
> —ARISTOTLE

In *Live at the Beacon Theater*, Louis tells the story of Jizzanthapuss, a six-year-old boy in his daughter's class. Louis confesses to hating this child with a grown-up hatred, as well as admitting that this feeling, and some of the actions that flow from it, is wholly inappropriate. Though Jizzanthapuss is by no means a blameless child, he is still a very young child, and therefore not an appropriate object of hatred or anger from a grown person.

Anger and hatred of various kinds are recurring themes of Louis's stand-up material and television work. Most often, Louis himself is the subject of these feelings, but he also reflects on being the object, and on situations where he merely observes someone else's anger at something else entirely.

Rats with Hooves

These feelings are natural, and we've all experienced them to a greater or lesser extent, but anger and hatred are not quite the same. To best understand the difference between anger and hatred, consider Louis's attitude toward deer. On *Chewed Up* he tells us, quite plainly, "I hate deer." But does he? Or is he simply angry with them? I think we can say, based on the rest of his routine, that both are the case. Louis is angry with deer—or rather, certain deer—but he also hates them. He is angry with specific deer for specific reasons. He hates deer, however, simply as a class of things.

Anger is the natural response to a perceived injury or offense, primarily toward oneself, but it can be extended to include others one cares about or even strangers. An injury or offense need not be directed at a person's body or self—someone who steals my computer has rightly earned my anger, in spite of the fact that my computer is a distinct thing from my self. Also, the injury or offense doesn't have to involve actually harming someone. We get angry just as often because some person or thing prevents us from doing what we want. As Louis notes, we often get angry when someone or something prevents us from doing our favorite thing (*Live at the Beacon Theater*). It generally involves the perception of the offense as well as a desire to strike back in some way. It can be momentary or lasting.

The primary difference between anger and hatred is that anger is a response to an action, where hatred is a response to the thing itself. Like its supposed opposite, love, hatred isn't about any particular act or event; both are based on our perception of and reaction to the very core of their objects. Also, where anger involves a desire to strike back, hatred goes further. Someone who hates wishes to destroy or humiliate the object of her hatred. The angry person's desire to strike back is a desire to even the score, to pay back the original offense as well as prevent future offenses. This is why the feeling of anger is often associated with justice and punishment. The person who hates has no such desire. Rather, she desires to eliminate the object of this hatred because there is no possibility of evening the score—there isn't any original offense that can be prevented in the future or made up for in any way. The object of hatred's only offense is existing. By its simple existence, the object of hatred somehow presents an ever-present threat of harm to the hater or to something that the hater identifies with (such as other people, animals, or possessions).

This analysis may not correspond to how we often talk about hatred or hate. Partially, this is because we tend to use those terms loosely, in a sense that more closely corresponds to the idea of being angry about something. Other times our professed hatred is real hatred, but the object is somewhat different from what we think. When someone says, for instance, "I hate traffic" or "I hate lines," neither traffic nor lines are the objects of hatred—rather it is that person's own participation in them that is the real object of hatred. More clearly, we sometimes say "I hate doing laundry" or "I hate vacuuming"—again, it's not the idea of clean clothes or carpets, or even the activities of doing laundry or vacuuming, that we are disagreeing with, but our own participation.

So, what Louis feels toward the deer who runs into his car—the one who "broke his own fucking neck"—is anger. It is a particular response toward a particular creature for a particular action. On the other hand, when Louis goes beyond responding to this particular action by this particular deer—when he hopes its deer wife dies of a broken heart and its deer children starve to death, when he fantasizes about shooting a baby deer in the mouth, or getting AIDS so that he can pass it on to deer—he has gone beyond anger. He is now in the realm of hatred. His feelings toward deer as a species are no longer about redressing perceived wrongs, but about the existence of deer. The only redress possible is the utter destruction of the entire species.

This may explain why moral philosophers have been more focused on anger. With anger, there are several ways it may be justified or unjustified. Anger may be justified, for instance, if the angry person's perception of the offense or injury and its cause is accurate. Assuming it is, we may then ask whether the degree of anger is justified by the offense, whether the anger is held onto for too long or not long enough, whether the angry person's willingness or unwillingness to reconcile is appropriate.

With hatred, however, only the first sort of justification seems possible: of the hater, we may only ask whether his perception of the hated object is accurate. That is, hatred can only be justified if the hated object merits hatred. There are no degrees of hatred, nor is it possible to hate something for too long or short a period of time. If an object genuinely merits hatred, the merit is based on what the object is, and the hatred will remain justified so long as the object exists—or exists in its present form.

Of Course . . . but Maybe

When we hold someone accountable for an action, it is assumed that that person had some measure of control over the action.

When Louis gets angry about the use of "the n-word," for instance, it is in part because the TV personalities who use that phrase have a choice between saying that and saying "nigger." By choosing to say "the n-word" they pass on responsibility for saying (or thinking) "nigger" to the viewers (*Chewed Up*).

The TV personality had a choice, and is therefore accountable—she could have said "nigger" or "the n-word." But what about Louis? The reason for his anger, he says, is in part because she's forcing him to say "nigger." He doesn't have a choice in the matter—but what about in getting angry? Do we have a choice to get angry? Now, if we are to say that anger and hatred may be justified or not, it seems that we are evaluating them from a normative standpoint—saying whether people are right or wrong to feel as they do. But then we are treating anger as akin to actions. If getting angry is akin to an action, then it follows that we must likewise say that someone feeling anger or hatred has a choice in the matter. But plainly we do not have such conscious control over our emotions. We can no more decide to be angry than we can to be invisible; and, likewise, it is impossible to choose to stop being angry.

But while we have little direct, conscious control over our emotions, there are other forms of control we do exercise in regard to them. I may feel angry but choose not to show it or act on it, for example. I may attempt to lessen my anger at some person by reminding myself of their good qualities or the good things they have done for me in the past, or by trying to better understand what led to the offense in the first place. When Louis, for example, gets into an argument with his younger daughter about "Pig Newtons," he controls his anger by reminding himself that she is a three-year-old and therefore not entirely in control of herself.

Hatred, likewise, can only be overcome by altering your understanding of the hated object—but this assumes that the perception of the object that caused it to be hated wasn't accurate to begin with. So now we turn to the question of what must be true of an object for it to merit anger or hatred.

White People Problems

If what we've said so far is accurate, then it follows that the justification of anger or hatred must begin with an examination of its object. Some kinds of things merit anger (and possibly hatred) and some don't. One of the things we enjoy about Louis C.K. is that he is frequently angry about things he really shouldn't be—and it is one of the things that he points out about other people. For example, there is the entire class of issues that Louis labels "white people problems" (*Hilarious*). These arise when "your life is amazing, so you just make shit up to be upset about."

Anger is the more complex emotion to justify, largely because it is a more complex phenomenon in general. Both emotions (if I am correct in calling hatred an emotion—it might be more correctly classified as an attitude) are reactionary. Anger and hatred don't simply arise from nothing. Rather, they are preceded by the perception that some harm has been done, either to oneself or to someone else. When Louis tells a story about getting angry, or making someone else angry, there is always some inciting cause. Anger and hatred do not arise from nothing. Anger is more complex than hatred because hatred perceives the harm as flowing from its object's very existence. If I hate something, I perceive it to cause harm to myself or others simply by being what it is.

On the other hand, anger is usually a reaction to a specific incident. When Louis talks about the idea of having sex with children, it may make us uncomfortable, but it does not make us angry. But an actual act of pedophilia certainly would. It's because of this specificity that anger is more complex than hatred. Specific events have specific circumstances in which they occur and specific causes that bring them about. It is these details surrounding the event that leads to anger that make that anger more or less justified.

The clearest case of justified anger is when one person knowingly and intentionally harms another (Gabrielle Taylor, "Justifying the Emotions"). In this case, the harmed person is completely justified in feeling angry. When a fellow driver tells Louis to "Suck a sack of dicks!" Louis accepts it because he knows that the other guy is completely justified. Louis intentionally cut the guy off, after all. There seem to be three components to such a case: there is a harm done; it is done by a person; and it is done intentionally. If these three conditions are present, then we have justified anger. But if we vary them, we do not thereby eliminate the grounds for feeling angry—we mitigate it. If we examine each condition separately, we will get a better idea of how anger can be more or less justified.

The "Awesome Possum" Incident

If anger is a reaction to a perceived harm, then two things follow: anger is only justified if the perception is accurate—if there has been an actual harm—and anger is only justified to a degree proportionate to the harm itself. Someone who gets angry when no harm has been inflicted, either to himself or someone else, is behaving irrationally. For instance, when Louis gets mad at the coffee shop hipster who won't acknowledge that he's wearing the same "Awesome Possum" shirt, his anger is unjustified because his perception does not match reality: the hipster is wearing an "Awesome Possum" shirt, but Louis isn't. So, there's nothing connecting the two of them, and therefore nothing for the hipster to acknowledge (*Shameless*).

But at the same time, any actual harm does not justify any degree of anger. If Louis's perception of the "Awesome Possum" incident had been accurate, then his response—feeling slightly offended—would have been entirely appropriate. On the other hand, his threats of physical violence toward the Cinnabon worker who was reluctant to sell him a Cinnabon (or a "fat faggot treat" as Louis calls it) is out of all proportion to the harm. Louis tells him "Dude, I'm eating that. That's what's going to happen next. You decide if we're going to be in the paper tomorrow, but that shit's going in my face" (*Chewed Up*).

These considerations are connected because accurately perceiving a harm includes accurate perception of the degree of harm inflicted, and hence of the degree of anger that may be justified. Aside from inventing things to be angry about, we also often get too angry about things because we perceive the harm as being greater than it actually is.

Two of These Fucking Things

These limits corresponding to the harm condition will, I think, seem reasonable to most people. So, too, will the limits set by the "intentionality condition," once we get to it. But before we do that, we must deal with the one condition that itself may seem controversial: that in order for anger to be justified it must be a reaction to a harm caused by a *person*. The reason the person condition may be controversial is because we can, and do, often get angry at non-persons. We get angry at children (Jizzanthapuss), at non-human animals (deer), even at inanimate objects (my phone) and abstract entities (Verizon). While it can feel good to cuss a blue streak at your phone when it won't work properly, it doesn't make a great deal of sense. The phone doesn't care. It is in no way affected by your anger. You will not teach it a lesson. It will not start to work properly once you yell at it.

But aside from the impact on future behavior, a justification of anger must take into account the question of desert—does the object of anger deserve it? In the case of the phone, the answer is clearly no. It didn't do anything but be a phone—and we can hardly blame it for that. It didn't choose to be a phone or to malfunction. It was just a phone, and as such, incapable of making choices and unaware of its circumstances.

The example of the phone also applies, though to a lesser extent, to animate non-persons. Children and non-human animals are not persons, in the sense that they are not rational, autonomous beings capable of making decisions and choices, and, consequently, of being held responsible for those decisions and choices. However, we should not deny that autonomy and rationality can be matters of degree. It makes no sense to get angry at an infant, because it cannot possibly have any idea what it is doing or how that affects others. When Louis gets angry with his younger daughter, for instance, for insisting that Fig Newtons are actually called "Pig Newtons" (*Hilarious*), he acknowledges that his anger is unjustified. As he puts it, "It's always your fault with a three-year-old. Always. Because they are just what they are. They can't help it. Just tape the windows—it's a fucking hurricane." It makes more and more sense to get angry as children grow up, learn more about the world, and acquire greater control over their actions. Only once a child is no longer a child—when she is mature and fully autonomous—are we completely justified in being angry with her for her actions.

With non-human animals a similar sliding scale can be applied. We are not as justified when we get angry at a puppy that pees on the carpet as we are when an already house-broken dog does, but no matter how mature or well trained, we are never justified to get as angry at a dog who pees on the carpet as we would at a person who pees on the carpet. Similarly, when Louis's younger daughter takes a crap on the carpet, there are limits to how angry he can get, because she isn't entirely responsible for her actions yet (*Live at the Beacon Theater*).

Worthless Piece of Shit!

With the introduction of the linked concepts of autonomy and responsibility, we come now to the intentionality condition. In order for the highest degree of anger to be justified, the person who inflicted the harm must have done so intentionally. Deciding to harm another person, directly or indirectly, correctly draws our ire. However, if the harm in question came about without any intention, as in accidents, we are less justified in our anger. We may still feel it, but it must be mitigated. The anger justified by an accidental harm is of a much smaller degree than the anger justified by an intentional harm.

However, like the harm and person conditions, the intention condition is not a zero-sum game. The highest degree of anger is justified by a clear intention to harm; the lowest by a harm caused with no intention. But there are various kinds of intentions that may lead to harm, and some of them mitigate justified anger—some even eliminate the justification of anger all together. For instance, consider the Cinnabon employee. We can impute several intentions behind his reluctance to sell Louis a "fat faggot treat," and each one justifies a different degree of anger. If his reluctance was based on simple dislike of Louis, then his intent was specifically to cause Louis harm—it was malicious. That would merit a high degree of anger. If, on the other hand, his reason is what he said—the treat in question was old and bad, and therefore not good enough to sell—then his intent was beneficent. That would merit no anger. Or, it is possible that he had a different intent. Perhaps he didn't want to sell it because he wanted to eat it, or because he was in a hurry to close. In that case, his intent would merit some anger, but not so much as malicious intent.

This does not mean that we're never justified in being angry with people who act based on good intentions. Quite the contrary. In extreme cases, the intention may eliminate the justification for anger completely. More often though, the good intention of the person who causes harm only mitigates the justification of anger. If someone lies to you in hopes of protecting you from the truth (a truth, in this case, that would harm you, but not them), you are justified in being angry—just not as justified in being as angry as you would be had they lied to you in order to gain some advantage at your expense.

This presents us with a strange scale. Certain intentions justify the highest degree of anger. A lack of intention justifies the lowest degree of anger. But, in certain cases, a particular intention can eliminate all justification for anger.

The Opposite of a Pedophile

If what we've said about the justification of anger is true, and our understanding of hatred is correct, then the notion of justified hatred would seem impossible, because it entails a contradiction. Hatred cannot be morally justified because it cannot be cognitively justified: the appropriate object for hatred cannot possibly exist. To see why, let's imagine a case of justified hatred.

Let's suppose, for the sake of argument, that Jizzanthapuss is an appropriate object of hate. This would mean that there is something about the boy's very existence that either is harmful, or continually threatens harm in a way that is more than merely potential.

In order for Jizzanthapuss to pose this kind of perfect threat, a threat that can only be dealt with through its destruction, he would have to be a being of pure malevolence. There would have to be no possibility of his having a nonharmful intention. More, the intentions that dictated his actions would have to be of the kind that justified the highest degree of anger—the intention to harm for the sake of pleasure in doing harm. If Jizzanthapuss were to be a justified object of hate, he could never be motivated by something as understandable as greed or laziness or inconsiderateness— these motivations would alter his intentions in way that mitigated the justification of anger, albeit only slightly. For example, think of the first offense Louis attributes to Jizzanthapuss: upon entering the classroom in the morning, the children are supposed to place their backpacks and other stuff neatly into assigned cubbyholes. Instead, Jizzanthapuss simply drops his stuff on the ground "so that he has more time for punching." Notice that Louis goes instantly to the most malevolent motive: Jizzanthapuss doesn't have time to put his stuff away because he has harm to inflict.

Now, let's play with this scenario a bit. What if Jizzanthapuss doesn't drop his stuff because he wants to hurt other children, but simply because he's lazy? That's behavior that needs to be corrected, but hardly cause for hatred. On the other hand, suppose the act of dropping his stuff on the ground isn't motivated by the intention to harm other children, but by the desire to inconvenience and embarrass his mother, who is stuck looking like a bad parent and having to clean up after him. (Admittedly, this would be a rather sophisticated plan for a six-year-old.) In this case, Jizzanthapuss may as well be Damien: a being of pure malevolence, and a worthy object of hate.

But Louis himself acknowledges that this is not the case. What prevents Jizzanthapuss from being a worthy object of hate is the fact that he is not a person. Being a six-year-old, Jizzanthapuss is not wholly autonomous, and therefore cannot be held entirely responsible for his actions or intentions. As Louis correctly notes, his mother is at least partly to blame for Jizzanthapuss's poor behavior.

The contradiction in the idea of a justified object of hate is between the person and intention conditions. A person is defined by autonomy; the ability to freely choose for oneself. However, to be a worthy object of hate is to be incapable of such autonomy. A worthy object of hate would have to be utterly incapable of having anything other than a purely malevolent intention behind its actions. Anything so determined by malevolence could never be a fully autonomous person, and thus could never be wholly responsible for its actions.

That's not to say that we can't imagine a person who, with full autonomy, consistently acts from malevolent intentions; we certainly can. And this person would certainly be worthy of anger in the highest degree for each harmful action he took. Nevertheless, he would remain unworthy of hatred because so long as he maintained his autonomy, he would retain the potential to act in non-harmful ways. No matter how unlikely, reconciliation would always remain possible.

This helps to shed light on the contradiction from the other side. Surely, it's worse to perform a harmful action when you could do otherwise. No one would deny that. But recall that hatred is directed not at individual actions or even collections of actions, but at the core of a being. To be able to do otherwise at all negates the possibility of being a worthy object of hate. At the same time, being unable to act in a different way, and thus having no or limited autonomy, likewise eliminates the justification for hatred. Thus hatred can never be justified.

I'm Glad He's Dead

If hatred cannot be justified, then it's wrong to feel it—whatever the circumstances and whatever its object, hatred is always evil, and generally results in as much harm, if not more, to its subject as to its object. Hate makes us bad people. To hate is to obsess over the object of your hatred, and over its destruction. Just think of the elaborate plan Louis outlines in respect to Jizzanthapuss, or his revenge against deer. In the case of the deer, Louis says he would gladly perform oral sex on men with bleeding penises in the hopes that he would get AIDS, which he would then pass on to deer by having sex with them. In the case of Jizzanthapuss, the plan involves causing the break-up of the boy's parents, getting into a homosexual relationship with the boy's father, leaving him and giving up his recently adopted homosexuality, and subsequently adopting homophobic views in hopes of making the father feel bad about himself. Both of these plans, aside from being ludicrously elaborate and needlessly vindictive, are also terribly self-destructive. Such is the nature of hate.

Anger can affect us in a similar fashion to genuine hatred, which is why some have lumped the two together as equally unjustified. Anger that is clung to too tightly, that is out of proportion with the offense or harm in question, or that lasts too long can distort one's character.

But we should not make the mistake of thinking that because anger is sometimes dangerous for its possessor it is therefore to be shunned in all cases. Quite the contrary, sometimes, as we have seen, anger is perfectly justified. Indeed, I will argue in the next section that sometimes not feeling anger, while not exactly wrong, indicates a moral deficiency.

First, however, consider that sometimes anger, even when justified, can have undesired consequences beyond the person who is angry. Louis notes, for instance, that the degree of societal anger at pedophiles is one of the reasons some of them become killers. If we didn't condemn pedophilia so strongly—if we didn't get so angry about it—then fewer pedophiles would feel the need to kill their victims in order to silence them (*Oh My God*).

What Kind of a Father Would I Be?

After putting forward this theory, Louis notes that it is one of the pieces of information he has that he has no idea what to do with. It's doubtful, for instance, that he would use it to mitigate his anger in the event that something happened to his own children. What kind of father would he be if he didn't get angry, indeed extremely angry, with anyone who harmed his children?

Some situations seem to demand anger as a response, and not feeling it seems to indicate that there is something wrong with a person. Someone who never gets angry may never have cause to, so a simple lack of anger is not especially noteworthy. But when someone plainly has cause to get angry and does not—well, that's just worrying.

For instance, let us return to Jizzanthapuss. Suppose Louis has just seen Jizzanthapuss hit another child. If Louis feels nothing about it, that may indicate a lack of sympathy. But suppose the child Jizzanthapuss hits is Louis's daughter. In that case, if Louis does not get angry—perhaps even very angry—we would be justified to conclude that he is not the best father. If he responds with no anger whatsoever, we might even be justified in going so far as thinking him a negligent father. Not getting angry with Jizzanthapuss wouldn't exactly be wrong, but it would indicate that something desirable was lacking in Louis's character. It would give evidence that there was room for improvement, and where that improvement might be necessary.

Suck a Bag of Dicks

In a similar fashion, if someone has harmed me or committed some offense against me, and I do not get angry, that indicates a deficiency on my part—specifically a deficiency of self-respect. As philosopher Immanuel Kant (1724–1804) says, "One who makes himself a worm cannot complain afterwards if people step on him" (*The Metaphysics of Morals*, p. 188).

This might explain Louis's reaction to being told to "Suck a bag of dicks!" (*Shameless*). Rather than get angry, Louis got curious. "I'm not mad," he says, "I was wrong." Partially this is because he had never heard the expression before; but it is also because the guy had a right to be angry at Louis. Louis had cut him off in traffic. The guy was just standing up for himself. He was in the right because Louis was, by his own admission, an asshole. Getting angry in this situation is part of how we insist that others treat us with due respect.

Again, this does not mean that I have a duty to get angry. I have a duty to stand up for myself—anger at the injustice of my treatment provides a motive for such action. I can just as easily fulfill my duty without getting angry, because I know I should, but that scenario seems to indicate a deficiency on my part. To stand up for myself because I know I should, rather than because I am angry at the treatment I have received, seems somehow impersonal. I can stand up for any random person because I ought to. But getting angry seems to indicate that I take the injustice more seriously, and more personally.

A New Way to Hurt Someone's Feelings

Anger gets a bad rap. There are plenty of real problems associated with it, but most of them arise from people being angry in the wrong way. They get angry at the wrong time for the wrong reasons at the wrong people. Many of us are guilty of this—certainly Louis is. He is also guilty of inspiring this kind of anger in others. On *Oh My God*, Louis tells the story of meeting his neighbor at his very nice building. The neighbor assumes that Louis doesn't belong there, and when he confronts Louis about it, Louis doesn't help matters by seeming to confirm his suspicions. The neighbor then asks the doorman to escort Louis from the premises, only to be informed that Louis does, in fact, live in the building. Louis's joy at the look of confusion and anger he receives from the neighbor is almost unseemly.

Neither Louis nor his neighbor was really in the right in this incident. The neighbor's initial anger at having a seemingly homeless man in his building would be better directed at the fact that there are homeless people, instead of at the idea of one resting near him. But his anger at being lied to by Louis was justified.

Anger is a necessary component of a moral life in the world we live in. So long as there is evil and injustice, anger will be needed and justified. But we should not lose sight of the fact that it needs to be controlled and regulated. In our own lives we should take care that those who get angry with us are not justified, and that when we are angry with others (or ourselves) we are justified.

II

Misery Is Wasted on the Miserable

4
On Being a Dead Person Who Hasn't Died Yet

MARK RALKOWSKI

> Most people are dead. Did you know that? It's true: out of all the people that ever were, almost all of them are dead. There are way more dead people. And you're all going to die. And then you're going to be dead for way longer than you were alive. It's like that's mostly what you're ever going to be. You're just dead people that didn't die yet.
>
> —LOUIS C.K.

Last year I started one of my classes by quoting this entire bit of Louis's. I told my students that most people were dead, that they were going to die, that they would be dead for much longer than they were alive, that *dead* was what they were mostly going to be as far as the universe was concerned, and that they were just dead people who hadn't died yet. Everybody laughed, which is interesting since these facts aren't obviously funny.

The moment I finished Louis's bit, a talented student named Eva Martin enthusiastically blurted out, "Marcus Aurelius!" She thought I was quoting from the *Meditations* of the famous second-century Stoic philosopher and Roman emperor Marcus Aurelius (121–180 C.E.), not Louis C.K.'s concert movie *Hilarious*, which originally aired at the 2010 Sundance Film Festival.

It was an understandable mistake. Louis often sounds like an ancient philosopher, and in this case he sounds a lot like the famous Stoic emperor. Louis calls us "dead people who haven't died yet." Marcus Aurelius wrote that each human being is "a little soul, bearing the weight of a dead body" (*Meditations*, 4:41).

What's the point of making this sort of observation, and why is it funny? Louis sometimes says that he uses humor to "help people" by taking them "to places where they have fear and foreboding, and making them laugh in that place" (*Talking Funny*, April 20th, 2011). "The areas I'm going into are touchy," he told *Fresh Air*'s Terry Gross on May 19th, 2014. "You feel a little sweat on the back of your neck when you get there, but if you stay there for a second, you can find something joyful and funny in it. And it's such a great thing to go to a scary place and laugh. I mean, what's better than that?"

It's hard to think of a more apt description of what Louis does with his writing. Whether he's talking about the inevitability of death, the unexpected benefits of divorce, or the pervasiveness of bad faith and sadness in American culture, Louis has a special talent for taking his audiences to the most uncomfortable places in their lives and helping them laugh there. As Louis's friend Marc Maron puts this point, "We all have this festering id full of devils and weirdness, and when we access it, voluntarily or involuntarily, it can be a frightening place, and it might make us feel ashamed of ourselves." But not if Louis is guiding us: he "just goes right in there and says, 'Don't worry, I got this. I got a flashlight. I know these people.'"

The purpose of ancient philosophy was not to make people laugh about these aspects of their lives. Plato, for example, thought laughter was bad for us because it could overthrow the rule of reason in the soul. He also worried that laughter was a vice that expressed scorn because it involved taking pleasure in the ignorance of others. Aristotle thought wit was an educated form of mockery and that amusement was a form of rest, while the Stoics shared Plato's worry that too much laughter was bad for a person because it was a threat to his self-control.

As Epictetus says in his *Handbook*, "Don't let your laughter be loud, frequent, or profuse" (Section 33). These aren't exactly ringing endorsements of comedy or humor. However, like Louis, many ancient philosophers *did* intend to help people. The main reason you should study philosophy, the ancients said, was so that you could become wise and live a good life. They may not have promised laughter, but they did promise happiness. (I also tend to think they laughed a lot more than they let on.)

It's a safe bet that Louis isn't presumptuous enough to promise happiness in exchange for laughing at his standup comedy or for thinking about his show *Louie*. He considers himself a comedian, an actor, and a dad, not a philosopher-king: "I'm just a comedian, you know? I think that's the bedrock of what I am. I do a lot of other things . . . I have a TV show and I act a little bit. But I'm a dad and I'm a comic. That's really mostly what I am" (*Charlie Rose*, May 7th, 2014). Still, a lot of Louis's comedy resembles Stoic meditations on death and loss, Epicurean reflections on the infinite value of the present moment, and existentialist challenges to see through our bad faith and take responsibility for our lives. It also doesn't change the fact that Louis has said several times that comedy has the power to disburden us of our excesses of fear. It takes us to the uncomfortable places in our lives and helps us laugh there.

The point of this chapter is not to unmask Louis as a closeted philosopher who has aims beyond making people laugh really hard. After all, as he told *Pitchfork* on June 20th, 2011:

> I'm not interested in other people thinking differently. I don't care. I'm not even educated; its something that I'm not qualified to do. I'm just like yeast—I eat sugar and shit alcohol. And there's a huge culture that goes with that. Alcohol creates massive shifts in world history, and it changes people's lives. People get pregnant because of alcohol. But the yeast doesn't give a fuck. The yeast isn't going, "I really want to help people loosen up and bring passion to Irish people's lives."

Some of Louis's best writing contains observations that are profoundly insightful and would have been appreciated in some schools of ancient philosophy. This can be true even if Louis doesn't care and is just the "yeast" shitting the "alcohol" that loosens us up and brings passion to our lives.

The Wisdom of Dr. Bigelow

Dr. Bigelow is an unforgettable character in Season Four of *Louie*. He isn't exactly a doctor—or he *is* a doctor but can't be bothered with the insignificance of most medical problems. He helps people by giving them perspective, not by treating their physical symptoms. And the perspective he offers sounds a lot like the ideas we are accustomed to hearing from Louis C.K.: every second without back pain is a lucky second; the only thing happier than a three-legged dog is a four-legged dog; enjoy heartbreak while you can—these ideas just as easily could have served as bits in one of Louis's standup comedy specials, or as fodder for a viral late night interview with Conan or Letterman.

When Louis decided to use these ideas in *Louie*, he put them in the mouth of a medical doctor. Louis calls himself the "yeast" that doesn't "give a fuck," and he denies having intentions to change the way people think. But his decision to use a doctor as the mouthpiece for these ideas suggests they're supposed to be helpful. They're supposed to be therapeutic for the people who internalize them.

In the first episode of Season Four, Louie goes to see Dr. Bigelow because he has injured his back and is having trouble walking. Instead of getting a medical opinion about what he can do to feel better physically, however, Louie receives philosophical advice about evolution. Dr. Bigelow encourages him to reconsider what it means to have a human body, how the body has evolved and continues to evolve, how it ought to be used given its "engineering" limitations, and how we ought to think about pain.

> Dr. Bigelow: The problem is, you're using it wrong. The back isn't done evolving yet. You see, the spine is a row of vertebrae. It was designed to be horizontal, and people came along and used it vertical. It wasn't meant for that, so the discs get all floppy, swollen, pop out left, pop out right. It's gonna take another twenty thousand years to get straight. Until then, it's gonna keep hurting . . . It's an engineering design problem. It's a misallocation. We were given a clothesline, and we're using it as a flagpole.
>
> Louie: So what should I do?
>
> Dr. Bigelow: Use your back as it was intended. Walk around on your hands and feet. Or accept the fact that your back is going to hurt sometimes. Be very grateful for the moments that it doesn't. Every second spent without back pain is a lucky second. String enough of those lucky seconds together and you have a lucky minute. (Louie, Season Four, Episode 1)

Louie doesn't get it. He thinks Dr. Bigelow is nuts and professionally irresponsible. Walk on your hands and knees? We're using a clothesline as a flagpole? Be grateful for any moment without back pain? What kind of help is this supposed to be? As Season Four develops, however, Louie learns to value Dr. Bigelow's philosophical advice. He even seeks it out for insight about how to deal with his most personal problems.

In "Elevator Part 3" (Season Four, Episode 6), for example, Louie runs into Dr. Bigelow in the lobby of his apartment building and he doesn't ask for a medical opinion. He actually hopes Dr. Bigelow can give him *more* philosophical advice. This time he wants to know whether he should keep dating a woman who is going to leave the country. Which choice will make him happiest? Not surprisingly, Dr. Bigelow doesn't engage Louie's problem directly or take it seriously. What Louie needs to do, Bigelow says, is change his perspective on the options that are open to him so that he can appreciate how fortunate he is just to be alive. It doesn't matter whether Louie dates the girl. Given how vulnerable human life is to disease and bad luck, he should be grateful for having the option at all.

> DR. BIGELOW: Here's what I can tell you. In medical school they tell you about thousands of things that could happen to the human body, diseases and maladies that you could never dream up. There's a thing where your bones dissolve and you become just a sack of organs. People are born sometimes with no eyes, with no face. They are rare, but there are neurological diseases that eat half of your brain. People are born sick and never know a moment of anything but pain and suffering.

> LOUIE: So . . .

> DR. BIGELOW: So, nobody cares whether you date this girl or whether you don't. Just pick a road and go down it, or don't.

Louie has exaggerated the burden of his choice because he has no perspective on how lucky he is. Compared to the profound misfortune that some people face, a choice like Louie's is something that one should treasure: how lucky Louie is just to be there, alive and healthy, ready to fall in love despite the risk of heartbreak.

LOUIE: But there's gotta be a way to decide which one is going to make me happier, to predict . . .

DR. BIGELOW: Take a look at this dog.

LOUIE: What's his name?

DR. BIGELOW: Doesn't have one. How many legs does it have?

LOUIE: Three.

DR. BIGELOW: Answer is it has plenty of legs. Had four; a coyote in Poughkeepsie chewed the other one off. Look at his face: perfectly happy, belly is full, just looking, waiting to see what comes next. Do you know the only thing happier than a three-legged dog? A four-legged dog. Now, if you'll excuse me this dog would like to get some air. (*Louie*, Season Four, Episode 6)

Louie wants to know whether he can be certain he's making the right choice. But Dr. Bigelow doesn't think this question matters. As long as Louie can learn from a dog's simple joy of being alive, his answer to the question, "Should I or should I not date her?" will simply be, "Yes, please!" From the three-legged dog's perspective, every option is a good option and every outcome is a gift that calls for joy and gratitude.

If we go on and on about the costs and benefits of our options, we are just refusing to make a choice. And Louis seems to fault this behavior for two reasons.

First, because it lacks perspective and fails to appreciate the real joy of living a life in which we *get* to make free choices.

Second, because it expects a level of certainty and cost-free living that simply isn't possible.

We can't help but lose out whenever we make a choice, because we can't *be* everything at once, and we cannot *do* everything at once. Making one choice always means not making the alternative choices. Louis's point is that there is an unrecognized benefit to seizing hold of one option and closing down the others.

In a 2014 interview with *GQ*, Louis explains a rule he lives by that sheds light on how he sees these issues. The overlap with Dr. Bigelow's advice is unmistakable: the point is to make a decision and *work*.

> These situations where I can't make a choice because I'm too busy trying to envision the *perfect* one—that false perfectionism that traps you in this painful ambivalence: If I do *this*, then that other thing I *could* have done becomes attractive. But if I go and choose the other one, the same thing happens again . . . My rule is that if you have someone or something that gets 70 percent approval, you just do it. 'Cause here's what happens: the fact that other options go away *immediately* brings your choice to 80. Because the pain of deciding is over. And when you get to 80 percent, you *work*. You apply your knowledge, and that gets you to 85 percent! And the thing itself, *especially* if it is a human being, will always reveal itself—100 percent of the time!—to be more than you thought. And *that* will get you to 90 percent. After that, you're stuck at 90, but who the fuck do you think you are, a god? You got to 90 percent? It's incredible!

You might think Dr. Bigelow and Louis are too glib. Situations that involve heartbreak are too painful to take this lightly. And so you might argue that Louis is offering a superficial or irresponsible wisdom: it may not matter to *others* or to the world as a whole whether you date a person, but it matters to *you* and it matters to *her* or to *him*.

This is where we see the transformative power of Dr. Bigelow's outlook on life, however. He is aware of love's risks. He just isn't afraid of heartbreak. He doesn't think it's anything to avoid. That's the "idiot's" way of thinking, the "boring" path to take through life. Dr. Bigelow identifies it with fantasy and going on a Disney ride.

> LOUIE: I'm too sad. Look, I liked the feeling of being in love with her. I liked it. But now she's gone and I miss her and it sucks. And I didn't think it was going to be this bad. And I feel like why even be happy if it's just going to lead to this? It wasn't worth it.
>
> DR. BIGELOW: Misery is wasted on the miserable.
>
> LOUIE: What?
>
> DR. BIGELOW: You know, I'm not entirely sure what your name is, but you are a classic idiot. You think spending time with her, kissing

her, having fun with her—you think that's what it was all about? That was love?

LOUIE: Yeah.

DR. BIGELOW: This is love, missing her because she's gone, wanting to die. You're so lucky. You're like a walking poem. Would you rather be some kind of fantasy? Some kind of a Disney ride? Is that what you want? Don't you see? This is the good part. This is what you've been digging for all of this time. Now you finally have it in your hand, this sweet nugget of love—sweet, sad love—and you want to throw it away. You've got it all wrong.

The pain hurts but it won't kill Louie. In fact, if he would just change his perspective on his suffering, he could even learn to find beauty in it. He could see it as a painful expression of a love that has added incomparable value to his life, regardless of how much it hurts no longer to be with the woman he fell for.

LOUIE: I thought this was the bad part.

DR. BIGELOW: No, the bad part is when you forget her, when you don't care about her, when you don't care about anything! The bad part is coming, so enjoy the heartbreak while you can . . . Lucky son of a bitch! I haven't had my heart broken since Marilyn walked out on me—since I was, uh, I was thirty-five years old. What I would give to have that feeling again. You know, I'm not really sure what your name is, but you may be the single most boring person I have ever met. (*Louie*, Season Four, Episode 10)

"Sweet, sad love" is what Louie has been digging for all of this time, Bigelow says. What does this mean? What could it mean *to be looking for* sad love? And why would Dr. Bigelow compare having fun with a person to being on a Disney ride? As Louie says, it seems like sadness is the bad part of love, not the benefit.

Dr. Bigelow's counterintuitive idea is that feeling sadness isn't a bad thing because our sadness just tells us what matters, as well as how much it matters to us. And we're blessed as long as things *do* matter to us. A sad person may suffer, but she also lives in a world full of value and meaning. She knows exactly who she is and what she wants. Dr. Bigelow's advice is to enjoy heartbreak while we can because there may come a time when we care a little less or don't care at all, and *that* is the deepest suffering of all: choices that seem equally unappealing, people who come and go and don't leave a trace.

As Dr. Bigelow says, he hasn't had his heart broken for decades, and he would give anything to feel that pain again. He longs for the time when life mattered enough for him to feel that deeply. Louie is "boring" and a "classic idiot" because, instead of whining and feeling sorry for himself, he should cherish his heartache as something precious and impermanent. He should see himself as a "walking poem." *Of course* heartbreak hurts—that's why Louie ought to enjoy it! And how can he feel anything but gratitude for having been given time with someone who meant so much to him? He wasn't entitled to her company, and he wasn't guaranteed to meet her. He also doesn't get to hold on to anything forever. That's just the "Disney" alternative to truly living, which always involves risk and loss.

A life without pain isn't something anyone should expect. "Who the fuck do you think you are, a god?" It also isn't something we should want. The German philosopher Gotthold Ephraim Lessing (1729–1781) once said that,

> If God were to hold all Truth concealed in his right hand, and in his left only the steady and diligent drive for Truth, albeit with the proviso that I would always and forever err in the process, and offer me the choice, I would with all humility take the left hand, and say: Father, I will take this one—the pure Truth is for You alone.

This isn't Bigelow's dilemma but it's close. For him, the choice is between being a pain-free god or a finite, vulnerable human being who suffers. Dr. Bigelow prefers being human. If we want to live a full and happy life, we must enjoy heartbreak while we can!

Misery Is Wasted on the Miserable

How could there possibly be wisdom in Dr. Bigelow's advice? He doesn't help Louie with his back pain; he tells him to get used to it. He doesn't help Louie deliberate about the costs and benefits of a difficult decision; he tells him his choice doesn't matter. And he doesn't relieve Louie of his emotional pain when he suffers from heartbreak; he tells him he should savor the misery of his "sweet, sad love" for as long as he can. How could this be good advice, or a source of wisdom, for anyone who is not a masochist?

Some ancient philosophers probably would have liked Dr. Bigelow's advice. After all, they offer similar perspectives—on having a body, on making choices, on dealing with loss—in their own writings. For them, philosophy was a way of life. It was not an academic discipline that only made sense to scholars. It was an art of living that related to the entirety of human existence. As Pierre Hadot explains this point,

> The philosophical act [for some ancient philosophers] is not situated merely on the cognitive level, but on that of the self and of being. It is a progress which causes us to *be* more fully, and makes us better . . . It raises the individual from an inauthentic condition of life, darkened by unconsciousness and harassed by worry, to an authentic state of life, in which he attains self-consciousness, an exact vision of the world, inner peace, and freedom. (*Philosophy as a Way of Life*, p. 83)

In other words, some ancient philosophies aspired to be therapeutic, and they were premised on the idea that human life is full of suffering that can be alleviated. For example, the Stoics and Epicureans taught that human beings suffer because their inner lives are disordered: we suffer from unregulated desires for things we don't need or can never acquire, and from excessive worries about things that we cannot change and must learn to accept.

The purpose of both Stoicism and Epicureanism was to "heal" our inner lives by transforming our modes of seeing and being. "No one can come too early or too late," Epicurus says, "to secure the health of his soul" (*Letter to Menoeceus*). And while the doctrines of Stoicism and Epicureanism were different, they both aimed to bring about a liberating transformation in the self by changing the way one looked at the world. "People are not troubled by things," Epictetus said, "but by their judgments *about* things" (*Handbook*, Section 5).

The Stoics thought people were most troubled by irrational desires that were rooted in false judgments. We want things we will never obtain, such as fame or a certain body type. And we try to keep things we are bound to lose, such as our youth or the people we love or our possessions. As Epictetus says, "You are foolish if you want your children and your wife and your friends to live forever, since you are wanting things to be up to you that are not up to you, and things to be yours that are not yours" (*Handbook*, Section 14).

A good Stoic, then, will try to obtain only things she can obtain, and she will try to avoid only things she can avoid. Everything else she will learn to accept with equanimity. "Do not seek to have events happen as you want them to," Epictetus says, "but instead want them to happen as they do happen, and your life will go well" (*Handbook*, Section 8). In other words, if we want to be happy, we must adapt our hopes and desires to events, and not expect events to conform to our wills. The Stoics called this "living in accordance with nature."

This apparently simple idea has transformative implications for any person who internalizes it. The only things that are *fully* under one's control are one's thoughts and choices. Everything else in life (such as whether we're sick or healthy, what other people do or don't do, what happens in the wider world, whether tragedy strikes, and so forth) is beyond our control, and so it is pointless—as well as costly to our wellbeing—for us to get emotionally invested in such matters. They are not "up to us," as Epictetus says.

> Some things are up to us and some are not up to us. Our opinions are up to us, and our impulses, desires, aversions—in short, whatever is our own doing. Our bodies are not up to us, nor are our possessions, our reputations, or our public offices, or, that is, whatever is not our own doing . . . if you think that only what is yours is yours, and that what is not your own is not your own, then no one will ever coerce you, no one will hinder you, you will blame no one, you will not accuse anyone, you will not do a single thing unwillingly, you will have no enemies, and no one will harm you, because you will not be harmed at all. (*Handbook*, Section 1)

The Stoics recommended that we constantly reflect on this distinction in an effort to change our "judgments about things" and transform our representations of the world, our inner lives, and our actions. "There is but one way to freedom," Epictetus says, and that is "to despise what is not in our power" (*Handbook*, Section 19).

To become a Stoic, then, was to have one's whole world turned upside down. Which is why the Stoics thought of education as a *conversion* from an ordinary, "human" way of looking at life, where what we value depends on our passions, to a "natural" vision of the world, where we see everything situated within the cosmic whole. The point was to re-place everything within the perspective of universal nature. As Marcus Aurelius says,

> Think of the whole of being, in which you participate to only a tiny degree; think of the whole of eternity, of which a brief, tiny portion has been assigned to you; think about fate, of which you are such an insignificant part. If you were to find yourself suddenly raised up into the air, and observed from on high the busy hodgepodge of human affairs, you would despise them, as you saw at the same time how vast is the domain of the beings inhabiting the air and the ether. (*Meditations*, Book 5, Section 24)

The idea behind a meditation like this is to reduce things to their true value by taking up a "view from above." The Stoics were materialists who thought the cosmos was subject to an endless pattern of generation and destruction: in the beginning all is fire; then the elements are generated; then the world is created, and eventually everything returns to fire, at which point the cycle begins again. Seen from this perspective, all human affairs—even the greatest accomplishments of an emperor like Marcus Aurelius—are trivial and unimportant.

> You have the power to strip off many superfluous things that are obstacles to you, and that depend entirely upon your value-judgments; you will open up for yourself a vast space by embracing the whole universe in your thoughts, by considering unending eternity, and by reflecting on the rapid changes of each particular thing; think of how short is the span between birth and dissolution, and how vast the chasm of time before your birth, and how the span after your dissolution will likewise be infinite. (*Meditations*, Book 9, Section 32)

Marcus Aurelius re-described *everything* from this perspective in an effort to detach himself from the objects of his desires and to free himself from his passions. He made the re-description of his world into a kind of spiritual exercise. For example, the fancy foods that he didn't need but often craved were "only dead fish, birds, and pigs," while the wine that tempted him was just "a bit of grape juice." The formal clothes that people admired so much were merely "sheep's hairs dipped in the blood of shellfish," while sex was nothing more than "the rubbing together of pieces of gut, followed by the spasmodic secretion of a little bit of slime" (*Meditations*, Book 6, Section 13).

When we take up this view from universal nature, even the most highly prized affairs in life appear "empty, petty, and putrid; a pack of little dogs biting each other; little children who fight, then laugh, and then burst out crying" (*Meditations*, Book 5, Section 33). Nothing human has any lasting value: "yesterday, a little bit of slime, tomorrow ashes or a mummy" (*Meditations*, Book 4, Section 48).

It isn't easy to look at the world this way, and it may not be obvious why anyone would want to. But that's only because we haven't experienced the benefits of "living according to nature." To be a Stoic was a daily challenge. It meant practicing an "art of living" whose goals were knowledge and freedom. We attain knowledge by transcending the limited perspective of the individual human being. And we enjoy freedom by eliminating our desires for things that don't depend on us. Why would we want either of these things? The ultimate aim for the Stoics—the reason one sought after knowledge and freedom—was to attain a condition of *apatheia*, a state of tranquility and imperturbability.

How to Live Like a Three-Legged Dog

Is Dr. Bigelow a Stoic? In many ways he is. In the scene from "Back", for example, he tells Louie to get used to his back pain because it's irrational to expect anything different from a body that has so many "engineering misallocations." Louie's trouble is not with his back. It's that he has unrealistic expectations about his body. What Louie needs to do, therefore, is adjust his expectations so that they accord with nature. And he can do that by taking up Aurelius's "view from above."

Marcus Aurelius thought he could reduce things to their true value by situating them in the context of universal nature. Dr. Bigelow asks Louie to do something similar by reconsidering the significance of human evolution. We can't eliminate the physical pain we feel, since that isn't "up to us," as Epictetus would say. But we can take control of the attitudes we adopt toward our physical pain, which are the deeper causes of our suffering. It's not our pain that troubles us, Dr. Bigelow suggests, but our judgments about our pain.

His advice in the scene from "Elevator Part 3" for thinking about the costs and benefits of a difficult decision is similar, although it is more Epicurean than Stoic. He tells Louie that the specific choice he makes doesn't matter as much as his attitude about his choice. "Just pick a road and go down it," he says. And repeat the exercise of taking up Aurelius's "view from above." Louie wants to know which choice will make him happiest, but Dr. Bigelow just reminds him that he could be suffering from unimaginable diseases and maladies.

Yes, Louie may get hurt if he takes a risk and a woman breaks his heart. But what does that matter since he has two eyes, a face, healthy bones, and a functioning brain? He "has it all" compared to many people in the world. He should be *grateful* for the opportunity to have his heart broken! Dr. Bigelow's Epicurean advice is for Louie to recognize that happiness must come from within, that his choice isn't really a burden, and that an average human life—one in which we are healthy—is all we need. It's greedy to ask for more, not to mention out of touch with the joyful wisdom of the three-legged dog.

You might think the scene from "Pamela: Part 1" proves that Dr. Bigelow is not a Stoic. He doesn't encourage Louie to cultivate a quieted mind. He tells him to embrace his heartbreak and enjoy it while he can. That doesn't sound like Stoic advice. It sounds like masochism. Wouldn't a Stoic warn Louie about the risks of love and even advise him against making himself vulnerable to that kind of disappointment and loss? After all, whether our relationships last and whether our love is reciprocated are not entirely "up to us." If Dr. Bigelow really were a Stoic, wouldn't he have advised Louie against entering into this doomed relationship in the first place?

People often think these kinds of things about Stoicism. It sounds like a cold and cerebral, philosophy, one that isn't fully human—a philosophy for Spock, the *Star Trek* character, but not for emotional beings like us. What good is a human life if it isn't open to meaningful human relationships, and what kind of meaningful human relationship doesn't leave us vulnerable to sadness, loss, and other passions that can disturb our inner calm? The Stoics sound like people who drop out of life because they are afraid of getting hurt, or like pessimists who look for happiness by lowering their expectations.

None of this is quite right, though, and Dr. Bigelow's advice to Louie can help us see that. The Stoics didn't think it was possible to live a life that is entirely free from pain. That would be an impossible goal. They also weren't pessimists about the future. They considered themselves realistic, and they thought most human suffering was a product of people being unwilling to deal with reality. We can't live a full life without experiencing loss, setbacks, and physical decline. The Stoics' exciting promise was that we didn't have to be victims of these changes or experience them passively. We could be like Marcus Aurelius and take control of the meaning of events by re-describing them.

This is exactly what Dr. Bigelow recommends to Louie when he encourages him to reconsider the meaning of his lost love. Of course he feels sad, but what is that feeling about? Where is it coming from? Bigelow's challenging suggestion to Louie is that he learn to see beauty in his pain. If he would adopt Aurelius's "view from above" one more time and step outside of his ordinary, everyday perspective on himself, he could see that his sadness is something impermanent that he ought to cherish. He could see how lucky he is to have had such a meaningful relationship at all, regardless of its premature ending. And if he could see *that*, he could accept his lost love with equanimity: it is just one part of a long life with many ups and downs and an inevitable end.

We might even say that, in this case, the "view from above" is really a view from the end of life, or a view from death. Dr. Bigelow is inviting Louie to reconsider the pain of his lost love from the perspective of being "a dead person who hasn't died yet." This isn't a matter of dropping out of life or lowering one's expectations. It's an insistently realistic and extraordinarily optimistic, welcoming acceptance of life's most painful experiences. Dr. Bigelow doesn't tell Louie that he shouldn't feel pain at all, and he doesn't counsel Louie against taking risks in love. He helps him reorient himself in his pain so that he isn't a victim of it. Louie cannot be entirely free from sadness. None of us can be. But he can free himself from overwhelming emotional disturbance.

Whether we're dealing with our aging bodies, difficult choices, or lost loves, Dr. Bigelow's Stoic advice remains the same: be realistic; adjust your expectations to nature, and step outside of your ordinary, human perspective on things. That perspective is shaped by unrealistic expectations and false judgments. Dr. Bigelow's point, like the Stoics', is not to give up on life or to find happiness by cynically lowering one's expectations, but to live life freely and realistically, and to enjoy new experiences and relationships without being crushed by life's inevitable challenges. According to Dr. Bigelow, the alternative is fantasy and Louie's pessimistic, defeated cry that "it wasn't worth it."

Dr. Bigelow is clearly a man after Louis's own heart. They share what Nietzsche liked to call, "courage in the face of reality" and "an unconditional will not to fool oneself." It's easy for us to wonder about the wisdom of Aurelius's "view from above." In reducing things to their "true value," for example, it also evokes questions about the meaning of life, such as whether it has any point. However, if we have learned anything from Dr. Bigelow, it's that *the poetry of human existence is in the impermanent things.* We "get it all wrong" when we hide from this fact. We don't live with purpose and joy because we pretend that everything we love the most will be ours forever. And while sadness is inevitable, it is also the most meaningful part of life that we ought to cherish.

Of Course Louis Isn't a Stoic, but Maybe . . .

I haven't tried to convince you that Louis C.K. is a philosopher. For one thing, he doesn't have a consistent philosophy or worldview. Sometimes he sounds like a Stoic. Other times he sounds like a hedonist who identifies happiness with pleasure. He certainly doesn't have the ethical aspirations that the Stoics had. They wanted to disburden people of their existential suffering; Louis finds humor in it. They wanted to help us live better lives; Louis wants to make us laugh really hard. Obviously, these are very different aims, and this shouldn't surprise us at all. As Louis said in the 2011 *Pitchfork* interview, he isn't in the business of changing the way people think.

But, still, there's a big difference between what Louis does and what most other comedians do. And it's a difference in content as well as style. In HBO's *Talking Funny*, Seinfeld asks Louis to do one of his bits, but Louis doesn't want to be put on the spot and so Ricky Gervais and Chris Rock pressure Seinfeld into acting out Louis's bit himself. He does the whole thing, step by step. But when he's finished, it's clear that something wasn't quite right. Jerry's version of Louis's bit changed it fundamentally. He didn't just do it badly. In a way, he didn't really do it at all.

LOUIS: That's a completely "Seinfeld-ed" version.

SEINFELD: Really?

LOUIS: I mean, you really polished it up. You made it nice.

SEINFELD: Really? . . . So, okay, now, just to finish the point, I love that joke—

RICKY GERVAIS: —But you made it like a joke. You made it like a joke. His was like his life is falling apart. That's the difference, really, isn't it?

LOUIS: When I do it I'm sputtering through it, and sweaty anger and energy, but you turned it into a beautifully crafted bit.

RICKY GERVAIS: And you could see the moves. Everything was clean. With Louis you don't even know the joke is coming. When Louis did it, I didn't think, "That's a joke." I just thought, "This is a man falling apart for my pleasure." This is a man spilling his heart out, telling me what a bad day he has had, and it's hilarious.

Ricky Gervais is right. Seinfeld can't "cover" Louis because he doesn't understand what Louis is all about. He took the tragedy out of Louis's bit, the sweaty, sputtering pathos of Louis's delivery, and made the bit into a *mere* joke. He made it into an intellectual observation with a punch line.

That's the kind of comedian that Jerry is. He's an intellectual who is very good at making apt but surprising observations of the most ordinary things. Louis does this as well, but what sets him apart from Seinfeld and others is his ability to make the tragic parts of our lives into the subjects of comedic study. Seinfeld, for example, can help us see new and interesting things in the act of driving ("you're inside but you're outside; you're moving but you're still—all at the same time"); Louis wants to talk about love and death, bad faith and sadness, divorce and raising kids as a single parent, and everything else that occupies the center of our emotional lives.

Most comedians don't know how to find humor in these areas, and wouldn't even try. Louis has built his career on these issues. We are dead people who haven't died yet; everything is amazing and nobody is happy; divorce is always good news; cell phones will prevent you from being a person; we love our beliefs but don't like to live according to them; of course we are appalled by slavery and subhuman working conditions, but maybe we're okay with them if they are necessary for making our technology—these are just a few of Louis's best known bits that need to be acted out, and probably need to be acted out *by Louis C.K.*, in order for them to have their full comedic force. They aren't just "jokes." They aren't just clever intellectual observations that surprise us and give us the pleasure of being reintroduced to the ordinary.

When one of Louis's bits goes viral, it's usually because he has touched on something universal and profoundly meaningful in the human experience. The "ordinary" that he lets us see anew is usually somewhere in ourselves: a repressed fear or desire, a bit of self-deception or undeserved self-congratulation, a feeling of fatigue with political correctness, an unwillingness to confront our mortality or our aloneness in the universe, etc. These are the kinds of issues that we normally hide from ourselves, so when Louis holds them up to the light the laughter can be especially intense.

Of course Louis isn't a Stoic, and of course he isn't a philosopher or a social critic who has aspirations to change the world. But maybe we can find something of practical, existential value in reflecting on some of Louis's best bits *as if* they were newly discovered meditations from Marcus Aurelius. Louis denies having the intention to change the way people think, but if you look closely at his yeast and alcohol analogy, he implies that *humor* can be a powerful change agent. Yeast doesn't care about the alcohol it produces or the people who drink the alcohol. But that doesn't stop alcohol from getting people pregnant and causing major shifts in world history.

Of course Louis doesn't promise that you'll be happy and experience the Stoic ideal of imperturbability if you internalize his comedy, but maybe he could. Maybe if you took some time each day to remind yourself that you're a dead person who hasn't died yet, that *dead* is what "you're mostly going to be" as far as the universe is concerned, "that you live in a great, big, vast world that you've seen none percent of," and that "even the inside of your own mind is endless" and "goes on forever, inwardly," it could help you see that the mere "fact that you're alive is amazing" (*Louie*, Season Two, Episode 5). Maybe it could even help you live a little more like a three-legged dog.

5
Just *Want* a Shitty Body

BEKKA WILLIAMS

> It's a hard thing to achieve, and I did. And I'm going to tell you how to have exactly the body that you want. You just have to want a shitty body. That's all it is. You have to want your own shitty, ugly, disgusting body.
>
> —LOUIS C.K.

> Do not seek to have events happen as you want them to, but instead want them to happen as they do happen, and your life will go well.
>
> —EPICTETUS

In a stand-up segment from the first season of his FX show, *Louie*, Louie explains the secret of getting the body you want: *Just want a shitty body*. It's a pretty funny joke. But it also illustrates a basic truth handed down from a Greek philosopher born in the first century A.D.—so long as you want only what you have or can get, you will not be disappointed.

The strategy of aligning your desires with the course of nature is a central part of the practical ethics of the Greek Stoic philosopher Epictetus. According to Epictetus, the best life for a human is a life without dissatisfaction. But there are two ways of going after such a life. We can either adjust our desires to the world, or we can try to adjust the world to fit our desires. As Epictetus stresses, the first option is much more promising. If I continually try to make the world fit what I want, I am bound to fail and be miserable. But if I simply change my desires to line up with what actually happens, I will always get exactly what I want! In the words of Epictetus, "Do not seek to have events happen as you want them to, but instead want them to happen as they do happen, and your life will go well." (We could call this the "love the one you're with" view of practical ethics. This helpful phrase is borrowed from the lyrics of "Love the One You're With," by Stephen Stills.)

The quotes at the beginning of this chapter illustrate one striking resemblance between things famously said by Louis C.K. and Epictetus. But of course, this is just one example, which might simply be an interesting and curious agreement. It would take much more to show that there is a real similarity between the philosophies of Epictetus and Louis C.K. If I want to claim a real similarity between Louis C.K. and Epictetus, you should expect more of me. And now I'm going to give it to you.

You Won't Always Be Lucky

Epictetus is a particularly well-known defender of Stoicism, which began to grow as a philosophy in the third century B.C. The Stoics tended to view philosophy not as an academic exercise, but instead as a practice. While they defended ideas in many areas of philosophy, one of the Stoics' primary focuses was on how we can make our lives go well.

The vast majority of the surviving teachings of Epictetus read more like a "how-to" book than a philosophical treatise. (Epictetus's short pieces of practical advice are commonly called aphorisms. To help you locate these online if you want (which you easily can; just search "Epictetus" with "Enchiridion"), I've included aphorism numbers wherever possible.)

For example, Epictetus tells us that when we consider going out in public, we should first remember what people are like. At the public baths, for example (remember that this was Greece, two thousand years ago), Epictetus tells us to keep in mind "what happens at baths—there are people who splash, people who jostle, people who are insulting, people who steal" (*Handbook*, Section 4). As Louis might put it, some people are going to be assholes.

So when going to the baths—or in modern cases, the pool—Epictetus is telling us that before we go we should remember that we'll have to deal with assholes; and if we go and this happens (which it almost certainly will!), we should not be upset.

We saw it coming, and we chose to go anyway. We had two choices: go to the pool and deal with assholes; or don't go to the pool. Going to the pool and dealing only with pleasant people wasn't on the menu, so we shouldn't be upset when we fail to get it.

Maybe everyone at the pool will behave, but this is not up to us. As Louie tells his daughter in "Pregnant" (Season Two), sometimes we're lucky. Sometimes we're not. If we're not lucky now, maybe we'll be lucky later. But this is just how it goes, and we shouldn't get upset.

When It Just Isn't Going to Happen

A crucial point for Epictetus, then—and for the Stoics in general—is that we must be careful to make sure that our impressions are correct, and try to make our beliefs and expectations line up with how the world really is. If we expect things to happen in a way that is contrary to the course of nature, we are bound to be upset.

This point is connected to the Stoic endorsement of causal determinism regarding the physical world. According to causal determinists, everything that happens is the *necessary result* of prior causes. In the words of Epictetus, "The nature of the universe was, is and always will be the same, and things cannot happen any differently than they do now" (Dobbin, p. 211).

Somewhat surprisingly, however, while the Stoics accepted causal determinism, they also insisted that our *internal states* are under our control. In particular, our desires, efforts, and thoughts about what's true and what's false *are* up to us according to the Stoics. But "our bodies are not up to us, nor are our possessions, our reputations, or our public offices, or, that is, whatever is not our own doing" (*Handbook*, Section 1). So, it's easy to see why they would recommend against becoming attached to outcomes in the real world. These are already determined (in most cases at least) by factors entirely outside our control. And if we want things that *will not happen*, we're obviously going to be disappointed.

However, Epictetus says, "If we try to adapt our mind to the regular sequence of changes and accept the inevitable with good grace, our life will proceed quite smoothly and harmoniously." There is an important peace and satisfaction in understanding that we couldn't have changed those things which aren't up to us. Or, as Louis puts it in *Live at the Comedy Store*,

> One good thing is that I've let go of any dream of getting in great shape. Like, it's like a relief. Just 'cause my whole life I've been like *someday*, I should really get in great shape. Now I'm like, "What? Why would I do that? That's not gonna happen." To me the bar, the level I want to reach, as far as the shape I'm in, I just want it to be so that if you find out that I died, you ask what happened.

By realizing what he can (and can't!) expect from his body, and accepting it, Louis has found contentment.

Play *Your* Role

Wanting things outside your control is risky. We see this with painful clarity when Louie is called into the office of Lars Tardigan and asked if he is interested in hosting *The Late Show* (but he's *not* offered the job). Louie's first reaction is to not let himself want it. After all, he reasons, "I'm not that guy. I'm forty-four and I'm, I mean, . . . You should get Jerry Seinfeld or somebody, right?"

At this moment, in recognizing that he may not be "the guy," Louie is acting in accordance with a word of caution from Epictetus: "If you undertake some role beyond your capacity, you both disgrace yourself by taking it and also thereby neglect the role that you were unable to take" (*Handbook*, Section 37). You should play *your* role—the role that nature has given you. Tardigan puts the warning even more strongly, saying that while there's a slight chance that Louie might get the gig hosting The Late Show, he probably won't. "You're gonna crack your head on the ceiling, and you're gonna go down. Probably for good."

The way Epictetus would put it, getting the job isn't up to Louie. But trying is. We can feel Louie start to really want the job at the end of his meeting with Tardigan, as dramatic music soars to help us along. And we're conflicted, because we know what Epictetus knew: desiring what isn't up to us is bound to lead to disaster.

Model Yourself on Cardplayers

It would be a mistake, however, to suppose that Epictetus would tell Louie not to go for it. A common objection to Epictetus, and

Stoicism more generally, is that it discourages effort and caring. After all, if I'm supposed to just want things to be the way they are, why bother to try—or even care about anything?

Epictetus, however, explicitly and emphatically objects, insisting that we *should* care and we *should* try. Caring and trying, he says, are simply part of our nature (*Discourses*, Book II, 5.6). But at the same time we should never forget that what ultimately happens is not up to us, and we should not be upset if things don't go our way.

This might seem paradoxical—or at least psychologically impossible for most humans. How am I supposed to try to succeed at something without caring whether I succeed? As Louis might put it: How do we not get carried away by our desires, without just not giving a fuck?

Epictetus says, be like a cardplayer. Cardplayers know that the chips themselves don't matter, and the cards don't matter. What matters is playing well. And that, according to the Stoics, is up to us. Winning is not up to us, so we shouldn't become attached to winning. (Indeed, as any good poker player knows, the thing about poker is that even the most perfectly-played hand can lose. Sometimes winning just isn't in the cards.)

Along the same lines, Epictetus instructs us that we should be like ballplayers. "You will find that skilled ballplayers do the same thing. It's not the ball they value, it's how well they throw and catch it that counts as good or bad" (*Discourses*, Book II, 5.15). If we are nervous or too concerned with how things will turn out, we have already screwed ourselves. We aren't happy, and we have also rendered ourselves unlikely to perform well.

Our Disgusting Bodies

In addition to his agreement with Epictetus about things that aren't up to us, Louis also echoes Epictetus in his straight-up admission that while we cannot escape the fact that we are situated in bodies, our bodies are disgusting. Louis says:

Take the body, the nastiest and least pleasant thing of all—which we nevertheless love and look after. If we had to look after our neighbor's body, we'd be sick of it inside a week. Imagine what it would be like to rise at dawn and brush someone else's teeth, or wipe their private parts after they've answered nature's call. Really, it's amazing that we can love something that on a daily basis requires so much of our attention.

Wait, no!! That was a fragment from Epictetus! (I got you though, right?) *This* is Louis (in *Chewed Up*), discussing his problems with wearing briefs: "This is all just mashed together; just upsetting, stingy, red, sweaty . . . just like . . . This looks like a pig's ass, when I'm naked."

Louie expresses similar disgust with his (and other men's) bodies in "Bummer/Blueberries" (Season Two): "I get so sick, when I fuck. I just gross myself out. I'm always on my back, and that's for her benefit. I just don't want to make a woman see this."

Both Louis and Epictetus know that we *just can't escape* our bodies . . . and that they're not up to us. And because this is true, they see that it isn't really our fault that our bodies are so disgusting. But at the same time, they both admit—and even insist—that our bodies *are* (fucking) disgusting.

If You Do It Shitty, Isn't It Worse *for You*?

Yet another agreement between Louis and Epictetus centers around the importance of performing well in whatever position is assigned to you. In "New Jersey/Airport" (Season Two), Louie says to twenty-year-olds:

> You should do your job, that's what I'm trying to say. *You should do your job.* Because it's your job. Because you're the person standing there doing that thing. So *just do it!* Do the shit out of it!! *Why wouldn't you?"*

And he's right! But Epictetus gives what may be an even better defense of Louie's view:

> Remember that you are an actor in a play, which is as the playwright wants it to be: short if he wants it short, long if he wants it long. If he wants you to play a beggar, play even this part skillfully. (*Handbook*, Section 17)

According to Epictetus, "What is yours is to play the assigned part well. But to choose it belongs to someone else" (*Handbook*, Section 17). As Louis says, when you're twenty years old (unless you're very lucky), others simply give you a job. You don't really choose it.

Once you're assigned the job (or role), Louie and Epictetus still agree: like it or not, your role is to *do the fucking job*. In Epictetus's language, that's the part that's up to you; and the fact that you were assigned the job is not. As Louie says: "You're wearing a vest that matches the building; just . . . do the thing that is the point of the place." Or, "Do the shit out of it!"

I Know That's Hard to Hear, but It's True

Epictetus's primary goal as a philosopher and teacher was to correct the mistaken impressions of others—*not* to be particularly agreeable or make others feel good. This is how one of Epictetus's students saw it: "Epictetus does not care at all if anyone should despise his *Discourses*, since in uttering them he was clearly aiming at nothing except moving the minds of his audience towards what is best" (*Epictetus: Discourses and Selected Writings*, p. 5) And for Epictetus, the most important thing was to correct our impressions, and to act in accordance with the way things actually are—so his aim was to move people toward the truth.

Louis gets this, of course, because he too is seen as a "truth-teller" by those commenting on his work. And it isn't hard to see why. He has tackled topics like sex, suicide, prejudice, and child molestation—in each case pointing out truths we'd rather avoid. He tells us the truth, even when the truth isn't pretty. Take just one example: child molestation. In "Dentist/Tarese" (Season One) during a stand-up segment, Louie says,

> So, here's the thing, if you have sex with a kid, you have to chuck them out because if the kid tells anybody, you're screwed. So I can't help but thinking that if we took down a few notches the hatred for kids-having-sex-people, at least you get the kid back.

Louie is probably right about this . . . however upsetting it is to hear, and however horrifying it is to think about. Indeed, Louie goes on to say, "Listen to me. I know that's hard to hear. *But it's true* . . ."

Like Epictetus, Louis—both in his real life and as Louie on his show—is also willing to tell us what we don't want to hear *about ourselves*. If his audience is out of line, he tries to correct them even if this is very unpleasant for them. In "Heckler/Cop Movie" (Season One), for example, Louie says to a particularly irritating heckler:

> Why were you the only one participating? Just think about that for a second; why was it just you? You know why? Because most people would *never* do that. Most people are polite, and they'd rather cut off their hand than hurt a show by talking. That's what . . . a good person wouldn't do that. So you must be a bad person.

Also consider Louie speaking to his daughter Jane about fairness in "Pregnant" (Season Two). In response to Jane's insistence that it isn't fair for her sister to get the only "mango pop," Louie says, "Right now she's lucky, and you're not particularly lucky. Maybe later you'll be lucky." This is exactly Epictetus's point—external things are not up to us, and we shouldn't be upset by them. (Sometimes we're lucky, and sometimes we're not. We don't control this.) Louie tries to explain to his daughter how things are in the real world, saying,

> She's a separate person from you. You're never gonna get the same things as other people. It's never gonna be equal; it's never gonna happen, ever in your life. So you might as well learn that now, okay?

Just as Epictetus would ask him to, Louie tells his daughter Jane exactly how it is, and how she should respond. *Life isn't fair*. And if she maintains her incorrect impression that it is, she will be repeatedly dissatisfied. Louie knows that he is failing to make Jane happy. He's just aiming to correct her impression of the world.

How the Fuck Do I Get Out of My Own Way?

If you're not already convinced that Louis's comedy often resembles and echoes the philosophy of Epictetus, consider the agreement between the two that we need to watch out for our own destructive inclinations.

Epictetus says that when you do something pleasurable, you should "be on guard." Then you should "bring before your mind two times, both the time when you enjoy the pleasure and the time when after enjoying it you later regret it and berate yourself; and set against these the way you will be pleased and will praise yourself if you refrain from it" (*Handbook*, Section 34). This way, Epictetus explains, we can correct our impressions and see pleasures for what they really often are—a trade-off involving later regret or dissatisfaction.

In a 2010 interview with Marc Maron, Louis talks about a time when he impulsively drained his bank account to buy a trumpet he could not (and never learned to) play, and then ejaculated onto the trumpet case in a peep-show booth . . . both of which he immediately regretted (realizing that "if he'd just jerked off first" he could have saved $1,400).

Later he spoke to his therapist about how to avoid doing things like this, asking "How the fuck do I get out of my own way?" Based on advice from his therapist, Louis tells Marc that he has taught himself to recognize when he thinks he wants something he doesn't *really* want. Citing a recent case in which he was impulsively researching motorcycles, Louis says, "I'm practiced now at stopping and going, 'Why are you looking at . . . It's got nothing to do with motorcycles." And, Louis says, "just the act of doing that cuts you off" (at least sometimes).

This is exactly what Epictetus advises—we must recognize that our desires are often based on mistaken impressions and a failure to consider the results that will necessarily follow if we pursue them. When we desire something, we must be sure to consider it for what it really is. (Remember the public pools!) The wise man, says Epictetus, "is on guard against himself as an enemy lying in wait" (*Handbook*, Section 48). Louis clearly views himself this way—and, at least sometimes, he has adopted Epictetus's approach to correct his desires.

Hey Letterman, Fuck You!

If I've been right so far, there are many ways in which Louis exemplifies the philosophical thought of Epictetus. But to finalize my case, let's return to the *Late Show* episodes.

In the penultimate scene of *"Late Show,* Part 3" we are devastated for Louie when he sees the news report that Letterman will not, after all, be retiring. But Louie is *not* devastated. He reacts exactly as Epictetus would have wanted. He knows he gave it his all—and as we see earlier in the episode, he made himself a real "option." Everything that was up to Louie, he did excellently.

But, as Epictetus always stresses, things beyond our character, desires, and efforts are not up to us at all. We can't control how things turn out. Sometimes things just don't go our way. If Louie had become fixated on not getting the job, he would have been miserable. But the source of this misery, according to Epictetus, would have been a false impression that getting the job was up to Louie. It wasn't. Outcomes never are.

Instead, Epictetus urges us to focus on what *is* up to us, and take satisfaction in excelling at these internal things. And that's exactly what Louie does. While everyone else at the bar with Louie is stunned and upset at the announcement that Letterman isn't retiring, Louie remains calm and composed. He sees that this wasn't up to him. But Louie's effort, illustrated throughout the *Late Show* arc, was up to him . . . And he kicked ass.

In the final scene, we see Louie standing quietly in front of the Ed Sullivan theater, facing the "Late Show with David Letterman" marquee. He blinks. We don't know what's coming . . . Is he going to cry? But then Louie grins. He raises his hands and cheers his own victory: "I did it! I did it!! Hey Letterman, I did it! Fuck you!" His effort was up to him—and it was excellent. The outcome was not—and Louie sees that. Epictetus would be proud.

6
You're Gonna Die

ETHAN MILLS

JANE: I have this weird thing in my head. It's like I get this weird feeling that I'm sweating, but on the inside of my face. And then, I get this weird thing where my eyes are all weird and I can see electricity, like I can see green lines going from a light bulb to all around. And then, I can see that everything is just electrons, colliding and floating and playing. And then, I feel if I just take one deep breath and then just wish hard enough I can just vanish into nothing, like I was before I was born.

DR. BIGELOW: I think you could use a glass of water. Sounds to me like you're dehydrated.

—*Louie*, Season Five, Episode 5

You're gonna die. It's right there in the theme song of *Louie* (at least in Seasons One through Three). Okay, technically it says that *Louie's* gonna die, but unless you're a vampire or robot, I hate to break it to you: this sobering existential fact applies to you, too. As Louis says in his special *Hilarious*, "you're just dead people that didn't die yet."

Most people think this is a depressing or fearful situation, but many philosophers, such as the Buddha and Epicurus, suggest different ways of accepting death without fear. Louis C.K. shows us that death can be funny, too. In *Hilarious*, he tells a story of attempting to comfort his daughter by telling her that they will both be long dead by the time the sun explodes. In *Louie*, death is discussed frequently, starting with the pilot, in which Louie claims that getting a puppy is simply an invitation to cry when the dog dies in several years.

Satisfaction Is Sooooo Boring

'I'm bored' is a useless thing to say. I mean you live in a great big vast world that you've seen *none* percent of. And even the inside of your own mind is endless, it goes on forever inwardly, do you understand? Being, . . . the fact that you're alive, is amazing, so you don't get to be bored.

—*Louie*, Season Two, Episode 5

Why do people get bored so easily? As Louie points out, there's no shortage of universe to learn about, and if you're bored with that, you always have your own imagination. At any given time, I have at least three dozen books to read, new episodes of *Louie* to watch, walks to take, work to do, etc. How could anyone ever be bored?

One answer comes from ancient India. Siddhartha Gautama lived sometime in the century before or after 400 B.C.E. and is better known as the Buddha (a title meaning, "one who is awake"). Sid (as I like to call him) would say that people are bored because of a fundamental characteristic of the human condition: *dukkha*. *Dukkha* is a word in the ancient Indian language, Pali (closely related to Sanskrit). It's usually translated into English as "suffering," but I think "dissatisfactoriness" is a better translation—a big, ugly word, for a big, ugly thing.

People are bored because they're constantly dissatisfied. For example, consider Louie's bit on researching Blu-Ray players:

Being a consumer is like a job. You have to make sure you have the best one. If you get a Blu-Ray player, you have to do research . . . You have to go on Amazon and read a review written by an insane person . . . 'I gotta get the best one.' Why? Who are you, the King of Siam, that you should get the best one ever? They're all the same, these machines. They're all made from the same Asian suffering. There's no difference. (*Louie*, Season Three, Episode 10)

There's a lot to be said about the global inequality between the suffering of Western consumers versus the "Asian suffering" Louie refers to, but the desire for consumer products produces the whole thing. We consumers think that Blu-Ray players or other products are going to make us happy, so we sometimes do things that might cause suffering to ourselves or others to get them (and given the continuing legacy of Western imperialism the people being harmed are often in poorer non-Western countries).

I'm sure many readers and I can relate to Louis when he talks about the effect these desires have on his eating habits: "I eat until I hate myself" (*Chewed Up*). Also, consider how dissatisfied we are with our cell phones: "The shittiest cell phone in the world is a miracle. Your life sucks around the phone" (*Hilarious*). As Louis says in *Live at the Beacon Theater*, "I have a lot of beliefs, and I live by none of them. . . . I just like believing them. . . . They're my little believies. . . . But if they get in the way of something I want or I wanna fuckin' jack off or something, I fucking do that."

But here's the rub: *these things don't actually make us happy*. Sure, the shiny new Blu-Ray player or a fancy iPhone will make you happy at first, but eventually your neighbor or an insane Amazon reviewer gets a better one, yours breaks down, a new format replaces Blu-Ray, the next iPhone comes out, or whatever. You get bored with the Blu-Ray player, iPhone, or whatever. And this makes us constantly want newer, better things. Rinse and repeat. The cycle continues.

But *dissatisfactoriness* isn't limited to Blu-Ray players and boredom. Here's what the Buddha says:

> The Noble Truth of suffering (*Dukkha*) is this: Birth is suffering; aging is suffering; sickness is suffering; death is suffering; sorrow and lamentation; pain, grief, and despair are suffering; dissociation from the pleasant is suffering; not to get what one wants is suffering . . . (*What the Buddha Taught*, p. 93)

Aging, sickness, death, sorrow . . . sounds a lot like an episode of *Louie*! According to most stories of the Buddha's life, his father prevented him from seeing sickness, old age, and death his whole life until one day in his late twenties he saw a sick person, an old person, a corpse, and wandering sage, thus setting him off on his quest for Enlightenment. This is why Buddhists often say that sickness, old age, and death are the three major sources of *dissatisfactoriness*.

Louie undergoes a seemingly life-altering transformation when he sees a homeless guy die in front of him, but, contrary to the Buddha's quest for enlightenment, Louie goes on a non-date right afterwards (*Louie*, Season Two, Episode 2). Louie summarizes the truth of *dissatisfactoriness* perfectly when he says about post-divorce dating, "I know too much about life to have any optimism, because I know even if it's nice it's going to lead to shit" (*Louie,* Season One, Episode 1).

Life Isn't All Puppy Dogs and Rainbows

You'll meet the perfect person who you love infinitely . . . you grow together, you have children, you grow old together, and then she's gonna die. That's the best-case scenario. That you're gonna lose your best friend. . . . and wait for your turn to be nothing, also.

—*Louie*, Season One, Episode 1

Louie and the Buddha agree that life isn't all puppy dogs and rainbows, and even if it were, those puppies are all going to die and there could be a hurricane coming after those rainbows. And one of the biggest bummers on the list of bummers is death.

But, wait, don't most Buddhists believe in an afterlife in the form of rebirth? Isn't *that* comforting? Wouldn't Louie wish to believe this, since he says that he envies people with faith (*Louie,* Season 4, Episode 10)?

Most Western people (especially the Shirley MacLaine, New Agey types) think of rebirth as a *good* thing: Hey, you get to live again! You've lived before! Cool! However, the cycle of rebirth is supposed to be a terrible, horrifying situation. You'd have to repeat junior high school countless times, with all the awkwardness and mistakes involved, like stealing your school's scales in exchange for drugs (*Louie,* Season Four, Episodes 11–12). So, in fact, rebirth would make our existential situation *worse.* You'd have to die again and again, and—far worse—repeat junior high again and again!

Diagnosing Dissatisfactoriness

Dukkha (that life is characterized by *dissatisfactoriness*) is known as the First Noble Truth. If that's all the Buddha had in mind, that really would be pretty depressing. But he has more to say. Here are the remaining Noble Truths.

2. *Dissatisfactoriness* is caused by unreasonable desires.

3. There is an end to *dissatisfactoriness*.

4. The path to the end of *dissatisfactoriness* is the Eightfold Path (right understanding, right thought, right speech, right action, right livelihood, right effort, right mindfulness, right concentration).

Even though Buddhism has a reputation for being irrational or mystical in the West, note how systematic and rational this is. Like a doctor, the Buddha diagnoses the problem (*dissatisfactoriness*), finds the cause (*desire*), and gives a prescription (*the path*). I don't want to get into the details of the Eightfold Path or whether the Third Noble Truth is really true (could human beings really completely get rid of *dissatisfactoriness*? I'm not so sure.)

Instead, let's look at death. The Buddha would say that our dissatisfaction about death, like our dissatisfaction about everything else, really comes down to a mistake: we expect things to be other than they are, and we form unreasonable desires. We are fully aware that we're mortal beings (or at least we intellectually assent to this), yet we seem to really deep down believe that we will live forever, as Louie says to his non-date in Season Two, Episode 5. Our fear and our dissatisfaction about mortality encourage us to deny it all together. The reason you're sad when a loved one dies is because at some level you really expected that person to live forever; the reason you're terrified at the thought of your own death is because you desire immortality. You think you're permanent, but Buddhists say that all things are impermanent (*impermanence* is one of the "three marks of existence" along with *dissatisfactoriness* and *non-self*). The problem is that your beliefs and desires rest on a false premise of permanence; *dissatisfactoriness* occurs when reality fails to live up to your ideas. When the Buddha got sick at the end of his life, some of his followers became agitated at his impending death. His last words to them were, "Transient are conditioned things. Try to accomplish your aim with diligence" (*What the Buddha Taught*, p. 138).

When Louie is sad after his girlfriend, Amia, goes back to Hungary, he talks to his doctor (who is far grumpier than, but perhaps almost as wise as, the Buddha):

Doctor Bigelow: So you, you took a chance on being happy, even though you knew that later on you would be sad. And now you're sad. . . . So, what, what's the problem?

Louie: I'm too sad. . . . I feel like why even be happy if it's just gonna lead to this?

Doctor Bigelow: Boy, misery is wasted on the miserable. . . . This is love, missing her. . . . You're so lucky. You're like a walking poem. Would you rather be some kind of a . . . a fantasy? Some kind of a Disney ride?" (*Louie*, Season Four, Episode 10)

As the doctor suggests, Louie needs to learn to accept the impermanence of his relationships, to be unattached to the Disney illusion of permanence, and he'll be happier for it. This is easier said than done. It's easy to merely intellectually assent to all of this. It's much harder to truly, deeply accept it, but this is just what the Eightfold Path is all about.

In some cases death, as the ultimate form of impermanence, could even be seen as a *good* thing, as when Louie says,

You don't live that long. Doesn't matter. I mean, life isn't that long. Eighty-some years. Buy some shit, use it, it breaks. Try to fuck somebody. Hope your shits don't hurt too bad. (*laughing*) I'm forty-four now. You start doing that math, and it's happy math now. Like, when you're in your twenties you're like, "How long will my life seem? I hope it seems like a nice long story, and I don't feel like I died too soon." You get to your forties and you're like, "I'm almost there, man. All right, yeah." (*Louie,* Season Three, Episode 9)

The Afterlife Doesn't Include You

Yeah, life is long and then it's over. And, uh, a lot of people wonder what happens after that. What happens after you die? It's a big question for human beings. What happens after you die? Actually, lots of things happen after you die; just none of them include you. 'Cause you're not in anything anymore. But there's all kinds of shit, there's the Super Bowl every year, and there's a dog catching a Frisbee . . .

—*Louie,* Season Four, Episode 1

But what if we had some kind of afterlife that really was permanent and blissful? Wouldn't that be a satisfactory answer to our *dissatisfactory* condition? For instance, many people believe in heaven or other heavenly realms. Louie says, however, "I don't think there's a heaven. I think there may be a God," at least since the *Back to the Future* movies. "But I don't think there's a heaven. I think that's the best news you're gonna get" (*Louie*, Season Four, Episode 10).

Like Louie, the philosopher Epicurus thinks there may be some kind of divinity, but denies the existence of an afterlife. Epicurus lived in Greece around 342–270 B.C.E. (not too long after the Buddha lived in India). The Epicureans were famous for living together in small communities while putting their ideas into practice as a way of life involving the pursuit of simple pleasures and overcoming unnecessary fears (such as the fear of death). Much like the Buddha, the Epicureans thought of their ideas as things to put into practice, rather than items for mere intellectual assent. So, if they don't completely cure you of your fear of death by the time you finish this chapter, don't worry. Like the Eightfold Path, it's a therapeutic process that takes time.

Unlike their contemporary "Epicureans," the original Epicureans didn't want lavish dinners or fine wines; given the right mindset, they claimed you could enjoy bread and water as much as elaborate feasts. You couldn't get an Epicurean to join Louie and his brother on a "Bang-Bang" of eating two full meals back to back, even if it was something as delicious as Indian-Diner (*Louie*, Season Four, Episode 3). Epicureans would point to the suffering Louie and his brother feel at the end of the "Bang-Bang"—as Louie says, clutching his stomach, "That was brutal." Is it really more pleasurable in the long run?

The other ingredient in the Epicurean life is to avoid unnecessary fears, since they cause suffering, too: *mental* suffering. Epicurus thinks the fear of death is irrational and unnecessary.

You should accustom yourself to believing that death means nothing to us, since every good and evil lies in sensation; but death is the privation of sensation. Hence a correct comprehension of the fact that death means nothing to us makes the mortal aspect of life pleasurable, not by conferring on us a boundless period of time but by removing the yearning for deathlessness. . . . This [death], the most horrifying of evils, means nothing to us, then, because so long as we are existent death is not present and whenever it is present we are non-existent. Thus it is of no concern either to the living or to those who have completed their lives. For the former it is nonexistent, and the latter are themselves nonexistent. (*The Art of Happiness, pp.* 156–57)

Epicurus is an atomist, which is the view that everything consists of tiny, indivisible particles. Unlike our modern idea of atoms, which can be cut to release a lot of energy, the ancient Greek word *atomos* actually means "uncuttable" (there were also atomists in ancient India, who imagined what they called *paramānu*—literally, "ultimately tiny things"). Epicurus thinks that everything in the universe consists of atoms, including us. At death, our atoms break up and are scattered back into the universe to later recombine into something else. Your individual consciousness ceases to exist.

These days God and the afterlife are closely connected in most people's minds, so it might seem odd that Epicurus—somewhat like Louie—thinks there are gods, but no afterlife. Epicurus sees the gods as examples of perfect blessedness rather than the vindictive, petty gods of Greek mythology. He was keen to point out that believing in stories like that makes people fearful and nervous (Zeus, for example, is hardly a paragon of mental health when it comes to his treatment of humans). So, says Epicurus, there are gods, but they don't interfere in our affairs and they don't provide us with immortality. Likewise, Louie is suspicious of contemporary conceptions of the divine: "I think if there is a God, it's probably not the one the way they describe Him in the Bible. They say He's our Father and we're His children. . . . Where's our Mother?" (*Louie*, Season Four, Episode 10).

Epicurus also thinks that the only way something can be good or bad is if it's a feeling of pleasure or pain. Epicurus's idea is that what it *means* to be good is to be pleasurable for somebody, and what it *means* to be bad is to be painful for somebody. The fact that being an Epicurean is a more pleasurable, and hence better, way of life is an objective fact about human beings, and likewise, having a more painful life of suffering is objectively bad (this idea—sometimes called hedonism—has also been taken up by the ancient Indian school of Cārvāka and in the contemporary ethical theory of utilitarianism).

Death Doesn't Matter

You don't live that long. Doesn't matter.

—*Louie,* Season Three, Episode 9

So, putting all of this together, the fact that death is the end of your consciousness is nothing to be afraid of, since the only bad thing, and hence the only thing worth being afraid of, is pain. When you cease to exist, you have neither pain nor pleasure. Dogs go on catching Frisbees without you, which the dogs no doubt enjoy immensely, but this has no effect on you. If you have no pain or pleasure, death can't be bad (or good). Furthermore, while you're alive, you're not dead, so what are you worried about? Nothing. So, either you are nothing, or you are not dead. Doesn't matter.

Think of it the two possible situations you could be in, like this:

SITUATION 1: YOU'RE ALIVE: You're not dead. Doesn't matter.

SITUATION 2: YOU'RE DEAD: You don't exist. Doesn't matter.

So, in neither situation does death matter to you.

Even if death isn't bad for *you*, you might worry about the effect your death will have on your loved ones. There I suppose some Buddhist non-attachment to desires might help. Sure, your death will harm your loved ones, and I definitely don't mean to trivialize grief, but life is, after all, filled with dissatisfaction that is caused by our desires. Maybe a little medicine from the Buddha or Louie's doctor could help others to move toward the acceptance stage of the grieving process.

All of this will happen after you're dead, so maybe Louis wouldn't care, just as he wouldn't mind his corpse being used to fulfill people's sexual deviances (*Live at the Beacon Theater*).

Death Is Nothing to Us, Except Maybe a Good Punch Line

One of my favorite story lines in *Louie* revolves around Louie's USO tour of Afghanistan (*Louie,* Season Two, Episodes 11–12).

His daughter sneaks a duckling into his luggage to keep him safe, and humorously enough, it does just that. As tensions are mounting between American soldiers and armed locals, the duckling escapes from Louie's bag. The tensions are instantly deflated and transformed into laughter when Louie trips and falls into a ditch while chasing the duckling across the desert scrub. Just as the image of a grown man falling into a ditch while chasing a cute duckling can defuse potentially violent tensions, so can Louis's comedic explorations of death defuse our most depressing anxieties.

The ideas of the Buddha and Epicurus can help us to be less scared, and the comedy of Louis C.K. gives us a position from which to reflect on the comedy of the whole situation. If philosophy and comedy can help make us a little less scared of death, a little more accepting of our situation in life, which might allow us to live our brief lives a little more joyfully, then, far from being useless amusements, philosophy and comedy are just what the doctor ordered, whether that doctor is the Buddha, Epicurus, Louie's grumpy doctor, or Louis C.K. himself. Or a duck.

Here we are thrust into a universe we neither completely understand nor control, with no direction and no answers, with a trajectory that leads inexorably to the annihilation of our brief moment of consciousness, a moment most of us, like Louie, waste eating ice cream in front of the TV. When you really stop to think about the human condition, it's actually pretty funny.

III

Raising the Grown-Up They're Going to Be

7
Because Nothing Can't Be!

JOSEPH R. KIRKLAND

> For this feeling of wonder shows that you are a philosopher, since wonder is the only beginning of philosophy.
>
> —PLATO

> You can't answer a kid's question. They don't accept any answer. A kid never goes, "Oh, thanks. I get it." They fucking never say that. They just keep coming. More questions. "Why? Why? Why?" Until you don't even know who the fuck you are anymore at the end of the conversation.
>
> —LOUIS C.K.

Louis C.K. has long drawn on his experiences as a father of two daughters to brutally hilarious effect as a comic. While he is, by all accounts, a doting dad offstage, the Louis we hear from onstage has no qualms describing kids as "buckets of disease that live inside your house" (*Chewed Up*). If there's a consistent theme to Louis's routines on parenting, it's that children are endlessly frustrating, annoying and, well, *childish*. Take the daily struggle of getting young kids dressed and out the door (*Shameless*).

Louis is able to get away with calling his own four-year-old daughter an "asshole" in front of thousands because he holds her to our expectations of reasonable behavior from full-grown adults for comic effect. The laughter he elicits from his fellow parents in the audience is the laughter of recognition. The routine works because every parent, however saintly patient, has found herself annoyed by the behavior of her children at some point. As TV critic Dustin Rowles puts it,

Once you have kids, there's little more satisfying than having your biggest complaints about parenting reflected back in a darkly hilarious manner. . . . If you ask Louis C.K. what makes him a successful stand-up comedian now, he'll tell you that it was becoming a parent. (*Louis C.K.'s Guide to Parenting*)

By taking off the kid gloves, as it were, Louis is able to subvert the idealized picture of children as pure and selfless angels. On his telling, kids are basically short, selfish jerks, especially when it comes to conversation:

They just talk whenever. They don't give a shit what you're doing or if it's a good time. I'm in a shoot-out with the cops, and she's telling me all kinds of shit. She doesn't care. Because she's *five*. They're self-absorbed people. (*Chewed Up*)

What a Wonderful World

Young kids *are* generally self-absorbed. They also have a (deserved) reputation for exhibiting a sense of curiosity that leads them to question most everything, a trait we actually call "childlike wonder." In his 2005 HBO special *One Night Stand*, Louis mocks the naivety of non-parents who assume that the incessant questions kids pose are a source of constant joy to their oft-beleaguered parents.

Observing a harried mother's dismissal of her child's innocuous question "Mommy, why is the sky blue?" Louis is reminded of his pre-fatherhood self smugly thinking, "When *I* have a child I will answer *all* of their questions and open their minds to the wonders of the world." For Louis, however, the childlike wonder that's so precious and endearing in theory can become maddeningly childish in practice:

More questions. "Why?" "Why?" "Why?" Until you don't even know who the fuck you are anymore at the end of the conversation. It's an insane deconstruction. . . . This goes on for hours and hours and it gets so weird and abstract. In the end it's like: "Why?" Well, because some things *are* and some things *are not.* "Why?" Well, because things that *are not* can't *be*! (*One Night Stand*)

It's fitting that Louis finds himself contorted into philosophical knots in trying to answer his daughter's wonder-full questions.

Both Plato and Aristotle, arguably the two most influential philosophers who ever lived, saw wonder as the driving force behind philosophical questioning. I sometimes joke with my students that philosophers are just adults who never stopped asking (potentially annoying) questions.

By gamely trying to resolve her series of increasingly frustrating "Why?" queries for once, Louis exposes the philosophical nature of kids' questions in general. What's more, in his attempt to take his daughter's increasingly abstract questions seriously, Professor C.K. ends up confronting a fascinating philosophical topic addressed by some of the very first philosophers: the meaning of nothing.

The First Philosophers

The very first philosophers in what is sometimes called the "Western" tradition (meaning, roughly, the intellectual tradition that began with the ancient Greeks some 2,600 years ago) are called the Pre-Socratics. They earned this title by having the audacity to exist before Socrates of Athens (around 470–399 B.C.E.) did.

These very first philosophers were largely unimpressed with the stories passed down through Greek mythology. Instead of merely accepting the shopworn conventions of tradition and custom, they sought rational answers to some of the most fundamental questions we can ask, the kind of questions we might expect from, say, an inquisitive (and therefore annoying) child. "What is everything made of?" "How does one thing change into something else?" "Where did everything come from?" "Why is there anything at all?" You know, precisely the sort of questions your kid might ask while you're just trying to get them to finish their goddamn French fries.

Philosophy is not the world's oldest profession, and it isn't a terribly lucrative one either. In fact, the very first philosophers were by and large amateurs, though not in the sense that they approached their work in a sloppy fashion or merely as a hobby. Rather, the Pre-Socratics were amateurs in the original, etymological sense of the word: they did the work because of a love for the work, not as a means to the end of a generous compensation package with fabulous benefits. Amateurs in this sense "do it for love, not money," and they were in luck: it turns out that there isn't much money to be made in asking questions of the form "Why does anything exist?" It's akin to something like an aspiring stand-up comic working the local open-mic night because, dammit, making people laugh is serious business, paycheck or no.

Falling for Philosophy

Scholars generally agree that Thales of Miletus (around 624–546 B.C.E.) was the first Pre-Socratic philosopher. Hailing from a port town on the coast of the Mediterranean Sea in present-day Turkey, Thales earned a reputation for an interest in astronomy and mathematics. In fact, tradition holds that Thales successfully predicted a solar eclipse in the year 585 B.C.E., an impressive feat that, nonetheless, failed to spare him from being the butt of quite possibly the first "absent-minded professor" joke ever. Plato writes:

> While he was studying the stars and looking upwards, he fell into a well, and a neat, witty Thracian servant girl jeered at him, they say, because he was so eager to know the things in the sky that he could not see what was there before him at his very feet. The same jest applies to all who pass their lives in philosophy. (*Theaetetus*, line 174a)

The Thracian servant would've appreciated Mel Brooks's classic line: "Tragedy is when I cut my finger. Comedy is when you fall into an open sewer and die." Thales, luckily, survived and was followed by a long line of subsequent philosophers in the West. All of them, in fact.

It was not long before the Pre-Socratics turned to metaphysical questions. Metaphysics is the branch of philosophy dedicated to the analysis of fundamental concepts like *being*, *existence*, *reality*, *change*, *time*, and so on. You know, the sort of "big ideas" that most people associate with philosophy in the first place. Some philosophers have argued that the central metaphysical question is this: "Why is there something rather than nothing?" That is, why does anything exist at all? Most of the world's great creation myths can be thought of as early attempts at wrestling with this question in a non-philosophical way. Some of these creation myths describe a god or gods creating the world out of nothing (what's called creation *ex nihilo*), but this kind of an answer merely raises the question: what is the nothing from which something (allegedly) was made?

Talking about Nothing in Particular

Imagine *nothing*. Got it? Good. But wait, what are you actually picturing in your mind? A vast black expanse isn't exactly nothing. Maybe some props will help. Here, take this pen and paper and draw for us a little bit of nothing. "Ah!" thinks the smart-ass (and comedian), "I will refuse to draw anything and win by default!" That's very clever, but in refusing to draw anything you haven't sketched nothing: you've just refrained from drawing in the first place. What if we cannot imagine *nothing* because it is literally impossible to do so? To put it bluntly: What the hell is *nothing*?

Nobody has had more to say about nothing than the Pre-Socratic philosopher Parmenides of Elea (around 515–460 B.C.E.). Elea was a Greek settlement located in present-day southern Italy, about a two-hour drive from Naples. Parmenides argued that the reason we cannot coherently think or speak of nothing is because nothingness itself is impossible. Something exists, he reasoned, indeed *must* exist, because it's impossible for nothing to be. Or, as an exasperated Louis C.K. himself put it to his curious daughter, "Why? Well, because some things are and some things are not. Why? Well, because things that are not can't be!" (*One Night Stand*).

The moment we try to think or speak about nothing we turn it into something! Even the word "nothing" isn't *nothing*: it's a word. Which is something. The very act of trying to define "nothing" renders it something, as defining 'x' involves stating what 'x' *is*. It reminds me of the old (and tired) observational comedy bit where every time a wife asks her husband what he's thinking, he replies, "Nothing." For Parmenides, if the husband truly were thinking of *nothing*, then he is actually not thinking at all. Presumably, the taciturn husband is simply choosing not to share his thoughts with his wife, not actually struggling to contemplate the meaning of non-being (though your marriage may differ).

In fielding those incessant "Why?" questions from his daughter, Louis appears to have stumbled onto the same insight as Parmenides, who argued, "That which is there to be spoken and thought of must be. For it is possible for it to be, but not possible for nothing to be." At first, it sounds like Louis the exasperated, accidental father-philosopher and Parmenides the Pre-Socratic have come to the same conclusion. However, it's where each goes from here that leads them into different philosophical camps altogether.

Giant Ants with Top Hats Dancing Around

A quick reading of Louis's "Why?" routine from *One Night Stand* suggests that both he and Parmenides agree that nothing can't be. Louis himself says as much when he agrees that "things that are not can't be." But the bit doesn't end there, and this turns out to be philosophically (and comically) critical. Just as Louis begins to give the impression that he and Parmenides are of the same mind, he pivots to the apparently *opposite* conclusion:

> Why? Because then nothing wouldn't be. You can't have fucking "Nothing isn't, everything is!?" Why? Because if nothing wasn't there'd be fucking all kinds of shit that we don't—like giant ants with top hats dancing around! There's no room for all that shit! (*One Night Stand*)

What Louis profanely articulates, here, is a rejection of what's called the Principle of Plenitude.

This principle is basically the idea, described most famously by historian and philosopher Alfred O. Lovejoy, of "the necessarily complete translation of all . . . ideal possibilities into actuality" (*Great Chain of Being*, p. 50). In plainer English, this is something like the idea that if something's possible, then it either *actually is now* or at some point, given enough time, will *become actual* and not remain merely possible forever. The former is sometimes called the "static" version of this principle, while the latter is called the "dynamic" version.

Louis insists, however tongue-in-cheek, that some things (say, giant ants with top hats dancing around) must remain merely possible for there to be enough "room" in the world for all of the actual things that do exist—say, the pile of soggy French fries his daughter has neglected to eat because she's asking too many goddamn questions over lunch.

If we assume that the universe is finite, then Louis's rejection of the Principle of Plenitude seems plausible. If there's only so much space in the world, then it would seem to follow that literally all possible things can't exist simultaneously. There just isn't, as Louis puts it, enough room for all that shit. Some things must remain non-existent to preserve a sufficient amount of space for the things that do exist.

This, however, wasn't Parmenides's concern. Where Louis's reasoning stems from the observation that there's (presumably) only a limited amount of room in the world for a limited amount of shit, Parmenides does not base his analysis on this—or any—empirical observation at all. Instead, Parmenides seeks to follow wherever logic leads him in the dissection of ideas like "being" and "nothingness," even if it leads him to conclusions that clash with what our five senses seem to reveal about the world. Nowhere is his disregard for so-called common sense clearer than in Parmenides's conclusion that change itself is impossible.

Don't You Ever Change

As bizarre as it may sound, Parmenides concludes that, because nothingness is impossible, change is impossible too. His logic goes something like this. What happens when something changes into something else? Well, the thing that changes is transformed from what it is to what it is not. Otherwise, it hasn't changed!

When a comedian tweaks a joke over several retellings before several different audiences, the final joke that emerges is different from the joke in its initial telling. In its initial telling, it is not the final version of the joke. But once it changes, it ceases to be what it was (the prior version of the joke) and has now become that which it was not (the final version of the joke). There's only one problem with this understanding of change, though. Change seems to require the possibility of "things which are not" (that is to say, nothing) which is precisely what Parmenides denies is possible.

This part of his argument can get confusing pretty quickly, but the basic idea is that since nothing ("that which is not") can't be, change can't really occur either. Now I know what you're thinking. You're thinking that he's playing with us. Who in their right mind can deny that things change? Who could deny that we're constantly surrounded by things—and persons—undergoing change? The indignities that come with aging are an especially rich comic vein that Louis has mined through the years, and it seems never to have occurred to Louis that he isn't really getting older (and fatter and balder) with age.

However, Parmenides doesn't deny that we *think* we see things (or ourselves) changing. What he denies is that what we *see* (our "ordinary experience") reflects the way things *really are*:

> For in no way may this prevail, that things that are not, are.
> But you, bar your thought from this way of inquiry,
> and do not let habit born from much experience compel you along this way
> to direct your sightless eye and sounding ear and tongue,
> but judge by reason the heavily contested testing
> spoken by me. (The first two lines here are from Plato's *Sophist*; lines 3–6 are from Sextus Empiricus, *Against the Mathematicians*.)

When forced to choose between logic and his own lyin' eyes, in other words, Parmenides sides with his logic, as crazy as the conclusion (namely, that change is impossible because nothingness is not) may make him seem. But what if he's right? What other strange conclusions follow regarding the real nature of things if we grant that change is logically impossible?

You Can't Get There from Here

If change is logically impossible—the testimony of our five senses notwithstanding—then what else does this reveal about the nature of "what is"? Well, for starters, motion seems ruled out, as motion is basically a change in something's location in space over time. When Louis walks across the stage, mic in hand, he changes his physical position in the hall relative to us in the audience. Or so it would appear to our senses. But if change in general is logically impossible, then change in one's location would be logically impossible as well. This, again, despite the fact that we think we see Louis schlepping across the stage! Motion—like all change—is, in reality, just an illusion, according to this Parmenidean logic.

Parmenides and his followers were well aware that these counter-intuitive conclusions would likely amuse (or infuriate) most people. His loyal student Zeno of Elea (around 490–430 B.C.E.) concocted a series of arguments (known as Zeno's paradoxes) to demonstrate that, despite our observations and common-sense feelings, Parmenides was right: change is ultimately an illusion. Aristotle summarized one such paradox (the "Race Course Paradox") like this: "That which is in locomotion must arrive at the half-way stage before it arrives at the goal" (*Physics*, VI:9, line 239b10).

Since Louis is not exactly the poster child for long-distance running, let's try a slightly different example. Picture a hungry post-show Louis at the Comedy Cellar in New York City, one-hundred feet away from the entrance to Ben's Pizzeria. Before Louis can get from the club to the pizzeria, he must first reach the halfway point—that is, before he can walk one-hundred feet, he must first walk fifty feet. And before he can reach the halfway point, he must first reach the quarter-way point—that is, before he can walk fifty feet, he must first walk twenty-five feet. And so on. Since we can keep halving the distance Louis must first traverse before he reaches the *next* halfway point an infinite number of times, it follows that—much to his chagrin, no doubt—Louis will never reach the entrance to Ben's Pizzeria, as it will take him an infinitely long time to traverse an infinite number of "halfway points."

Of course, we do *see* people walking and arriving at their destinations all the time. But, as Parmenides is quick to remind us, why assume that what we think we see is the whole (or real) story? Thus, as much as it may pain common sense (or those of us not named Parmenides or Zeno), it follows that change is impossible, and that whatever is, is one and unchanging. In some ultimate sense, then, there aren't really a plurality of discrete beings subject to change, there remains only pure Being itself: one, eternal, and unchanging.

Nothing from Nothing Leaves Nothin'

As we've seen, Louis concludes that "nothing can't be" by appealing to something like the Principle of Plenitude. Parmenides, on the other hand, concludes that nothingness itself is logically impossible and thus eternal and unchanging

Being, alone, is. In other words, Louis does not deny the coherence of the idea of non-being; he just argues that it's impossible for everything to exist at once. Parmenides, in contrast, concludes that everything, in fact, does exist, though our common notion of "everything" is deeply confused due to the faith we place in our senses. For the Pre-Socratic from Elea, whatever is, is. There's literally no other option.

If our brief exploration of nothing has left you frustrated, wondering what the practical import of all this questioning might be, you would not be alone. Like the Thracian servant mocking poor Thales at the bottom of the well, many of the contemporaries of the Pre-Socratics dismissed these metaphysical questions for being out of touch with so-called "real world" concerns. You may be unable to refute Zeno's paradoxes, but if you fail to show up for work, your boss is unlikely to accept the excuse that you require an infinitely long commute just to make it there (though some days it might feel that way). It's telling that Louis ultimately fails to resolve his daughter's series of "Why?" questions, falling back on the timeless parental trump card—and I'm paraphrasing here—eat your French fries *because I said so*.

Indeed, the entire exchange between Louis and his daughter is framed around his attempt to get her to finish her meal. She's not eating her French fries because she's evidently too busy asking her father to probe the limits of language, thought, and reality itself. Feeding your kids is a very real parental responsibility that Louis has riffed on elsewhere:

> When your kid won't eat, you just go crazy. Because you have a physical need to feed them, it's an instinct. And when they're sitting there just looking at their food, you're like, "Just fuckin' eat it! You'll die, you idiot. Eat the food!" "I don't like it." "It doesn't matter, put it in your face. They have your footprint at the hospital. They know I have you. I'm not allowed to let you die, you piece of shit. Eat it! You have a Social Security number, you're on the grid, motherfucker. Eat. If you're skinny, I go to jail. Do you understand?" (*Chewed Up*)

Being may, in fact, be one, eternal, and unchanging, but in a certain pragmatic sense, it doesn't matter. Child Protective Services aren't going to listen patiently to a lecture on Parmenidean logic if your child is malnourished due to neglect. Nor should they.

But he isn't merely a comedian, either. He's a father. And given how misanthropic his comic persona is, and how often his children serve as comic foils in his routines, it's easy to forget that Louis the person views "dad" as his primary role. Louis described his reaction to becoming a parent in an NPR interview in 2015:

> I realized that a lot of the things that my kid was taking away from me, she was freeing me of. There was this huge pride in having a kid and also that I didn't matter anymore. The greatest thing about having a child is putting yourself second in your own life. It's a massive gift to be able to say you're not the most important person to yourself. . . . If you can be useful, which means to somebody else, not to yourself, if you can be useful, it just makes you feel better. So I live in service for my kids, that's the first priority and then things like my career, they feed into that, they're part of that, because I'm providing for them but also it's just not that important. If something's not important, it's more fun.

I suspect that the palpable frustration Louis experiences as his discourse on nothingness builds isn't solely due to the apparently interminable nature of such metaphysical questioning. If anything, it seems due to the fact that, in his dogged attempts to answer each new "Why?" he's pelted with, he's increasingly failing to fulfill his paternal responsibility to see to it that his kid is fed: "If you're skinny, I go to jail," after all.

Parents have obligations that their young charges are only remotely aware of, if at all. Louis the adult caregiver bears the weight of responsibility that comes with parenthood: feeding, sheltering, clothing, protecting, and nurturing his children, and that's just for starters. If he fulfills his obligations well, then his children can enjoy the luxury—indeed, the privilege—of indulging in that childlike wonder that some of us thankfully never outgrow. "The unexamined life is not worth living," said Socrates. But I'm also reminded of a line attributed to playwright Bertolt Brecht: "Bread first. Then ethics."

Now eat your French fries.

8

Should Jane Get to Be Bored?

Daniel Addison

> **Howard Stern:** Don't you have to be angry to come up with good comedy? Don't you have to be really pissed off at the world and see all of the stupidity in it?
>
> **Louis C.K.:** No, I think it comes from curiosity. I think it comes from a playful curiosity.
>
> —Louis C.K. on *The Howard Stern Show*, May 2014

Remember the opening scene of "Country Drive" in *Louie* Season Two? Louie's driving his daughters out of the city. His youngest, Jane, repeatedly expresses her boredom. She then asks, "Why won't you answer me?" Louis responds by admonishing her.

> Because "I'm bored" is a useless thing to say. I mean, you live in a great, big, vast world that you've seen none percent of. Even the inside of your own mind is endless; it goes on forever, inwardly, do you understand? The fact that you're alive is amazing, so you don't get to say "I'm bored."

Many viewers find Louie's response admirable. They see him as aiming to instill in his daughter a sense of wonder with which she should approach both the world external to her mind and the world contained within it. This sense of wonder should *replace* her boredom—in a sense, *cure* it.

Perhaps, though, we should be worried by Louie's response. Perhaps a child's boredom is not something a parent should

93

attempt to "cure" at all. Perhaps Louie's attempt to do so is something we should condemn rather than praise.

In his provocative article, "Louis C.K. Is Wrong about Boredom," Mathew Remski suggests that the appropriate response to Louie's remark is indeed condemnation rather than praise. Remski thinks that Jane's "yearning boredom is about paralysis of limitless possibility." She is expressing existential angst, and a more spiritually evolved father would be able to enter into it with his daughter. Such a father would be able to take his time in letting this boredom be, such that he and his daughter might experience and examine it together. He would feel its depths and ponder its meaning with her.

But Louie doesn't let this possibly fruitful boredom be. He tells his daughter, "you *don't get to say* 'I'm bored'," and Remski thinks this shows that Louie is unevolved as a father. He isn't evolved as a father because he hasn't figured out how to deal with his own anxiety. As Remski says, Louie's "famous admonishment, now scoring big hits through the new-age blogosphere, that his fictional daughter . . . shouldn't be allowed to be bored, is not a borderline-spiritual encouragement for her to seize the day. *It's a transference of anxiety*."

Remski thinks Louie can't endure his own anxiety. "He's not saying, 'You don't get to be bored' to his daughter, but to himself." And this leads him to misinterpret his daughter's words. When Jane says she's bored, Louie takes it to mean that she's uninterested, but that's not what she is saying. "Her boredom and his boredom belong to different categories. Her yearning boredom is about paralysis of limitless possibility . . . Louie's boredom is the anxious boredom of the adult: he doesn't know what to do with himself, time is wasting away, and he fears he's forgotten how to feel wonderment, so he demands his daughter feel it for him."

The more important consequence of Louie's intolerance of his own anxiety, however, is that it triggers his admonishment of Jane, which Remski views as an act of psychological violence.

The answer pretends to kindle the girl's wonderment, but it actually burns the tenderness of her question. She's asking a question about how to manage emptiness, and the answer is to overwhelm her with stuff. Instead of letting it be an open moment in which the parent can share in the revelation of uncertainty that the child makes new for him, Louis crams irritated gumption and panicked work ethic down her throat, guilting her with what she already knows but was too innocent to accept, guilting her for naming a condition to which we dare not confess, guilting her for being so rude as to ask for help. We laugh because he releases the valve on our own guilt over doing the same thing.

If Remski's right, then indeed we should admonish Louie's admonishment, rather than praise it. "We have to let our children be bored, so they can explore safely the endless horizons of time, and softly confront the abyss." Remski thinks that this is "the punch line that Louie . . . speaking for the cultural unconscious, can't afford." If we laugh, it's because we too can't handle our anxiety. If we laugh, it's because we're guilty of sharing Louie's thought that our children's boredom must be repressed under the thought that "the fact that you're alive is amazing," as Louis instructs his daughter. His admonishment manifests our nasty tendency to ruin our children by imposing upon them our panicked propensity to run from the abyss, to avoid rather than explore it, and to cover up our awareness of it with "amazing" things—with accomplishments and achievements and ever-forward moving productivity. Rather than encourage Jane to take time with her boredom, as Louie should too, he thus seeks to banish it from existence.

But you can't take time if you're terrified by your own boredom. You have to move things along. Be rushed, maybe, in the way that you were rushed as a child. You can't tolerate your children taking time or else they will expose how your own forward movement is in a state of perpetual derailment. So there's no surprise when a father overpowers his daughter with an answer several cynical clicks north of her intellectual paradigm.

Does Louis Really Run from the Void?

Remski's charge is a challenging one, but I don't think this take on Louie's admonishment is really consistent with Louis's general outlook on life. Remski takes his criticism of Louie the character to apply to Louis the man. But Louis the man isn't the type to run from the void.

To see this, consider first Louis's response to a young man's question during his AMA on reddit. The questioner expressed despondence at the futility of it all. He asked Louis how he managed to keep plugging away when success wasn't immediately forthcoming. In his response, Louis tells the kid not to avoid his feelings of despair. He encourages him to enter into those feelings and to explore them. He advises him not to give in to the temptation to escape from them—not to give in to the need to "feel okay all the time."

> You'll be fine. You're twenty-five. Feeling unsure and lost is part of your path. Don't avoid it. See what those feelings are showing you and use it. Take a breath. You'll be okay. Even if you don't feel okay all the time.

It's even clearer that Louis values and is willing to experience the depths of despair from something he says during an interview with Conan. He doesn't want his daughters to have cell phones, he explains, because then they'd miss out on the benefits that come through experiencing the void, the despair, the aloneness, and the nothingness. Cell phones are bad for us, he argues, because they facilitate our escape from these hard-to-endure yet spiritually rich experiences—because we reach for our phones to avoid the void.

> You need to build an ability to just be yourself and not be doing something. That's what the phones are taking away, is the ability to just sit there [*taps chair*], like this. That's being a person. Right? No one can [*do that anymore*]. You gotta check [*buries into an imaginary phone and presses its buttons*]. Because, y'know, underneath everything, in your life, there's that thing—that empty, forever empty, y'know what I'm talking about? Yes? Just that knowledge that it's all for nothing and you're alone, y'know it's down there. And sometimes when things clear away, you're not watching anything, you're in your car, and you start going 'Ohhh no, here it comes! That I'm alone!' like it starts to visit on you, y'know just this sadness. Life is tremendously sad, just by being in it.

It's our inability to experience the void, Louis says, that's responsible for our "murdering each other with our cars" by texting and driving. "Because we don't want to be alone for a second. Because it's so hard." He then tells us of a time when he was driving and a song came on the radio that made him sad, and he resisted the urge to escape the empty nothingness by playing with his phone.

> So I started getting this sad feeling and I was starting to reach for my phone, and I said you know what, don't. Just be sad. Just let the sadness—stand in the way of it, and let it hit you like a truck. And I let it come, and I started to feel, oh my god. And I pulled over and I just cried like a bitch. I cried so much. And it was beautiful. Sadness is poetic, you're lucky to live sad moments, and then I had happy feelings 'cause of it, 'cause when you let yourself feel sad your body has like antibodies rushing in to meet the sadness. So I was grateful to feel sad, and then I met it with true profound happiness. It was such a trip. And the thing is, because we don't want that first bit of sad, we push it away . . . (*Conan*, 2013)

When we look at moments like these, it's pretty clear that Remski doesn't need to criticize Louis for failing to confront existential angst head on. Louis is all about those confrontations. He wants his daughters to develop "the ability to just sit there," and to be able to learn from what their feelings are telling them, just as Remski wants us to let our children be bored and let them take their time.

If this is Louis's attitude, however, Remski is probably wrong to find a flight from anxiety and an act of psychological violence in Louie's "you don't get to be bored" admonishment of Jane. But if Louis isn't running from his own anxiety, and if that isn't how we should understand his reaction to his daughter's boredom, how should we think of it? Why did Louie admonish Jane for being bored? What kind of adult is Louie trying to encourage his daughter to become, if he's not merely attempting to "overwhelm her with stuff" or "cram irritated gumption and panicked work ethic down her throat"?

Louis's Love of Learning

Every human being, by nature, desires to know.

—ARISTOTLE

Louis's own love of learning is plain enough. As he told Charlie Rose in a 2014 interview, "My favorite thing to do is learn." When responding to a fan's observation, "it seems you like to learn," during his AMA on reddit mentioned above, he writes, "I do love to learn. It's all I feel like I'm ever doing. It's really the best you can do in life, is learn." It's the best we can do in life! It almost sounds like Louis is taking a position on an ancient debate that Socrates started when he asked everyone he talked to about "the best life for human beings." Louis's answer: a life of learning. That's when we are at our best as a species.

If we look now at Louis's famous "Everything is amazing and nobody is happy" bit from *Hilarious*, we can see how this idea of "human beings at their best" informs other parts of Louis's comedy. In this bit, Louis's criticism of humanity, especially the current generation of it, is explicit and obvious. He rails against people for being blind to the "amazing" things around them. But what really motivates this criticism is Louis's idea that we *ought* to be in a state of wonder or perplexity (at the mere fact that we are alive, or that there is anything at all instead of nothing, or that we are able to sit in "chairs in the sky" like characters in a "Greek myth"), and we would be in that state if we would approach the world as humble and receptive students of its wonders, some of which are in our own minds, rather than as bored consumers waiting to be entertained.

If this is right, then when Louis counters Jane's boredom with "the fact that you're alive is amazing," he isn't setting her up to inherit what Remski sees as Louis's own panicked retreat from the disturbing experience of nothingness. He's encouraging her to appreciate the state of perplexity that is very similar to boredom. Plato and Aristotle, we'll see, have similar thoughts.

How Dare You Bitch *about Flying!*

People on planes are the worst. . . . "I had to sit on the runway for forty minutes." Oh really? What happened then? Did you fly through the air, like a bird, incredibly? Did you soar into the clouds impossibly? Did you partake in the miracle of human flight, and then land softly on giant tires that you couldn't even conceive how they put air in them? How dare you—bitching about flying! "I had to pay for my sandwich." You're flying! You're sitting in a chair in the sky! You're like a Greek myth right now. "But it doesn't go back very far and it's squishing my knees." (*Hilarious*)

In this admonishment of his generation Louis pokes fun at people who simply incorporate the results of technological achievements into their needs and desires. You might think Louis's criticism of his flying companion, the one who got upset at losing something "he didn't know existed thirty seconds ago," merely singles out for criticism our tendency to experience more frustration at losing a thing than we experienced happiness in acquiring it—the sort of behavior that behavioral economists call "loss aversion." Louis is definitely taking issue with that, but I think what really gets Louis riled up here is simply that this generation isn't philosophical enough: he's flabbergasted at their complete lack of a sense of wonder. As is clear from the beginning of this tirade, he finds his generation's lack of wonder all the more egregious given that we have so much more to wonder at than all previous ones.

Underneath Louis's seemingly pessimistic diatribe against "the shittiest generation of piece of shit assholes that ever lived," then, is a recognizably philosophical optimism. He's criticizing what we are on behalf of a conception of what we could and should be—what we are when we are at our best as a species. But what justifies this criticism? What allows Louis to hold that we *ought* to wonder? Why *should* we recognize the amazingness of all the amazing things around us? Why would we be better—or at least less shitty—if we did?

The Desire to Understand

As a lover of learning, Louis is like Aristotle. Philosophers in general are quite inquisitive people, but none more so than the one Dante calls "the master of those who know" (*Inferno*, Circle 1, Canto 4, line 131). According to all the ancient reports on his character, Aristotle was ferociously engaged in all areas of human learning. This feature of his personality displays itself in his books, too, where he relentlessly plugs away at a problem until he arrives at a satisfying explanation. A healthy curiosity animates these works, a sense of wonder at the thing he seeks to explain. Throughout he's guided by the questions, "What is this thing? How did it come to be as it is? What kind of activities or functions are specifically characteristic of this kind of thing? What capacities are essential to its being as it is?"

Aristotle esteems intellectual activity above all else. He even reveres it: he singles out our capacity to contemplate and understand as the divine element within us. In doing so, Aristotle thus doesn't merely take Louis's love of learning to the extreme. He also develops his whole philosophy around Louis's thought that "the best you can do in life is learn." Aristotle doesn't think that his interest in explaining things is something unique to himself. He thinks human beings in general have a natural desire to understand, and that the activity of learning is a defining characteristic of human nature. As he says in the famous opening line of his *Metaphysics*, "Every human being, by nature, desires to know."

We naturally desire to know, Aristotle explains, because, being the rational animals that we are, it's natural for us to wonder at how things work. In the broad sense of the term that includes finding scientific explanations for things, we philosophize, he explains, in response to this wonder.

> It is owing to their wonder that men both now begin and first began to philosophize; they wondered originally at the obvious difficulties, then advanced little by little and stated difficulties about the greater matters, e.g. about the phenomena of the moon and those of the sun and the stars, and about the genesis of the universe. And a man who is puzzled and wonders thinks himself ignorant . . . therefore since they philosophized in order to escape from ignorance, evidently they were pursuing science in order to know, and not for any utilitarian end. (*Metaphysics*, p. 982b, lines 12–19)

Aristotle's account of "human beings at their best" is based on his understanding of us as essentially knowledge-seeking creatures. Since it is the capacity for doing philosophy and science that makes us the kind of beings that we are, our deepest happiness will come by actualizing this capacity. It's when we're actively doing science and philosophy, he thinks, that we're truly being the kind of being that we are; in engaging in this activity we're actualizing our potential.

Because Aristotle grasps us as essentially knowledge-seeking creatures, he holds a very low opinion of the mere pleasure seekers. The beasts in the fields can live the lazy life of mere pleasure too. Aristotle disdains the humans who only go after pleasure because in living the life they choose they only actualize their capacity to be animals, not their capacity to be rational animals.

> The many, the most vulgar, would seem to conceive the good as happiness and pleasure, and hence they also like the life of gratification. Here they appear completely slavish, since the life they decide on is a life for grazing animals. (*Nicomachean Ethics*, p. 1095b, lines 16–20)

Louis's worldview shares these elements of Aristotle's. His tirade against the current generation is based on similar ideas about what our nature consists in. It takes us to task for how radically we've failed to realize this nature. For Louis, we're not "the worst people so far" merely because "we don't even know what's involved" in how the technology to which we're addicted works.

The more egregious issue is that we don't even experience the wonder concerning how such things work that would naturally lead us to desire to understand them. We're ignorant of "what's involved," but not even wondering how our phones work, not feeling puzzled by how they do what they do, we fail to recognize our own ignorance. We are thus content to rest in rather than "escape from ignorance." At the very least, if the wonder could be restored, Louis hopes we'd appreciate anew how "amazing" it is merely that these things can do what they do.

On Being Amazed at the Shit in the World

In his tirade, Louis compares himself favorably to the unamazed "noncontributing product-sponge cunts" with whom he shares the planet: "*I'm* amazed at the shit in the world" (my emphasis). As we've just seen, it's this sense of wonder that Louis most fundamentally aims to restore with his chastisement. See how this comes through most clearly in the fictional dialogue at the end of the bit. To meet her finicky complaints, Louis simply reiterates the sense of wonder the person he's criticizing ought to possess. "How *dare* you—bitching *about flying*! 'I had to pay for my sandwich.' *You're flying!*" Like Aristotle, Louis loves learning, possesses a sense of wonder, and judges us harshly if we fail to do the same.

What accounts for this feature of Louis's character which singles him out from his peers? An answer can be found in the way Louis talks about his most important teacher—his mother.

> My mother was a math teacher and she taught me that that moment when you go "I don't know what this is!" when you panic, that means you're about to figure it out. That means you've let go of what you know and you're about to grab on to a new thing that you didn't know yet. (*Letterman*, 2014)

We'll appreciate the philosophical import of this lesson Louis learned from his mother by comparing it to the teaching of Aristotle's most important teacher—Plato. Aristotle studied under Plato for twenty years in the Academy Plato founded. The influence, as you'd expect, is deep and far-ranging. One key thing Aristotle inherits from his teacher is the thought that, when approaching a philosophical problem, it is important to clearly state and fully experience the perplexity—in Greek, "*aporia*"—that leads to it. The influence can be seen in Aristotle's remark, "For those who wish to solve problems, it is helpful to state the problem well" (*Metaphysics,* 995a, line 27).

The significance of *aporia* in Plato's own work, however, more obviously illuminates the point of Louis's tirade. Plato wrote dialogues in which Socrates would typically play the leading role. Socrates would seek the definition of a certain moral term with the person after whom the dialogue is named. He seeks the definition, for example, of piety in the *Euthyphro*, courage in the *Laches*, and virtue in the *Meno*. In each dialogue, Socrates's conversational partner would begin believing the task an easy one: asked what virtue is, Meno responds, "It is not hard to tell you, Socrates" (*Meno,* p. 71).

In each dialogue, however, Socrates examines proposed definitions and eventually shows his partner to be committed to contradictory beliefs. His partner sees that his various beliefs about the moral notion in question are in conflict with one another, and this undermines his naive belief that he knows the nature of that thing. In this way Socrates brings his partners to the state of perplexity or *aporia*, and they have to either leave the conversation or confess now that they don't in fact know what it is—piety, courage, or virtue—that they've been talking about. It is likely that the historical Socrates was executed for doing exactly this to the leading men of Athens. It is understandable, if not forgivable, that those whose social standing hinged on being recognized as experts did not take kindly to having their actual ignorance revealed. One of the official charges reflected their dislike for this man's way of bringing listeners to *aporia*: corrupting the youth.

With these historical realities in mind, Plato set out to defend Socrates in his writings. In the *Meno*, for example, Plato's character Socrates examines a slave boy and brings him to perplexity. Plato's Socrates goes out of his way to make clear the benefit received by those brought to this state. (I've added emphasis where we'll find the point of Louis's tirade reflected, as I'll explain after the quote.)

> SOCRATES: At first he did not know . . . even now he does not yet know, but then he thought he knew, and answered confidently as if he did know, and he did not think himself at a loss, but now he does think himself at a loss, and as he does not know, neither does he think he knows.
>
> MENO: That is true.
>
> SOCRATES: So he is now in a better position with regard to the matter he does not know.
>
> MENO: I agree with that too.
>
> SOCRATES: Have we done him any harm by making him perplexed and numb . . . ?
>
> MENO: I do not think so.
>
> SOCRATES: Indeed, we have probably achieved something relevant to finding out how matters stand, for now, as he does not know, he would be glad to find out, whereas [this was not true] before . . .
>
> MENO: So it seems.
>
> SOCRATES: Do you think that before he would have tried to find out that which he thought he knew though he did not, before he fell into perplexity and realized he did not know and longed to know?
>
> MENO: I do not think so, Socrates.
>
> SOCRATES: Has he then benefited from being numbed?
>
> MENO: I think so.
>
> SOCRATES: Look then how he will come out of his perplexity while searching along with me. (*Meno*, p. 84)

We can now gather together the elements of our defense of Louis's "You don't get to be bored" admonishment of his daughter Jane. It is an ordinary and obvious thing that without much ado we apply the terms "good," "bad," "virtuous," "courageous," "pious," or their more modern equivalents. We think we know what we mean. But Plato's Socrates seeks to shatter our naive and lazy belief that it's an easy thing to specify what it is we're referring to with these terms. His stated goal in perplexing us is that we wonder what we mean when we speak as we do, so that we may try and "would be glad to find out" what this is. For Aristotle, this wonder is our "natural" state—the state we ought to be in so that we might actualize the potential we possess that makes us what we are, the potential to engage in the activity of philosophical and scientific theorizing about the perplexing, amazing, wonder-worthy world in which we live.

Louis's admonishments of his generation ("How *dare* you— bitching *about flying!*") and of his daughter ("You don't get to say 'I'm bored'") aim at the same philosophical end. The problem Louis has with his daughter's boredom is the same as the problem he has with his generation's failure to wonder: in both cases there's a failure to see the world aright. Seen aright, the world is an amazing, that is, a *perplexing* place. As the glance at Plato's Socrates brings home, however, we see the world as we should—from a state of perplexity, wonder, or *aporia*—by meditating on the obvious, on the everyday ordinary objects or thoughts forever before our eyes.

When Louis encourages Jane to see the world as amazing, then, he isn't forcing on her his own anxiety-induced need to be overwhelmed with stuff. He isn't stuffing a panicked work ethic down her throat. He means rather to encourage her to wonder. Encouraging her to wonder is not encouraging her to run from, but rather to face the nothingness—"that empty, forever empty . . . that knowledge that it's all for nothing and you're alone, y'know it's down there." He thus tells the twenty-five-year-old, "Take a breath." "Can you just take a little breath?" he rhetorically asks the noncontributing product-sponge cunt.

It's by facing the nothingness that one achieves *aporia* and comes to see the world as amazing. To rightly recognize our phones and planes as more perplexing than our unthinking assumptions lead us to believe, we need some release from the urgency of our desire that they perform their functions immediately. This release would put some reflective distance between ourselves and our tools, and this space would allow our rational nature to wonder how they work. Achieving this distance requires taking a meditative breath.

Remski is right to stress the importance of letting a child's boredom be, of sticking with rather than fleeing the experience of nothingness that such boredom involves. He is wrong though when he sees an anxious fleeing from this nothingness in Louis's "You don't get to be bored" admonishment of his daughter Jane.

The experience towards which Louis urges Jane with his admonishment is not opposed to the experience of nothingness, as Remski thinks. The experience Louis hopes she'll have is rather the reward for sticking with this nothingness, "seeing what those feelings are showing you," and coming out the other side. What he hopes she'll experience is the full-blown philosophical wonder that puts one square on the path towards a life of speculative joy.

If we look into Jane's receptive eyes in the shot of her face as Louis delivers his admonishment, we can see the seeds of this future experience being sown.

9
What Fuckin' Chance Does a Kid Have?

JOSEPH WESTFALL

For parents, especially parents of young children, one of the most appealing aspects of Louis's humor is his willingness to confront, reflect upon, and address some of the secret ambivalences characteristic of parenthood—ambivalences, sometimes manifest as regrets or concerns, that few parents admit to themselves, much less to anyone else.

As a father, Louis appears to have genuine firsthand experience of such things; as a reflective human being, he seems to have thought them through; and as a writer and comedian, he has managed to express them in hilarious, sometimes disturbing, but often poignant ways. In so doing, Louis makes it easier for all the rest of us to recognize these facts about ourselves, too.

His keenest (and most frequent) observations about children and parents fall into two loose categories: on the one hand, he often talks about the "true nature" of children, that is, that they (especially as infants) are largely unknowable to their parents, and furthermore, that once you get to know them, they are not unmitigatedly good people; on the other hand, parenting is hard in a variety of ways that makes having children seem, on at least some significant occasions, like it has ruined your life.

Taken together, these truths—as Louis sees them, and as incompatible as they seem—constitute the emotional basis of the relationship between parents and their children. Or, perhaps more to the point, the conflict here—between loving your kids as the greatest experience you could ever possibly have and despising them for destroying the very possibility of your happiness—ultimately indicates that the emotional relationship to your children is not a good or stable basis for the activity of parenthood at all.

Kids, of course, can only relate emotionally to their parents, which is why they are so often, as Louis puts it, "fuckin' assholes." When parents respond in kind, they are no less assholes—but, unlike their children, parents have the ability and thus the responsibility to parent from a perspective that honestly takes into account their children's immaturity, and refuses to blame the kids for being kids. That said, he is still willing to call them out—from a perspective of honesty and seriousness—for being the little assholes and douchebags that the great majority of children are.

You Just Have to Wait

At first blush, Louis's depiction of the parental relationship to and understanding of children seems rather negative. When his youngest daughter was still a baby, for example, he noted, "We have a baby, and I don't—I don't really know the baby, to tell you the truth, because she hasn't said anything. . . . I like her, she's fine, but I don't know her. How do I know what she's really like? Maybe she fuckin' hates Jews. I don't know. I don't know nothin' about her" (*Shameless*). As he often does, Louis plays on our usual assumptions—in this case, of the innocence of babies—to make what seems after the fact an obvious point: we have no idea what kind of person any infant will become, nor do we know what (if anything) babies are thinking now, as babies. As far as any adult knows, babies might be racists.

This is not the rosy picture of infanthood that we typically hear from new parents or in our culture in general. But it also lacks the sense of certainty characteristic of the views of, say, St. Augustine, who famously consigned all unbaptized infants to Hell—not, as some theologies would have it, exclusively for an inherited sin, but because babies are themselves (according to Augustine) evil people.

All the same, for Louis as for Augustine, if there's one thing to be said of infants, it is that they do not—cannot, developmentally—consider the needs of others. "Babies are selfish. They just, '*Waah!*' No baby every goes, '*Waah!* But how're you doin', though?'" (*Live at the Comedy Store*). And this view of infants as mostly unknown, basically selfish beings informs

Louis's understanding of older children, as well. "The other kid we have is a girl, she's four, she's also a fuckin' asshole. . . . I say that with no remorse. Fuckin' asshole. She's a douchebag. She is! Fucking jerk" (*Shameless*). Of course, it being Louis, the analysis does not end there. "That's the thing: nobody ever calls her on her bullshit. That's how she got to be an asshole in the first place" (*Shameless*). And a year later, when his four-year old was five, Louis returned to the very same theme: "They're self-absorbed people. They have no ability—no five-year-old ever goes, like, 'No, go ahead and finish. I'll tell you after. It's fine'. They just can't" (*Chewed Up*). Ultimately, then, for Louis, it's not just that kids are selfish assholes—but that they are developmentally constrained to be selfish assholes.

If adults acted like children do, they would be (rightly) reprimanded for their bad behavior. But children have no choice in the matter, and thus are not exactly responsible for acting in the offensively self-absorbed ways they do. This puts adults who interact with children—and parents, most of all—in the position of having actually to understand something about children's psychological and personal development. The "good" parent, on this view, will be the one who takes into account the fact that the child is a child, and as such incomplete, not fully developed, not fully responsible for saying and doing the things he or she says and does. This point becomes very clear in a story Louis told about his youngest daughter when she was three years old. Without getting into the details of the story (the famous "Pig Newtons" incident), we can see already in the set-up the significance of Louis's point here:

> The three-year old, here's her deal: she's a three-year old. That's really it. She's three years old. The other day, I got into a fight with her. Whose fault is that? I'm forty-one. And she's three. It's always your fault with a three-year old, always. Because they are just what they are. They can't help it. Just tape the windows, it's a fuckin' hurricane. Just wait. Any time you're like this with a three-year old—"*Don't you underst——*you're an idiot. That's you being an idiot. "*Don't you understand?*" No, I don't, Dad. I haven't developed enough. You just have to wait. (*Hilarious*)

Thus, given the nature of kids, Louis seems to counsel patience to parents. And yet . . .

I Love Her—but I Wish She Was Never Born

Louis is the first to note that having children radically dimin-
ishes the quality of a person's life—at least by the standards
one would have used before having kids. In a musing with
which nearly every parent can agree, he notes, "The one thing
I truly regret about my children is that they don't respect
sleep" (*Live at Carnegie Hall*). More than this, however, parenthood for Louis entails the loss of perhaps all the simple
pleasures of life—so much so, that it becomes difficult to see
how the life of a parent is actually worth living. "I love my kids
and I'd die for them, but my life fuckin' stinks. It just does.
What it is when you're a parent—all the pleasures are gone.
Nobody fucks you ever again. That shit's just over. You don't—
you can't sleep. You don't sleep, you don't eat meals, you just eat
at the sink, fast, standing up" (*Chewed Up*). All of the freedom
and autonomy that is typically associated with adulthood—"I
shit with the door open; that's my life," Louis notes
(*Hilarious*)—comes to an end with the introduction of children
into one's life, he seems to argue, such that caring for the children and attending to their needs becomes one's whole life.

Of course, many parents argue that, even if this is to some
extent true, having children provides compensatory pleasures
and a new, higher sense of satisfaction with one's life. And,
without doubt, that he is profoundly moved by his children is
evident in Louis's comedy. All the same, however, he makes an
important observation that many parents likely experience,
but few are willing to discuss openly.

> It's hard having kids because it's boring. That really is the hardest part
> of having kids. Ask any parent, "What's the hard part? Is it looking
> after their healthcare? Is it making sure that their education—?" No,
> it's just being with them on the floor while they be children. It's just
> . . . they read Clifford the Big Red Dog to you at a rate of fifty minutes
> a page, and you have to sit there and be horribly proud and bored at
> the same time. (*Live at the Beacon Theater*)

How boring is parenthood, exactly? In describing playing a
board game with his youngest daughter, Louis notes how
slowly she counts the spaces she needs to move her piece on the
board. In his retelling, eventually Louis grows frustrated

enough to interrupt the girl's effort. "Just go here," he says, to which his daughter responds in earnest, "Daddy, I'm learning." To great comic effect—but also successfully communicating the centrality of boredom in a parent's life—Louis imagines his retort: "I know. You're gonna grow up stupid because I'm bored. I can't take it, baby. I can't. I can't watch it. I am bored more than I love you" (*Live at the Beacon Theater*). Parenthood, then, on Louis's comic view, both deprives the parent of all of the basic pleasures of human existence, and replaces them with boredom and the frustration that derives from boredom.

What, if anything, then, does parenthood have to recommend it? The answer, for Louis, is overwhelmingly straightforward and immensely powerful—but not without ambivalence, all the same. Referring again to his youngest daughter, Louis confesses something I think most parents feel, at least occasionally, despite the fact that few parents would be willing to admit it to themselves or others: "I love her, I love her—but I wish she was never born."

> Any honest parent will tell you that they live with that ambivalence. And it's torture. You look at your beautiful child's face, and you have two feelings at the exact same time. I love my daughter in a profound way. I cry at the drop of a hat when I think about her. This kid has made me love her so much that it's—it's made me more able to love other people. I can love people that are dead that I didn't love properly. Her love for me makes my love transcend time and travel through space. This kid is amazing. You cut a tomato on a plate and she smiles like you've just fucking adopted her from Zimbabwe or something. She's an amazing creature of pure beauty and love—and I regret every single thing that led to her birth. That's how you feel! Cause it's fuckin' hard! (*Live at Carnegie Hall*)

The difficulty of parenthood leads, for Louis, inevitably to boredom and occasional feelings of regret—as well as the potent and transfiguring sort of love he poetically describes. But this ambivalence is not optional: if you have children, you will sometimes wish you hadn't. The difficulty of it all, however, does not justify bad parenting. Despite the boredom you should still spend time with your kids; despite your ambivalence about the value of their very existence, you should still love them— and meet your responsibility to raise them well.

Some Parents Are Okay, Some Parents Are Douchebags

For Louis, at least as he presents himself in his stand-up and television comedy, good parenting really comes down to two basic things: first, you have to do what you can to keep your children safe; second, you have to keep the goal of parenting (and childhood, for that matter) always in mind. From the outset, the first of these two elements of good parenting is quite apparent; in infancy, it is in fact probably the only thing a parent really needs to do. As Louis notes, "It's not a very complicated relationship with a baby. It's just somebody I have to make not die. That's really what the whole thing is. And I'm better at it sometimes than others" (*Shameless*). Admitting on occasion his fatherly foibles does not prevent Louis from presenting himself, in general, as an attentive and protective dad—one who has mastered, more or less, the art of making his kids not die. And as obvious and apparently important as this part of parenting is, he does note that it has not always been the case that parents understand—or choose to enact—their roles as protectors and preservers of their children's lives. He makes this point when comparing the contemporary understanding of parenthood to that of his own mother:

> It's a lot of work having kids, especially now, as opposed to the past. Because in the past, you just had your kids and they just did their thing and you did your thing. That's what it was like for me. I'm amazed at that now. Because I have a five-year old and an eight-year-old, my oldest daughter is eight years old. And when I was eight, my mother, she would go to work and I would go to school. We were like roommates. There was no—so you just go, "See ya later! Maybe I'll have a child when I get home from work, I don't know." I would go to school and then I would just wander around town. And I would do weird shit. (*Live at Carnegie Hall*)

And it's in making this point—that his mother left him to his own devices at a very young age, which was not only unsafe, but also left him free to engage in all sorts of "weird shit"— that we see the transition from the first element of good parenting (making your kids not die) to the second (raising them well).

In contrast to the style of parenting customary (on Louis's view) of his parents' generation, Louis offers a snapshot of his own parental practice:

> But now, my kids, I take them everywhere. I'm responsible for every second of their lives. I'm with them all the time, watching them do their thing. I take them to soccer. "Yeah, you—you're playing soccer right now. I know you're playing—are you done, okay? Let's move, let's go over here. Was that fulfilling, was that strengthening and confidence—?" You have to do everything with them. (*Live at Carnegie Hall*)

Thus, despite the boredom, the frustration, and the ambivalence, a parent must be consistently present in their child's life—and must, present and attentive, make an effort to insure that the child's psychological as well as material needs are met. Pam, Louie's friend/love interest in the series, *Louie*, suggests at one point that Louie is "father of the year" just for showing up, being visible in his daughters' lives (*Louie*, Season One, "So Old/Playdate"). To be sure, this is important—and more than some fathers, including Louie's own, actually do. But this isn't enough.

The new model of parenting, the model upon which Louis bases and judges his own performance as a father, requires not only presence and protection, but also attention—and not just any sort of attention. Too many parents today, he thinks, attend to their children in the wrong ways. Talking to Conan O'Brien about giving cell phones to kids, Louis observed, "Some parents really struggle with, 'All the other kids have the terrible thing so my kid has to'. No. Let your kid go and be a better example to the shitty kids. Just because the other stupid kids have phones doesn't mean, 'Okay, well my kid has to be stupid otherwise she'll feel weird'" (*Conan*, 2013). He makes a similar point on stage, with regard to the choices parents make for their kids:

> I like kids. Parents, I'm not crazy about. Most parents—like, this whole country, our thing is the children. We have to do it all for the children. And meanwhile, nobody gives a shit about how they raise their kids. People put minimal effort into it. They have—their kids, they're like consumers of their kids, like they want to call customer service, "Why does he play videogames all day? I don't understand why he plays

video—" Maybe because you bought him a fuckin' videogame. You idiot! Throw it away! Who told you that was a good idea? A developing mind [*mimics mindlessly playing videogames*] . . . Fuckin' idiots. (*Hilarious*)

The point here is, in part, that parents must find another standard than their children's desires and the social acceptance they will or will not receive from their classmates and peers to guide the decisions they make regarding what their children do or do not do, have or do not have, and ultimately become or do not become. Echoing most classical philosophers on the question of ethics and upbringing, Louis suggests that it matters how you raise your kids—because they will very likely become the people you raise them to be.

The irony, as he noted in the videogames example, is that despite the fact that our children end up doing exactly what we let them or encourage them to do, as parents we end up disappointed they didn't turn out better. "We give them MSG, sugar, and caffeine, and weirdly they react to those chemicals. And so they yell—'Aaagh!' And then we hit them. What fuckin' chance does a kid have?" (*Hilarious*). The temptation to give in to a child's demands, or simply to copy what the other parents are doing—whether out of laziness, boredom, frustration, thoughtlessness, or even genuine ignorance and confusion—is very great. A sort of herd instinct overtakes some parents, inclining them to believe that, so long as everyone else is doing it, it must be all right for the kids, in the end. And the pressure to conform is at least as great on parents as it is on their children, since that pressure comes not only from the other parents but from one's own children, as well.

You're Not Raising the Kid in Front of You

In the conversation Louis had with Conan O'Brien about cell phones, we see something of the parenting philosophy Louis will ultimately espouse coming through. Louis's main argument against giving kids cell phones—despite their obvious appeal to parents as a means of staying in communication with (and keeping tabs on) their children—has to do, not with their safety in the present (in which case he might favor them), but with their development into adult human beings.

You know, I think these things are toxic, especially for kids. It's just this thing [*mimics texting*]. It's bad. And they don't look at people when they talk to them, and they don't build empathy. You know, kids are mean. And it's because they're trying it out. They look at a kid, and they go, "You're fat." And then they see the kid's face scrunch up, and they go, "Oh, that doesn't feel good to make a person do that." But they've got to start with doing the mean thing. But when they write, "You're fat," then they just go, "Mmm, that was fun. I like that." . . . The thing is, you need to build the ability to just be yourself and not be doing something. That's what the phones are taking away. It's the ability to just sit there, like this. That's being a person, right? (*Conan*, 2013)

Good parenting (as we've already seen) involves both attending to your child and keeping that child safe. While it is perhaps arguable whether having a cell phone might keep your child safer than not, and despite the fact that this is a widespread perception among parents in this country, Louis rejects the potential increase in safety for what he takes to be a much larger gain in maturity and development. Without cell phones, his daughters are less able to contact their father when they need him—but they are more able to become real, authentic, adult human persons.

We see this trade-off again in a more recent interview, wherein Louis explains how he tries to prevent his children from becoming spoiled in spite of his rather substantial wealth.

I really try to be aware of not letting them grow up weird or spoiled, which is easier to do here [*in New York*] than it is in L.A. My thirteen-year old daughter leaves the house at 7:15 every morning and takes a smelly city bus to school way uptown. It's like eight degrees out, and it's dark and she's got this morning face and I send her out there to take a bus. Meanwhile, my driver is sitting in a toasty Mercedes that's going to take me to work once both kids are gone. I could send her in the Mercedes and then have it come back to get me, but I can't have my kid doing that. I can't do that to her. Me? I earned that fucking Mercedes. You better fucking believe it. ("Crabby, Epic Love Letter")

Again, here, we see Louis weighing safety and comfort, on the one hand, against a certain sort of upbringing on the other.

And this cuts right to the heart of the philosophy of parenting—and of childhood—implicit in the thinking and comedy of Louis. Although the thirteen-year-old girl waking up at 7:15 in the morning would, in some very real sense, be much better served by a ride in the Mercedes, the adult she will become someday would not be. "When you're raising kids," Louis reminds us, "you're not raising the kid in front of you, you're raising that grownup that they're going to be later" (*Live at the Beacon Theater*). This insight into the job of the parent is rooted in Louis's understanding of the nature of the child as essentially in flux, becoming an adult, and it runs throughout his comic and serious statements on children and their parents.

Every parent can understand the mixture of love, sympathy, and frustration that seems characteristic of the mother of "Jizzanthapus," a child who enters his classroom and—rather than putting away his own things—just throws his things on the floor and leaves it to his mother to pick them up and put them away. Louis notes that the reason the kids are asked to put away their own things is to help them to learn to manage the material world maturely, taking care of their own belongings and avoiding creating unnecessary messes for others. We might see even more deeply that these lessons derive ultimately from a learned respect for the rights of different people to inhabit the same spaces without causing each other unnecessary harm—and thus need not be surprised by how quickly Louis reaches what seems at first like an extreme conclusion: "I hate his mother. Because you hate a weak parent when you're a parent. Because it's like you're raising Hitler, motherfucker! Do your job. Get in there!" (*Live at the Beacon Theater*). The line from Jizzanthapus to Hitler runs directly through his mother's decision to choose to treat her child as *nothing more than* a child, rather than raise him with the adult he will someday become in mind.

Another instance where we see Louis's parenting philosophy playing out in an especially sophisticated (if comically crude) way is in his reprise of the discussion—this time in his FX series, *Louie*—of talking to children in an angry, berating manner. Recall that, earlier, in the set-up for the "Pig Newtons" anecdote, he noted that, when you end up in this sort of argument with a three-year-old, it's *your* fault. The three-year-old is just being a three-year-old. Left at that, of course, Louis would seem to be promoting the same bad parenting philosophy he sees in Jizzanthapus's mother: treating his child like she's nothing more than the three-year-old she is.

Yet we see that Louis's understanding is deeper than this when he returns to the same sort of situation, two years later:

> I was talking to my daughter the other day, and I was talking to her like this [*demonstrates angry bent-over berating*], so I was bent over, and I was talking like *this*. I have no idea what I was talking about. I think I even forgot while I was saying it. I just was upset, and I was talking to her like this, and she's looking up at me with this face like coping, like looking at me like, "I, uh, . . ." And I realize, I'm her first asshole. Like, I'm the first one. (*Louie*, Season Three, "Telling Jokes/Set-Up")

Here, the same scenario—forty-something father berating a young child—becomes the opportunity for the father to realize something important about his daughter. She will not always be this young. And although it's normal for parents and children to mature out of such antagonisms, the impression left on the child's mind by her father being an asshole will last much longer than even the memory of the argument will. By being an asshole to his daughter, Louis helps his daughter along the way to becoming the kind of woman, in the future, who attracts and is attracted to assholes. No father can just be an asshole to his daughter; in being an asshole now, he is always also becoming his daughter's *first* asshole—the first in a line of assholes that in some important sense owes its very existence to that first one, her father.

No parent can prevent all harm from coming to his or her children. Every parent is alternatively bored and frustrated by his or her children, and sometimes ambivalent about having become a parent at all. Given these facts, every parent makes mistakes that inevitably make things worse rather than better for their children.

You cannot parent without at least sometimes, at least in small ways, making your children's lives worse. But that harm need not be so devastating as to ruin those children's lives. The difference between succeeding and failing as a parent, between good and bad parenting, is not the difference between protecting or failing to protect your children from harm. Rather, for Louis, the difference lies in recognizing that children are not simply children.

Adults are more or less everything they are ever going to be. But children are in a constant state of becoming something else, something more, some as-yet-to-be-determined adult. Understood in this way, children are not simply there to be protected, coddled, and enjoyed. The parent's job is not only to do those things, but most importantly, to help to determine the adult they are going to become—to prevent their own Jizzanthapusses from becoming Hitlers. And to try to understand childhood—and thus parenthood—well enough to deal with the assholes their children will sometimes inevitably be, while preventing themselves from becoming the first in a long line of assholes with whom their children have to deal.

If we can do that—protect them now without losing sight of how we are shaping what they will become in the future—then it might just be possible to give our kids a better fuckin' chance.

IV

That Knowledge
that It's All
for Nothing and
You're Alone

10
On "Crying Like a Bitch"

ROBERTO SIRVENT AND JOEL AVERY

> Wherever there is life there is contradiction, and wherever there is contradiction the comical is present.
>
> —SØREN KIERKEGAARD

It's hard to watch Louis C.K.'s standup without thinking of the Danish philosopher Søren Kierkegaard (1813–1855), who was pretty funny in his own right.

Imagine the sad Dane on stage in a dank Copenhagen nightclub delivering one-liners like: "People demand freedom of speech as a compensation for the freedom of thought which they seldom use." Or consider Kierkegaard organizing a routine around the notion that people would sin less if they stopped going to church. He actually wrote that as part of his notoriously scathing critique of the Danish church. Can't you hear Louis saying the exact same thing?

Perhaps there's no big distinction between philosophy and comedy, at least when they're performed by people like Kierkegaard and Louis. These wise sages don't just want us to *think* about life. They want us to live it. *They want us to do something*. Kierkegaard's main criticism of Hegelian philosophy, which was a dominant school of thought in his day, was that it was too abstract and didn't deal with the actual lived existence of human beings. Kierkegaard grew tremendously frustrated by this. He noticed a huge gap between philosophizing and existing, between thinking and doing.

As "Louie," Louis C.K. expresses some of the same frustrations, though he doesn't explicitly attack philosophical discourse

—you never hear him say, "Why couldn't Hegel get his fucking act together?"—he goes after sitcoms. And he does this by creating a show that looks like a sitcom at first. He even copies the Seinfeld pattern of opening and closing with stand-up. But once we start watching, we realize this isn't a typical sitcom. In "Oh Louie / Tickets," Louie has a role in a TV show where he's supposed to play an inconsiderate lout who constantly ignores his wife's pleas that he use a bottle-opener to open his beer. What's the gag, you ask? The gag is supposed to be that the husband is such a lovable asshole that the wife responds to his sickish behavior with "Oh Louie, I love you!" Louie wants no part of this sitcom trope. This is not the way he wants to do comedy. So he suggests that what should happen instead is that "she leaves and he has to deal with his shit."

Like Louis, Kierkegaard used pseudonyms in his work. There's a philosophical point to this strategy. The point in examining their works isn't to tease out what Louis and Kierkegaard really think so much as to ask what we, the readers, the viewers, are going to *do* as we confront their stories. This philosophy sweats and farts and has awkward sex because this philosophy is lived in real, messy, human bodies.

A Walking Contradiction

"We live on the edge of existence and nothing, and we have no respect for that." Louie makes this observation in "Bummer / Blueberries," but we'd be forgiven for thinking that he was quoting Kierkegaard. According to Kierkegaard, we're caught in the contradiction of treating life seriously on the one hand while recognizing the humor of all of the contradictions we must live with as human beings. Human existence is made up of extreme opposites. The tensions between body and soul, time and eternity, possibility and necessity, and finitude and freedom, consumed Kierkegaard's thoughts and occupy much of his writing. If you ever read his work, you'll probably accuse him of being all over the place. This is no accident. That's humanity for you in a nutshell.

Of course, "Louie" illustrates these tensions in less genteel ways than the upper-class Dane did. But we think Kierkegaard would have laughed along with us watching "Subway / Pamela," where Louie struggles to listen to a brilliant violin solo on a subway platform while an obese and apparently homeless man stands behind the violinist and strips down to take an impromptu shower with a water bottle. We already know what Louie has said about looking out for one another, so he's not simply irritated by the fact that this man's ugly body is distracting him from fully appreciating this beautiful music (though there is that, of course!). "Louie" doesn't present us with some moralistic main character. Far from it. Instead, we notice another tension in this scene. What Louie can't reconcile is that he lives in a society that produces so much beauty, and yet leaves so many of its people behind. This scene captures something of the irony we encounter daily which begs for a greater response.

Louie doesn't just encounter contradictions in the world around him. He embodies them. Louie is constantly talking about the body. *His* body. His farts, his fat, his age. He is constantly talking about jerking off. Constantly. And the rest of the time, Louie is picking up his kids from school, talking to them about racism, and protecting them from thugs. So we face the contradiction of the good father who makes his living telling dirty jokes. Louie is a walking contradiction. As are we.

Funny Because It's True

Kierkegaard believed that existential suffering and anxiety exist because of the contradictions we encounter in life. Our lives are played out in these contradictions. For Kierkegaard, the comic is present in incongruity. Louie constantly ushers us into encounters that show us life's comedy. So how are we to react to the absurdity we encounter? Laughter is a good start. The stand-up comic, by making us laugh, can draw our attention to the contradictions of life and their attendant suffering. Of course, laughter isn't enough. Many of these contradictions are serious, causing genuine suffering, and require more of a response.

But where do we draw the line between the comic and the obscene? Are we allowed to laugh at tragedy? We love to watch people falling down stairs or slipping on ice. But what happens when a madman runs in front of a garbage truck and is decapitated, as we see in "Bummer / Blueberries"? And can you imagine a greater incongruity than the title of this episode? Is this some kind of cruel joke? But if we look closer, we see Louis C.K.'s comedic genius at work.

Let's look at this scene in its proper context. Louie is on his way to a date. And it's with an actress who sees this date as potentially beneficial to her career ("He could be something at some point."). Prior to the horrific accident, we might suspect Louie of trying to play the date in just as calculating a manner, hoping to get laid. One less night jerking off. (Who are we kidding?). But after watching the garbage truck tragedy unfold, Louie is unable to simply skate along the surface of life, ignoring its depths. Dropping all pretenses, he opens up to his date. "I'm sick of this bullshit life," he says. Does this mean Louie will finally do something?

This Bullshit Life

Kierkegaard wrote about the various ways that we respond to the suffering which contradiction brings. He termed the lowest response as that of the aesthete. The aesthete's whole existence is focused on avoiding pain. To avoid suffering and maximize pleasure, the aesthete seeks instant gratification. This means living in constant turmoil. In a world fraught with contradiction, suffering is a constant threat, driving the aesthete to make all sorts of attempts to escape to a fantasy world where there is no risk or vulnerability. Of course, this escape is not possible. Eternal happiness cannot be found without confronting and living with suffering. The aesthete knows this, but remains stuck in a cycle of trying to escape it.

In "Moving," Louie exemplifies the aesthete's vain pursuit. Deciding that he and his girls need to move, he finds himself seduced by a townhouse he could never afford. He's blind to the absurdity of his dream, unable to hear his accountant's voice of reason, and becomes pathetic in his conversation with the realtor. In his fantasy, Louie is convinced that "buying this house would fix everything." Where's the irony, you ask? In his attempts to flee his problems in pursuit of an ideal life, he flees meaningful engagement with his actual life. As his friend Pamela puts it, "You're so afraid of life that you're boring." Louie knows she's right. In his standup routine at the end of the episode he admits, "I only have courage for a perfect life." Irony all the way down.

Thinking Too Much and Too Little

Let's take a closer look at the 'aesthetic' way of life. Kierkegaard spends much of his writing portraying and evaluating different ways of life, or spheres of existence. It's hard to watch Louie and not think immediately of Kierkegaard's first sphere of existence: the aesthetic life. What does it mean to live the aesthetic life? There are two actual 'types' of aesthetes.

The first type of aesthete lives for the moment and tries to satisfy as many desires as possible. All that matters to this person is immediate gratification. He takes no time reflecting on his desires, no matter how childish or selfish they might be. This person also tends to get lost in the crowd. He is simply doing what everyone else is doing. He therefore looks to the outside to ground his identity. There is no distinction between the person's *environment* and his *self.* The self is merely doing what his environment tells him to do. So there is no freedom. This type of aesthete is a slave to his desires and to his environment. He doesn't think about either. He just follows them. He does as he's told.

The second type of aesthete doesn't reflect too little but too much. He's constantly dwelling on the past and fantasizing about the future. He's not fully present. By thinking in this way, he loses touch with what is *real* and what is *there*. By constantly fantasizing, he deprives himself of making any real-life commitments. He's not pursuing anything other than his thoughts. He's only *thinking* about stuff. The goal of life, according to this aesthete, is to constantly think, deliberate, and fantasize. Kierkegaard challenges the aesthete with the following: So what if your brain is constantly active if you're not taking any steps to actually *do something*? This second type of aesthete is no freer than the first type. The irony is that in seeking freedom in so many possibilities ("I can have vanilla, strawberry, chocolate, or mint chocolate chip") he is now *unfree*, unable to make a decision.

The life of the aesthete (both types) is captured brilliantly in the episode "Something Is Wrong." Louie wants to break up with his girlfriend, but he just can't bring himself to do it. "What's on your mind?" she asks innocently. "Nothing, there's nothing," Louie replies. But of course there *is* something on his mind. There's *a lot* on his mind. He wants to break up with her.

Or does he? He doesn't want to commit to her, but he also doesn't want to commit to breaking up with her. He's fine just thinking about both options. But he doesn't want to commit to either. Each possibility requires an action. It requires that he *do* something. So instead, Louie just thinks and thinks and avoids making a choice. His girlfriend calls him out on it: "You're doing your mouth thing. You're trying not to say something." If we're going to be perfectly honest, it's not that Louie's not trying to *say* something. He's trying not to *do* something.

After initiating a guessing game to read Louie's mind, she finally finds out that he wants to break up with her. Louie maintains his passive-aggressive streak and essentially makes his girlfriend break up with herself. She can't believe he's putting her in that position. And in an attempt to try to make it easier for him, she says he can just sit there and stay silent for seventeen seconds if he wants to break up. It doesn't get more passive than this. After seventeen seconds, she gets up and says, "Here, why don't you eat this salad when you're done with your ice cream." In other words, let me know when you're ready to be an adult. Let me know when you grow a pair.

That's Louie the "overthinking / I don't want to make a decision" aesthete. Now it's time for Louie the "immediate gratification/seize the day/no reflection needed" aesthete to step to the plate. After seeing his car demolished for violating some impossible-to-understand parking signs, Louie happens to walk by a motorcycle shop. Like a child eyeing the newest remote-controlled racecar at Toys "R" Us, Louie sets his sights on buying some new wheels. Of course, Louie doesn't really *think* about whether this is a wise choice. He's overcome by his childish whims, and no reason or reflection will get in his way. Sure, it may *seem* like he's putting some thought into it. But he's really not. The salesman shows Louie all his scars, which at first appears to turn off Louie. "That's crazy," he says. "I've got kids."

"But how much is it?" he asks. Louie pauses, pretending to weigh the pros and cons in his head when his immediate desires have already made up his mind for him. Then, when he's told he can park it anywhere, he's immediately convinced. This is the selling point. When Louie woke up that morning, he had no special desire for something he could park anywhere he wanted. But because of recent events, he can't help but have that desire. And he can't help but be overtaken by that desire. "So it's actually smart to buy a motorcycle," Louie concludes. Sure enough, he buys it, gets in an accident, and finds himself in an emergency room getting scolded by his doctor. "You know there's nothing dumber than riding a motorcycle," the doctor says. "It's just stupid."

Something Is Wrong

We see Louie wearing *both* aesthetic hats in the final scene where his now ex-girlfriend helps him get situated back at home after his accident. In a time of rare vulnerability he asks her to stay, but his girlfriend tries to call him out of this destructive and paralyzing sphere of existence (the aesthetic life). "Do you realize that you might be wasting four years of both of our lives because you can't say, ''Bye, see you?' right now because in this second that feels weird?" Louie here is driven with his immediate urge—wanting someone to make him feel less lonely—and he is not able to see past this. He cannot foresee any long-term consequences. He cannot reflect past his immediate needs and desires. The *here* and the *now*.

Paradoxically, Louie also suffers from *too much thinking*. He still can't get himself to break up with his girlfriend. He's paralyzed in thought. Seeing this, she begs him to just *do* it. Make a call, Louie. In all of this, it is Louie's girlfriend who helps us see what life looks like outside of the aesthetic sphere of existence. Not only does she foresee the long-term implications of staying together, knowing full well that it will sting in the short-term. She's also able to make the breakup happen. She actually does something.

We can imagine Kierkegaard watching this episode (appropriately titled, "Something Is Wrong") and thinking to himself, "Yes, indeed. Something *is* wrong." But what exactly is it? According to Kierkegaard, it's Louie's lack of choice. The problem with both types of 'aesthete' is that they both avoid making a decision. There's no real choice made by either. One is a slave to his desires or to what everyone else is doing. The other thinks but never acts. The first is a child that never seems to grow up. The second doesn't realize that a mature person takes active steps to form his self in the choices he makes. This is why Louie looks so much like a child in this episode. He doesn't want to make a choice for himself, which is why he feels so relieved when his girlfriend makes it for him. But Kierkegaard asks us to follow *our* choices, not those of others and not those of our petty childish desires.

The closest Louie gets to making an actual choice comes at the very beginning of the episode. Here, Louie and another man stare puzzled at the impossible-to-understand parking signs placed next to their cars. They stand there for a while until Louie gives up. He's done overthinking it. He doesn't know whether he can park there or not, so he makes a decision. "I gotta go," Louie says, while the other man sticks around deliberating about what the signs mean, putting off any decision he might have to make. Move his car, be late for an appointment. Leave his car, risk getting towed. Decisions, decisions, decisions. Here, the other guy plays the role of the overthinking aesthete, paralyzed with possibility, not making a decision. Louie, on the other hand, makes a decision and risks the consequences. Here is what it means to choose. Yes, Louie pays the consequence—his car is demolished—but at least he made a choice. In doing so, he shows a glimpse of what it means to push forward out of the aesthetic way of life. Embrace risk. Make a choice. Do something.

To Be or Not to Be . . . a Famous Glamour Monkey

For Kierkegaard, the ironist is always aware of and pointing out how difficult it is to be a human being. The joke is always found looking at the gap between the inner (your self-image) and the outer (your actual behavior). This contradiction comes out in "Eddie" when a long lost comedy buddy pays Louie a visit. Eddie is at the bitter end of a frustrating career and life, intent on drinking himself to death. In one of his rants, he zeros in on Louie's modest success and accuses him of selling out. This doesn't jive with Louie's sense of himself as a comic struggling to string tours together to support his family. And it runs counter to Louie's sense that even if his life is shit, at least he's telling the truth about it.

Eddie challenges Louie: "I just thought we do this shit to get off and find truth, not to become famous glamour monkeys!" In

Eddie's vision, Louie is the glamour monkey and Eddie is still pursuing the truth (which has taken a nihilist turn for him). Eddie is hard to be around because he is constantly calling people out, telling the "truth" of their inadequacies, delusions, and so on. But Eddie can't do more than that, and in this regard, he plays Hegel to Louie's Kierkegaard. Eddie's truths are abstract. They don't connect with the lives of the people he's criticizing, or offer them anything more than the criticism. There's nothing to be done in response to Eddie's shtick. And Louie calls him out on it.

Kierkegaard and Louie C.K.'s comic genius lies in pointing out incongruities and contradictions. This is what they're looking for. But the ultimate point is *doing something*: finding a way to live in the incongruity and contradiction of human experience, living a life of responsibility and trueness to one's self in a world fraught with risk, vulnerability, and suffering. For both of them suffering cannot and should not be avoided, if only because it allows us to be fully human.

Everything's Not Okay . . . and That's Okay

This is the difference between irony and comedy for Kierkegaard. Irony spots the problem—the suffering that's part of being human. But it stops there. Comedy, however, recognizes the *implications* of this guilt, anxiety, and suffering. Irony tells us that contradictions exist; comedy tells us that these contradictions aren't going anywhere. They're here to stay. They're permanent. They're what make us human. Denying the contradictions of human existence is itself a contradiction, as we saw in Louie's absurd pursuit of his dream home.

"The more one suffers, the more sense, I believe, one gains for the comic," Kierkegaard once wrote. But Louis may have said it even better in an interview with Conan O'Brien. "I cried like a bitch," Louis admits, describing the overwhelming sadness and emptiness he felt by listening to Bruce Springsteen.

> I cried so much, but it was beautiful, it was poetic, you're lucky to live sad moments. And then I had happy feelings because when you let yourself feel sad, your body has antibodies, it has happiness that comes rushing in to meet the sadness. So I was grateful to feel sad, and then I met it with true, profound happiness.

11
Louis C.K.'s No-Bullshit Philosophy

Marie Snyder

> Underneath everything in your life there's that thing: That forever empty . . . That knowledge that it's all for nothing, and you're alone. It's down there. And sometimes when things clear away . . . it starts to visit on you: this sadness. Life is tremendously sad.
>
> —Louis C.K.

On an episode of *Conan*, Louis C.K. described pulling over his car and crying—"like a *bitch*"—triggered only by Bruce Springsteen's "Jungleland" playing on the radio. He told Conan about the poetry of sadness hitting us like a truck: "You're *lucky* to live sad moments!" Conan's original question had actually been about cell phones though, so Louis went on to explain why one hundred percent of people text and drive:

> People are willing to risk taking a life and ruining their own because they don't want to be alone for *a second* because it's so hard. . . . Because we don't want that first bit of sad, we push it away. You never feel completely sad or completely happy. You feel kinda satisfied with your product, and then you die. You need to build an ability to just be yourself and not be doin' something. That's what the phones are taking away is the ability to just sit there. Like this. That's being a person.

What Louis is describing can be used to understand the existentialist ideas of Jean-Paul Sartre. Existentialism gets a bad rap as a depressing free-for-all because it encourages these very feelings of angst to rise up within us, and it suggests we make our own decisions about morality. We might picture the

131

existentialist as a rare species, members found wearing all black, looking glum, and carrying around copies of *Nausea* to show off the extent of their internal suffering. But existentialism, especially through Louis's warped sense of humor, can be incredibly freeing. If we can acknowledge our aloneness in this meaningless life without distracting ourselves from the sadness, then we can begin to live authentically: honestly seeing who we are, our choices, and our responsibilities to the world.

That Forever Empty Thing

For there disappears with God all possibility of finding values in an intelligible heaven. . . . We are left alone, without excuse. . . . condemned to be free.

—JEAN-PAUL SARTRE, "Existentialism Is a Humanism"

Sartre might not sound like much of an optimist at this point but it's early yet. Sartre is one example of an atheist existentialist. There are Christian existentialists who find all the answers in God, but the atheists think that's a cop-out. Louis does claim to believe that *maybe* there's a God but that there's definitely no heaven, so he might still be in Sartre's good books. Without that heaven, without the final *judgment* of God, according to Sartre, we're left to determine our own values as individuals. We've been thrown here onto this earth without any idea of what we're actually *for*, and now we have to figure out meaning for ourselves all by ourselves.

It's no wonder we push this aloneness away by grabbing for our phones to text "Hi!" to fifty people. A horrible feeling of anxiety can settle in when we recognize we've been abandoned to our own devices. It might be no coincidence that both Louis and Sartre were raised without a father in the home. Maybe they're more aware of that sense of abandonment and more willing to get into it more deeply than the rest of us cowards.

We also push away our aloneness by attempting to hook up with somebody. *Anybody.* But Louis tells us the problem with that in *Live in Portland*.

Everyone wants to find somebody; everyone who's alone. But you're alone *anyway*. You're alone. You're alone in the darkness. Even if you're with someone, you're alone. And you should be okay with being alone; otherwise you'll drive them away. But that's a different conversation.

This isn't an argument for being single; it's a concern about a misguided belief that companionship can stave off aloneness. Louis recognizes that, even if we're joined at the hip to the love of our life finishing one another's sentences, no matter what we do to distract ourselves from the reality of it, we are still alone with ourselves. Even with the tightest bond, we still have moments when we don't feel completely understood. The path towards figuring out what we're doing here can be approached through exciting debates and discussions among friends and lovers, but the conclusions we come to about ourselves and the world, we necessarily come to alone. We have no other recourse than to accept the human condition as one of profound isolation whether living alone or surrounded by people.

Who're You Calling Absurd?

Life is absurd. We're free to create our own values, and it gives us the willies to be alone in this. It means thinking all the time, and that's really hard. In our search for meaning in our lonely lives, we come up against a world that doesn't care about us.

We want some clarity, but the universe is irrational. We need to find meaning in life, but the world offers us nothing, so we shut down. But to cope with this we need to wake up from living like automatons in the day-to-day grind and see how radically free we really are! Any people who've had that "walking dead" feeling as they run through their day can see the benefit of this way of thinking.

In recognizing this absurd freedom, that it's all for nothing and we're alone, it can be an anguishing experience to derive our own meaning. In *Live at the Comedy Store*, Louis tells us the meaning *he's* found in life as he addresses his two daughters:

> You and your sister don't have kids. I can cover all of this, and then we all die. That's my goal. I want to make enough money that we can just lock the door and eat the food . . . People overthink this life shit. They get all knotted up. (Hipster voice): 'I don't know what to do with my life, like, what I should be. . . . like what should I, like, do, with my, like, life?' (Pointing to his mouth): Just get food and put it in here! Put

food in here! That's IT! . . . It doesn't have to be more complicated. Do it until you're dead.

Every other creature in the world is content to just eat, reproduce, and die. Suddenly we get in the picture, and we expect more. It's hard to consider the possibility that Louis's right—that it's not complicated. Unlike most other animals we can imagine ourselves in the future; we have a sense of time that extends beyond our lives. The time limit on our existence makes us anxious to do something fulfilling, something to complete our journey.

But what? If the other animals are here to serve us, and if there's no God, then what are we supposed to be *serving*? The existentialist answer is to figure it out for yourself. The anguish and the beauty of existentialism is that the meaning we choose to follow is up to us. That's terrifying because what if we can't figure it out or get it wrong? Yet it's also freeing because we get to take a stab at it for ourselves.

Acknowledging that we're born without any purpose and have a limited existence here can sound depressing, but recognizing our mortality and *appreciating* the finite nature of our lives can also shake us awake. We don't have time to waste! It's ironic that knowledge of our impending death is one thing that separates us from most other animals, yet it's something many of us deny. We mourn for other people when they die but in a way that keeps us detached from our own eventual demise. But it's coming, and, according to existentialism, we should drag ourselves out of denial to look at it.

Louis often makes fun of death. In *Live at the Beacon Theatre* he complains about people who want something done with their ashes: "You're dead! I'm not going to run errands for you after you're dead. You don't matter anymore." And later he comes up with an idea to help people who have sexual compulsions by offering up his own dead body for their use: "I want to be the Willie Wonka for perverts."

But Louis also recognizes the importance of discussing death. In *Live at the Comedy Store* he explains how "a dog dying is an opportunity for your kids to deal with death. It's like a dry run for grandma." Even children have to understand how to express their feelings around death. His first encounter with the concept went like this:

> I found out when I was seven that everybody dies. My grandfather told me. He said, 'EVERYBODY DIES!' I wasn't even talking to him. I was just trying to blow out the candles.

Louis makes fun of death, yet he clearly sees that "life is tremendously sad." We have moments that catch us off-guard as we grieve the fact that our lives will end. It'll all be gone. For Sartre, death is just the final stage of life. It's the point when we become what we will be without any further potential. Because there is an ending, the choices we make take on a greater significance. Each choice could be our very last, and how we are just before we die is how we are. Period.

At death we become just a collection of facts, a thing that might live in people's memories and only as accurately as their interpretations of us recall. When we ignore this fact of our lives and lie to ourselves about our own mortality, then, according to Sartre, we're not being *authentic*, a pivotal existentialist idea we'll get to next.

Sitting There Being a Person

Because exploring the sad bits about life is all a little upsetting, we distract ourselves from any sign that we're about to recognize our own mortality or our own aloneness in the world. And nothing's a better distractor than stuff. We fill our lives with the next new thing so we can think about how bright and shiny it is rather than despair over the shortness of life. Who wouldn't?

Yet in *Hilarious*, Louis explains that our outrageous sense of entitlement and our obsessive consumerism are making us deeply unhappy. We've "created such a high bar of stimuli that nothing can compete anymore." We get a sense of emptiness when we follow the path of shopping and prettifying our lives to impress our friends. We *know* something's missing from these choices. We want more than just to feel "kinda satisfied with your product." Sartre explains:

> Man cannot escape from the sense of complete and profound responsibility. There are many, indeed, who show no such anxiety. But we affirm that they are merely disguising their anguish or are in flight from it. (p. 5)

We might act like it doesn't bother us, but those doubts are there.

Distractions keep us from the angst and anguish that can come with contemplating our "knowledge that it's all for nothing and you're alone," but flight from conscious thought and self-reflection keep us from knowing ourselves too. We can't ever entirely escape the feeling that we're alone and life is too short, but what we *can* do is embrace our reality with greater honesty and live life more fully. To the existentialists, what they call 'living *authentically*' is important as a way of understanding ourselves honestly, of taking responsibility for our choices, and of determining our own morality for ourselves and society.

Living authentically requires honest self-awareness. Most of us fall into two traps: ignoring the facts of our lives to see only an idealized version of ourselves and ignoring the limits to our potential. We lie to ourselves about what we're really like, and we're surprisingly convincing.

Sartre uses an example of an inauthentic waiter being very waiterly: stiff and over-accommodating to the point that he's no longer an authentic self; he's no longer a real person when he's playing at being a waiter. But Louis seems to do a great job of avoiding this trap. In his stand-up acts, Louis gives us a sense that there's a real person on the stage. Now it's entirely possible that he's just really good at playing the part of a comedian *acting* like a real person. As the audience, we can't really know for sure. We have a sense when someone's being *in*authentic, but if they appear authentic, we don't always know if that's really real or not.

But we also get a sense of who we are through the goals we have, our potential. A woman might think of herself as a comedian because she devotes her life to it. But if she's not funny, then 'comedian' isn't part of her identity the way she might like it to be and calling herself one would be inauthentic. We have potential that might *be* us one day, but we also have limits to this potential. Most people can smell inauthenticity in others, but the trick is noticing when we do it *ourselves*. Above all else, we must be ruthlessly honest with ourselves about who we are.

Louis says, "You need to build an ability to just be yourself." To get to the freedom in this absurd situation in which we've been thrown here without a purpose, we have to have the courage to face reality head on, to ignore the distractions when that angst starts to surface, and to honestly admit who we are to ourselves. But that's just *one* piece of living authentically.

Existentialism Is a Free-for-All? No It Very Isn't

Being authentic also involves taking responsibility for every choice we make and recognizing that everything we do *involves* a choice. This is a philosophy that stops our children from blaming us when they forget to do their homework. It stops our partner from blaming us after giving up on that dance career. But it also stops us from blaming any decision we make on an internal compulsion or an external manipulation. We have no excuses for our behavior. None.

If we all lived authentically, we'd never hear claims like, "It's not my fault," "Everyone else is doing it," "I have to look out for me," "What else could I do?," or "I didn't have a choice." And wouldn't that be *lovely*?

More than just avoiding all that annoying whining, living authentically can give us a profound sense of freedom. This philosophy offers a subtle yet significant shift in attitude that changes everything! If a friend drags you to a comedy club, that very phrasing of "being dragged" relinquishes your responsibility over whether you enjoy the evening. It becomes your friend's fault if it sucks and the evening is ruined.

That might *feel* like freedom from responsibility, but there's a *greater* freedom to be had. If you recognize that you made a choice to go with your friend, to relieve your boredom, to make your friend happy, or even because going out is less painful than arguing, then as soon as you acknowledge your choice, you can feel the freedom that comes with *wanting* to be there rather than *having* to be there.

Whatever the reason guiding the choice, living authentically puts you back in the driver's seat of your own life. And honestly acknowledging that you're making a choice can open the door to making different choices. You have an option to say, "No, thanks," and hang up the bloody phone! It might take a while for friends to get used to the new you, but you're worth it.

Sartre goes even further to say that our actions are our way of showing the world what we think is moral:

> When we say that man is responsible for himself, we do not mean that he is responsible only for his own individuality, but that he is responsible for all men . . . in choosing for himself he choose for all men. . . . one ought always to ask oneself what would happen if everyone did as one is doing. (pp. 4–5)

Louis says something similar, in *Beacon Theatre*, when he's discussing a moron cutting across traffic to make an exit. Louis is very clear: "You should act in a way that, if everybody acted that way, things would work out." Nothing can be better for any one of us unless it's better for us all. This is the burden of our authentic freedom.

According to Sartre, we're in this alone, so we have to create our own morality and meaning that dies with us, which is freeing but also anxiety provoking. This anxiety propels us towards distractions as a solution, but the honest solution is living authentically, which means honestly acknowledging who we are, recognizing we make all our choices in life, and being responsible for creating a path for everyone. Louis's comedy fits well with each of these points. Except when it doesn't.

Of Course Authenticity Is Important, Of Course It Is, but Maybe . . .

We're so obsessed with perfection and permanence, a life of lifetime warranties, that we might start to think, "Okay, if I'm going to do this authenticity thing, it's going to be all the time and forever." But we *can't* do it all the time. It's just not possible to remember it while we go about our day. We regularly stop reflecting on things, stop thinking, whenever we immerse ourselves in routines or stuff or gossip. But, to the existentialists, it's important to bring ourselves back to it whenever we can.

"Bad Faith" is a term that refers to any time we're not being authentic: when we're self-deceptive, when we're distracted by the shiny things cluttering up our lives, or when we avoid taking full responsibility for our choices. In bad faith, we make excuses for our words or actions. In authentic existentialism, since everything is permitted, we are left without any excuses, or, as Louis might say, "No bullcrap."

We all fall into bad faith from time to time and have to be re-awakened from our "fallenness," a term used to describe when we believe we're merely being tossed about by life instead of being active agents of it. We falter when we buy cellphones despite knowing how they're made. In *Live in Portland*, Louis berates us because, "People are suffering immeasurably far away so you can leave a mean comment on a YouTube video while you take a shit!"

We've made a choice that we know isn't the right choice because we've allowed ourselves to slip into a denial of our knowledge. We're following the lead of others who are also living in bad faith, instead of thinking for ourselves. And Louis falters right there with us. He recognizes that our morals shift depending on how we feel in the moment, and that they almost *completely* disappear whenever we drive a car, swearing at total strangers in a way we would never do in any other context.

One type of excuse we use is convincing ourselves it's just the way we are. Sartre tells us, "There is no such thing as a cowardly temperament . . . what produces cowardice is the act of giving up or giving way" (p. 12). I think it's safe to say Sartre would hold the same standards for a *horny* temperament. Nowhere do we see Louis's *fallenness* more than when he's talking about sex.

Louis pretends he has no choice when he says his behaviors are due to "a flaw in the human male." In *Live in Portland*, he says:

> If you're a woman and you asked any man on the planet Earth, and say, "Would you just squeeze my tit for a second?", one hundred percent of us will go, "Oh yes, absolutely." Doesn't matter who we are, what we're doing. I could be doing heart surgery, "What? Oh ya. Oooo." We love tits to a fault. Men love tits. We love tits more than we are good people. It's a higher driving force than our morals.

Louis believes that men, by *nature*, stop being good people when provoked by the option of touching a woman's breast. He talks about sexual desire as an unsolvable problem for all men. In *Live at the Beacon Theatre*, he explains,

> Some things I'm sick of, like the constant perverted thoughts. It makes me into an idiot. I'm jacking off to morons. It's a dumb part of life I'm sick of. And it's all day too. It's really a male problem. Women

try to compete: '*Well* I'm *a pervert. You don't know.*' You *get* to have those thoughts. I *have* to have them. You're a *tourist*, I'm a *prisoner* there.

This raises an interesting question about whether or not our thoughts are our choice. But even if thoughts aren't things we choose for ourselves, giving in to them *is* a choice. If it's within our will to act courageously when we don't feel brave then it's within our will to ignore the urge to jack off when we *do* feel aroused. It's in bad faith to suggest otherwise.

Sartre was not moralistic, though: "We can judge . . . that in certain cases choice is founded upon an error or by any man who takes refuge behind the excuse of his passions . . . it is not for me to judge him morally, but I define his self-deception as an error" (p. 16). For Sartre, what we choose is up to us, but we must be honest about being in the driver's seat of all our decisions. There are no good excuses for our behavior, but Sartre understands that we fall back into inauthenticity regularly. It is what it is. As soon as we see we're in a state of fallenness, we can arouse ourselves from this position in order to live authentically again. Until the next time.

There's a Whole Spectrum of Responsibility Out Here

Louis shows us another piece of Sartre's theory when he talks about sex. According to Sartre, even falling in love is a choice. We might feel excited being with a person, but that's not love; it's just a feeling of excitement. Then we make a choice around how to act given that this feeling exists. But we don't choose by chance. We want people around us who see us in the way we want to be seen: people who really *get* us. That "getting us" is yet another way we understand ourselves. Relationships aren't about having someone who keeps us company because we're all alone in this anyway. They're about helping us figure out who we are.

Alone, we can only really know ourselves to an extent. We need other people to show ourselves to us. In reflecting us back to ourselves, like a mirror, we more clearly see who we really are. But some mirrors distort our image, and others have bad lighting that makes us look ghastly, so we toss them aside. It's important to our sense of self to have intimate relationships with people who get us. But then we change, and our opinions of each other change, so we're constantly adjusting the lighting to provoke the judgment we want from the other.

In doing this dance, we ride a line between possessing the other and trying to avoid completely controlling them. We play push-me, pull-me. We want the other to love us freely not because they promised they would, but not too freely that they'll leave. That can be a tricky balancing act. And it's so vital because without that connection, we lose a chance to understand ourselves better. Sartre famously rode the line by maintaining an open relationship with another existentialist, Simone de Beauvoir, that allowed him to be reflected by more people yet keep that deeper reflection at home.

People debate whether Sartre is being realistic or pessimistic here. I really think he's onto something. Do you ever get a little excited (yet nervous) to see what follows the words, "You know what *you're* like?" For better or worse, we *want* to see how others see us on the off chance we'll be validated by their views. Now, when they give us their honest opinion, we still have a choice to accept it or reject it. It's in bad faith to accept or reject these opinions blindly, without some personal deliberations. We are being authentic only when we look at the opinions of others, consider them against our own examples of ourselves, and are brutally honest with ourselves when rejecting or accepting them based on how well they actually fit with who we are.

Louis shows us that brutal honesty when he accepts a label of "pervert" for so frequently acting on that urge to jack off to morons. He is in bad faith when he insists his acts are not within his control, but he acts authentically in explaining the legitimacy of accepting this pervert identity. Then he gets at a greater concern with the way we connect these days in *Live from Carnegie Hall*:

> Sex has a really weird role in our lives now because sex isn't really about love. It's not even about lust for another person. It's just about cumming. We're just cummers. That's all we care about now. We're so proud of it: 'Look at my hot load of cum!' It's not a *load*. It's a teaspoon at the most. It's a child's dose of Tylenol. Most people, when they have

sex, there's nobody even there. It's just porn now. That's all we do is jack off to porn. That's the whole country's sex life.

This isn't a moralistic position against pornography; it's an existential concern that, for many, sex is less about a struggle towards finding an other who can show us ourselves in a way that fits and more about an act completely empty of connection. Without intimate relationships, we lose an important method of gaining greater self-awareness. We need to turn off the computer and talk to other real people in order to get ourselves reflected back at us if we want to live a fully authentic existence.

Luckily, we're works in progress! There's no way to pin us down, to decide who we actually *are,* until we die. For Sartre, as for Louis C.K., continuing to think about who we are and why we do what we do, whether painful or hilarious, is vital to this process of developing the authentic self and living with absurd freedom during our brief stay here. They both recognize that you need to take the courageous step to feel the sadness of being alone in a meaningless world and then work towards living life authentically: being yourself and taking full responsibility for all your choices with no excuses. You can choose to be distracted by things and feel kinda satisfied with your product, or you can choose to tap into the radical freedom of existentialism. The choice is yours.

12
Confronting the "Forever Empty"

BRANDON POLITE

During his September 19, 2013 appearance on *Conan*, Louis C.K. recalls a particular moment in which he experienced profound sadness. He was driving his car, listening to Bruce Springsteen's "Jungleland," when he was suddenly and unexpectedly struck by what he called the "forever empty," or the knowledge that deep down "it's all for nothing and you're alone." Rather than attempting to ignore this forever-empty feeling, as he says he normally would, Louis made the conscious decision to both welcome and confront it. Because he let himself be sad, he claims that he experienced a moment of "true, profound happiness." Louis concludes from this that we all should respond in a similar manner whenever we feel this sort of sadness. Normally, he says, "because we don't want that first bit of sad, we push it away," which he had first wanted to do by texting people not to feel so alone. But when we push it away, Louis argues, we miss out on the sort of meaningful and worthwhile moments that being more mindful and self-controlled would allow us to have.

These are some pretty heavy and heady ideas for a comedy bit on a late night talk show. The intellectual territory that Louis explores both in this bit and elsewhere was carved out and mapped by existentialist philosophers during the first half of the twentieth century.

Free to Be . . . You and Me

What Louis describes as profound sadness closely parallels how existentialists understand *anxiety*. According to German existentialist philosopher Martin Heidegger, when we're anxious we no longer feel *at home in the world*. Our ordinary mode of being in the world is replaced with a feeling of *alienation* from it. Our concerns and projects lose the meanings and values we ordinarily attribute to them, and, similar to Louis listening to "Jungleland," we're confronted with the possibility of our own deaths and the *nothingness* (or forever emptiness) that is their defining feature. Being aware of the nothingness that surrounds us and lies beneath everything we do, Heidegger thinks, reveals that meaning and value lack an objective foundation. From his perspective, then, Louis was right: every project we undertake, goal we pursue, and concern or care we have will ultimately be all for nothing.

But if value doesn't exist out there in the world, then where does it come from? The absence of an objective source of value, according to French existentialist Jean-Paul Sartre, whose work built upon Heidegger's, means that we possess the *radical freedom* to create it for ourselves. It also means that we're free to create our *selves*. We do not each possess a self prior to or independent from our actions, in Sartre's view; instead, our selves come into being as a result of our choices, especially the roles we choose to adopt and projects we choose to undertake. We choose and thus exist *authentically*, according to Sartre, whenever we commit to our roles and projects both consciously and passionately. This requires taking full responsibility for every action we choose to perform. (With radical freedom comes radical responsibility.)

That we're free to choose what to do and who we are may sound rather uplifting—the stuff of every high-school graduation speech. Yet, Sartre believes that most of us will fail to live authentically most of the time. To be fully authentic *at every moment* would require reviewing our possibilities and committing to one of them and thereby taking responsibility for ourselves. The mental and emotional effort this would demand would be almost impossible to sustain under the best circumstances; however, as nearly all of Louis's work attests to, the world provides us with anything but the best circumstances. It's much easier to give up our freedom and responsibility for ourselves. We do this whenever we thoughtlessly or indifferently accept values, play roles, or pursue goals that others (family, society, religion)—including our past selves—have set for us. Whenever we give up the tasks of value-creation and self-creation in this way, according to Sartre, we live *inauthentically* and act in *bad faith*.

Get Ahold of Your Self!

Louis's immediate reaction to feeling sad was to text a bunch of people. He did this not out of any concern for them or to reaffirm his commitment to them, but solely as a means to escape his own thoughts. Louis claims that anyone who texts while driving is similarly uncomfortable with being alone. People are willing to go so far as "to risk taking a life and ruining their own," he says, "because they don't want to be alone for a second, because it's so hard." Louis believes that we respond in inappropriate ways to being alone, among which he also includes masturbating and overeating, in order to keep the forever-empty feeling at bay. These actions thoughtlessly reproduce culturally specific behaviors designed for just this purpose. From the existentialist perspective, in performing them we deny our radical freedom and thus our standing as self-creators and value-creators. A mode of existence whose central concern is to avoid even a moment's discomfort, which Louis believes our culture promotes, results in a life where, as he puts it, "You're never feel completely sad or completely happy. You feel just kinda satisfied with your products, and then you die." Existentialists would say that such a life is governed by bad faith.

Now, it's not *what* Louis is committed to—namely, to being sad—that matters for his act to count as authentic; rather, it's *that* he is committed to it in the right sort of way: both consciously and passionately. The deep satisfaction he experienced as a result of this commitment indicates why existentialists believe we should strive to be authentic at all times and why doing so would result in a life that's truly worth living. By taking control of himself and choosing his sadness, Louis transformed what would have otherwise been an unpleasant moment into a deeply meaningful and worthwhile one—one that, had he grabbed his phone, he would have missed out on altogether. "I was grateful to feel sad," he says, "and then I met it with true, profound happiness."

Louis says that this happened because our bodies send in happiness "antibodies" to counteract the sadness. This suggests that his happiness was entirely beyond his control—a mere biochemical inevitability. As a result, someone might argue that Louis didn't create meaning from his sadness by means of a conscious choice, which means his experience wouldn't count as authentic from the existentialist perspective. To this objection, Sartre would respond that our emotions are entirely the result of our choices. Even if we don't fully *choose* them, we are *responsible* for them. So long as Louis took responsibility for his original choice to feel sad, which he appears to have done, then his experience can count as authentic.

Whatever the case may be, Louis says that his experience was "such a trip." This is actually a good metaphor for how existentialists view human existence. We come into the world as if thrown into a car that we didn't get to choose from the lot and that's traveling down a road we didn't choose to take. (This imagery captures Sartre's notion of *facticity*: those facts about the world—such as natural laws and our social situation—and our bodies—such as our race, sex, and sexuality—that place constraints on what we're free to do. We can't overcome gravity, for instance; and in many places gay couples can't get married.) Outside of the car, we're surrounded on all sides by a vast, empty abyss. The question our existence forces upon us, then, becomes: Do we act as if the abyss isn't there and follow a route that the world would be all too happy to lay out for us, effectively becoming *passengers* in our own lives? Or, do we instead take control of the wheel and make our own way through the abyss and, in the process, remake it into something worth traveling through?

Taken purely as a metaphor, the second option is clearly more appealing than the first. But if as a result of striving for authenticity you've ended up literally living out of your car and, unlike Louis, can't afford to pull over from time to time and appreciate the ride—loneliness and all—then you might come to view the second option with considerable pessimism. To aim for authenticity is to be constantly mindful of life's absolute pointlessness and the fact that everything you're struggling for will ultimately become nothing upon your death. If you struggle within the abyss for too long without transforming your life into something that you can find value in, then the struggle itself can lose its value and all that remains is emptiness and despair. To reach this point would be to transform yourself into the forever empty: an endless vortex (or *eddy*) capable of sucking the meaning and value out of everything you encounter. This is precisely what appears to have happened to the character Eddie Mack on *Louie*.

Despair

We meet Eddie in the episode that bears his name (Season Two, Episode 9) when he unexpectedly reappears in Louie's life after a twenty-year absence. Eddie and Louie started out doing stand-up comedy together. But when Louie started booking high-profile gigs, like *Letterman*, Eddie accused him of selling out and effectively ended their friendship. "I just thought we'd do this shit to get off and find truth," he tells Louie, "not to become famous glamour monkeys." After the two parted ways, so did their careers, with Louie achieving a level of success that Eddie couldn't reach. Whereas Louie's career led to his relatively stable life in Manhattan, Eddie struggles on the road from one smalltime gig to the next, living out of his car in what he calls the "sewers of America."

The reason for Eddie's reappearance is that he's decided to give up the struggle, not with comedy, but with life. Eddie can no longer find meaning or value in anything, himself least of all. He acts the way he does—antagonizing strangers, railing against water, chastising Louie for not having been a hero on 9/11, and so on—not out of any commitment to the values his words and actions express, but seemingly for no reason at all. He's not even sure why he's come to see Louie. The reason he comes up with is that Louie's the one person he's chosen to say goodbye to before killing himself.

Eddie sees the abyss that underlies the human condition in the way that Louis (the real guy, not the version of himself he plays on *Louie*) claims he did when listening to "Jungleland." But whereas Louis could find or create something of value in that moment, Eddie can't bring himself to try anymore after a life that's fallen well short of his expectations. "That's the worst part," he says, "when the want goes. That's bad. I mean, suffering is one thing, or not having is one thing, but when you just don't care anymore. . . ."

Eddie's choice to commit suicide possesses some of the hallmarks of authenticity: he acknowledges life's ultimate meaninglessness and consciously chooses a response to it. What's missing from his choice, however, is *passion*. It isn't normal for human beings not to care. As Heidegger would say, to be human *is* to care. Eddie's not caring, then, is evidence that he's sick. Eddie also fails to recognize alternative possibilities as genuinely open to him. He's reached the point where he believes that "the only prescription that's gonna improve his life is death."

This is clearly false. He could seek professional help—preferably, from a better doctor than the one who prescribed him suicide pills. There's also nothing to stop him from trying out other careers or pursuits besides stand-up comedy until he finds something worth committing to. Eddie's suggestion that it's too late to make such a change because he's now in his forties reveals his bad faith, since he's denying both his radical freedom and his responsibility for who he is and who he can be.

Rather than seeing it as an invitation to continually re-create himself and his values, therefore, Eddie sees the nothingness his feelings reveal to him merely as a relief from the burdens of existing. On the next season of *Louie*, over the course of the "Late Show" trilogy (Season Three, Episodes 10–12), we watch as Louie struggles against becoming precisely this sort of person.

Avoiding the Eddies

After Louie's terrific appearance on *The Tonight Show*, CBS offers him the opportunity to audition to replace David Letterman, who's stepping down as host of the *Late Show*. At first, Louie isn't sure that he wants to take it. Not only is it something that he can't really see himself doing, but actually landing the role would negatively impact the two most important roles he already plays: father and stand-up comedian.

We know from Season One's finale ("Night Out," Episode 13) that the one thing Louie prides himself most on, apart from masturbating, is being a father. To host the *Late Show*, he would have to give up most of the time he currently devotes to Lilly and Jane, which makes him understandably reluctant to commit himself to the pursuit. But when Louie meets Janet, his ex-wife, at the beginning of Part 2, to explain why he "can't" take the opportunity, she immediately recognizes what he's really after: he wants her to say that he can't give up his time with their daughters because she needs him to do his share. By pointing out that he's trying to shift the responsibility for his choice onto her, rather than accepting it as his own, Janet exposes Louie's bad faith.

As if this weren't bad enough, Janet goes on to suggest that if he doesn't get the job, his twenty years of struggling on the road as a stand-up would have been for nothing. The Chairman of CBS, Lars Tardigan, made the same point when offering him the opportunity in the first place. The only hope that Louie has of pulling himself out of the "rapidly decaying orbit" around which he's "circling failure," Tardigan explains, is if he tries out for and lands the *Late Show*. But as Tardigan makes absolutely clear, Louie's chances of landing the job are slim.

Regardless of how he chooses, then, Louie's career is most likely heading down the drain. He now has to contend with the possibility of sliding into an even more serious form of bad faith than the one he engaged in with Janet. Once his career finally reaches the sewer, Louie could very easily get sucked down into the eddy of nothingness and seek out Eddie's prescription for his own life.

While Tardigan is clearly manipulating Louie to get a cheaper option than twelve-million-dollar "slam dunk" Jerry Seinfeld, it's unclear how much Tardigan's words push Louie to pursue the *Late Show*. Pulling him in the opposite direction is his relative comfort with the moderate success he's achieved in his career. While he's not a major star, Louie possesses a quality that's more valuable to him: *integrity*. As Dane Cook noted near the end of "Oh Louie/Tickets" (Season Two, Episode 7), Louie's earned a reputation as a "comedian's comedian," meaning he devotes himself to his craft and doesn't pander for laughs. Because he bases his material solely on what he and his peers find funny, with little concern for how a mainstream audience might respond to it, Louie performs himself onstage authentically. Earlier in that same episode, we learned that because of this self-conception, Louie once gave up a shot at getting a sitcom to air because it wasn't the "really honest, real show" he'd hoped it would be. Like Eddie, then, Louie strives to "find truth" through comedy.

This same concern appears to underlie Louie's anxieties about replacing Letterman. As Jay Leno explains to him when they talk on the phone, hosting a late-night talk show means performing fourteen minutes of new material every single night. In order to take over the *Late Show*, then, Louie would have to let a team of writers come up with most of his material. He'd also have to adapt the version of himself he plays onstage to cater to the expectations of a mainstream audience. As producer Jack Dall explains to Louie after his first screen test, among other things, he's going to need to lose weight, lose the beard, and put on a suit and tie. But Louie is deeply uncomfortable with reproducing his predecessors and broadening his appeal in order to achieve mainstream success. He's most afraid of losing the version of himself he performs onstage, his *comic persona*, which has afforded him a relatively comfortable life offstage, within a new role that could make him the sort of "famous glamour monkey" that any truth-seeking comedian would loathe. So, although Louie doesn't want to end up like Eddie, he seems unsure whether he wants to become anything else.

Playing with Your Self

In response to Dall's demand that he change how he presents himself onstage to be more appealing to a mainstream audience (that he *doll* himself up, as it were), Louie insists that he's "not gonna become a different person" in order to take over the *Late Show*. Standing up for himself in this way might seem to be what authenticity demands: a passionate re-commitment to himself as the overweight, bearded schlub that he is. (As Louie himself says onstage in Season One, Episode 3: "I'm going to tell you how to have exactly the body that you want. You just have to want a shitty body.") Yet, Louie is effectively refusing his capacity to change by telling Dall that he's not going to do what he knows it would take to achieve the role he's pursuing. This leads us to wonder why he's pursuing it in the first place and, thus, to what extent his pursuit constitutes a genuine choice. If Louie doesn't really want to host the *Late Show*, why doesn't he just stop pursuing it altogether? It's as if he's being compelled by forces beyond his control—whether they're internal or external is unknown—which would mean Louie is still operating with the bad faith Janet exposed before he ever started training with Dall.

From what we see of Louie's training sessions, pretty much all he does is fail. He has poor comic timing, he's awkward on camera, and he can't conduct an interview without making the guest cry. But after Janet brings their daughters over to wish him good luck the night before his test show, something changes in Louie. Lilly and Jane made him a crayon portrait of him on TV, hosting a show called *Daddy Night Live*. At that moment, it appears as if Janet's advice at the restaurant finally sinks in. "Nobody needs a father that much," she said. "The girls need a role model. They need to see you live and succeed."

As he kneels on the floor, overwhelmed by his daughters' gesture, Louie begins to recognize that he has to commit himself to them in a new way. Rather than being their daddy, Louie has to become the sort of person they can look up to: a self-realized, authentic individual whom they can emulate to live meaningful lives. If he can't become this person, regardless of whether he becomes the host of the *Late Show*, he will have failed as a father. Whether it's personal or professional success, Louie has to at least *try* to attain it to become the sort of father he really wants to be. While this will result in him being less present in his daughters' lives, it will be because he has committed himself to them in the right sort of way—unlike his own absent father, who, as we see in "In the Woods Part 2" (Season Four, Episode 12), simply gave up his commitment to Louie altogether.

In order to recommit to his daughters properly, therefore, Louie has to commit to the task of becoming a late-night talk show host. This means he's going to have to adapt his comic persona for a mainstream audience: from the T-shirt and jeans wearing, foul-mouthed truth-seeker to a suit and tie wearing, amiable commentator on the day's events—a role he fully embraces and embodies during his test show. In doing so, he thrives in areas he was formerly reluctant even to try. He commits to weak material—jokes that he probably didn't write himself. "It's a really unique thing to be reading jokes off cards," he says, presumably after one bombed, "because you just see your death in front of you." Despite believing that a joke will end up producing silence (the sound of nothingness), he nevertheless commits to it as fully as one he believes will resonate with the audience. He's also able to deal with vulgar topics in ways that are palatable to a mainstream audience without having to sacrifice the humor. When he admits to guest Susan Sarandon that she was the first person he ever masturbated to, for instance, he simply says that he "had himself a little time" and lets the audience fill in the details. This euphemism is even funnier than had he told her more crudely that he "jerked off" while thinking about her.

In these ways, Louie is able to conform to a mainstream audience's expectations without forfeiting his identity. He accepts his capacity to change (unlike Eddie) and commits to becoming a suitable replacement for Letterman. He pours himself into playing this new role after resisting a final temptation to relapse into bad faith, which Jerry Seinfeld offers him immediately before the taping. Instead, Louie uses Seinfeld's attempt to sink him into despair and throw him off his game as fuel for what could very well have been the single greatest performance of his career.

Laughing into the Abyss

But as Louie finds out soon afterward, he never really had a shot at the job in the first place. Tardigan was merely using him as leverage to negotiate a lower salary for David Letterman's next contract. Despite his obvious disappointment, Louie neither succumbs to despair nor attempts to distract himself from the loss. Instead, in defiance of the fact that everything he's struggled for was all for nothing, Louie directly confronts the source of his loss by heading to the Ed Sullivan Theater, home of the *Late Show with David Letterman*. Then, in an act reminiscent of the real-life Louis as he listened to "Jungleland," Louie transforms the nothingness his loss represents into something worth having struggled for, changing the meaning of his failure to become the new host of the *Late Show* into a form of success he wasn't originally seeking. "I did it! I did it! I did!" he shouts at the building. "Hey, Letterman! I did it! . . . Fuck You!" He's not going to end up like Eddie, as he had feared. Nor did he become the fame-seeking sellout that had threatened his and Eddie's shared commitment to finding truth through comedy. Although he may have lost out on becoming the next Letterman, he now knows he can become whatever Louie he chooses to become so long as he passionately commits himself to the task.

The sense of freedom that comes from this knowledge and the moments of deep satisfaction it makes possible are precisely why existentialist philosophers, such as Heidegger and Sartre, urge us to strive for authenticity in every moment of our lives.[1]

[1] I would like to thank this volume's editor, Mark Ralkowski; my friends, Krista K. Thomason and Aaron Harper; my colleague, Bill Young; my former student, Ruth Amerman; and my wife, Katie Koca Polite, for their various roles in helping me conceive, think through, and write this chapter.

V

Did You Look in the Downstairs Bathroom?

13
Why? Why? Why?

JOEL WALMSLEY

It's a delightful coincidence, as I put the finishing touches to this chapter, that today is *both* UNESCO's "World Philosophy Day" and the UN's "Universal Children's Day."

Children make excellent philosophers because, as Ronnie de Sousa points out, philosophy just *is* the kind of activity that attempts to preserve into adulthood the 'childish' trait of persistent questioning. In a recent interview with the online magazine *Pensées*, de Sousa says:

> . . . a grown-up continues to ask the sort of questions that children ask: "What for? Why? Is it really? How do you know? Why does it matter?" You know, these are all typical philosophical questions that pretty much define the field, and all it is to be a philosopher is to keep asking those questions past the age of four.

Given Louis C.K.'s frequent discussion of his daughters' pronouncements, it's therefore hardly surprising that much of his comedy is regarded as highly "philosophical."

If you're not already familiar with Louis's famous "Why?" routine from the HBO special *One Night Stand*, I highly recommend that you watch the routine for yourself in one of its various online manifestations. I recommend the same thing to my own philosophy students. The point—and the humor—behind the routine is that children are almost *never* satisfied with the answers that parents provide to their questions; attempting to answer all of their why?-questions leads one down a never-ending path (or, as a logician would say, an "infinite regress") of incessant follow-ups.

In this respect, Louis's "Why?" routine connects with a prominent theory in the philosophy of science, and identifies one of its major problems. There's a substantial philosophical literature that takes the why?-question as its starting point; specifically, it is commonplace to regard *explanations* (in both scientific and everyday contexts) as "answers-to-why?-questions."

Louis's routine simultaneously anticipates a potential problem with this account—the infinite regress—together with two potential solutions to that problem. Although we often think that why?-questions should be given "Because"-answers, in some cases—in order to stop a never-ending series of follow-ups—it may be more appropriate to reply with something analogous to Louis's "Shut up and eat your French fries, godammit."

In other cases, as he suggests elsewhere in the same special, there simply may not *be* a "because"-answer; the best way to answer a why?-question is just to say "Why not?" It's quite remarkable that a three-minute "bit" can cover all that ground, but as we'll see, that's testament to the philosophical richness of Louis's standup.

Why "Why"?

In a famous 1948 essay with the forbidding title "Studies in the Logic of Explanation," the philosophers Carl Hempel and Paul Oppenheim jump in at the deep end with a similarly grandiose statement. They say:

> To explain the phenomena of the world in our experience, to answer the question 'why?' rather than only the question 'what?', is one of the foremost objectives of all rational enquiry; and especially, scientific research in its various branches strives to go beyond a mere description of its subject matter by providing an explanation of the phenomena it investigates. (p. 135)

They go on to develop a theory of the logical structure of explanations—an account of how we ought to *answer* why?-questions—that we don't need to go into here. But their idea that explanations are answers to why?-questions has stuck. It's now widely adopted as a useful rule of thumb or operating assumption that guides philosophical theories concerned with the nature of explanation.

But why why?-questions? Hempel and Oppenheim hint at one reason for this focus in the above quotation: it's the emphasis on answering *why*?-questions (rather than merely *what*?-questions) that distinguishes genuine explanations from "mere descriptions." Answering a what?-question (ideally) tells you something about the way the world is. But more often than not, we want more.

Why-questions force us to dig a little deeper—we don't just want to know *that* certain things are the case, we want to *understand* them more thoroughly. And this connection—between why?-questions and genuine understanding—goes all the way back to Aristotle (384–322 B.C.E.). As he puts it in his *Physics* (Book II, Chapter 3):

> our inquiry is for the sake of understanding, and we think that we do not understand a thing until we have acquired the *why* of it.

In other words, putting this all together, the goal of explanation is the generation of understanding, and answering why?-questions is how we achieve that goal.

This is exactly what's going on in the routine with Louis's daughter's persistent questioning. Here are the opening lines of the dialogue:

DAUGHTER: Papa, why can't we go outside?

LOUIS: Well, 'cause it's raining.

DAUGHTER: Why?

LOUIS: Well, water's coming out of the sky.

DAUGHTER: Why?

LOUIS: Because it was in a cloud.

DAUGHTER: Why?

LOUIS: Well . . . clouds form when there's . . . vapor.

DAUGHTER: Why? . . .

As things get going, Louis's daughter already knows *that* she can't go outside, but seeks an explanation for *why* that's the case. And she learns *that* it's raining, but wants to discover *why* the rain has occurred. And she finds out *that* clouds form when there's "vapor," but wishes to understand *why* that general meteorological truth holds. We'll return to this ongoing exchange in due course; it's a long way from being finished! For now, note that in addition to the important and intimate relationship between explanation, why?-questions, and understanding, the opening lines of the dialogue illustrate three further philosophically interesting features.

First, there seem to be two types of why?-question that we can ask. One is to ask for an explanation of why a *particular* thing occurred—when Louis's daughter asks "Why is it raining?" she's asking for an explanation of a specific event or state of affairs. The other is to ask for an explanation of why, in general, certain patterns or regularities can be expected to obtain—when she asks "Why do clouds form when there's vapor?", she's asking something about types of events or the laws of nature that describe them. As it happens, the theory of explanation put forward by Hempel and Oppenheim says that a good explanation should use *both* of these categories of information: to explain something is to show how it follows from the specifics of the situation together with the regularities that govern those specifics—it's raining because *in general* clouds form when there's vapor, and in this case that vapor has caused water to come out of the sky. These different aspects of the logical form of scientific explanation seem to be well-captured in the opening exchanges of the dialogue; Louis has already latched onto something significant in the philosophical literature.

Second, however, it's important to keep in mind that explanation has a practical or pragmatic goal—the generation of understanding—and thus will require different things of the answer depending on the intended audience. The way we answer the why?-questions of a child will be different from the way we answer the why?-questions of a meteorologist on the same subject. Louis's shrugging and uncertain reference to "vapor" seems to indicate that while he's not certain that this is *the* correct explanation, it might be good enough to provide *an* explanation; it might be enough to stop his daughter's barrage of questions if it's sufficient to generate understanding on her part. . . . Except, of course, this doesn't usually work with children (or perhaps, even, with philosophers). As Louis puts it: "A kid never goes 'Oh, thanks, I get it'."

This leads into the most important, third, point both for the humor of the dialogue and for the problem with this philosophical theory of explanation. When we explain something by citing *either* specific states of affairs *or* the general regularities that govern them, we do so by providing answers that are themselves susceptible to further questioning. It's all very well to know that the water is coming out of the sky because it was in a cloud, and it was in a cloud because there was "vapor," but we can always still ask for more. Louis's "Why?" routine suggests that children are particularly well attuned to this fact.

It might seem that this demand for further answers—in this case—is simply due to the peculiar obstinacy displayed by Louis's daughter (and children or philosophers in general) in her incessant questioning. But actually, this is a very general problem that arises once we regard explanations as "answers-to-why?-questions." For any *answer* to a why?-question, one can always ask a *further* why?-question of it. I propose to call this the possibility of an "explanatory regress" in the literal philosophical sense of "a series of statements in which a logical procedure is continually reapplied to its own result without approaching a useful conclusion"; the humour of the "Why?" routine—and Louis's exasperation—stems from observing this explanatory regress unfold.

This Goes on for Hours and Gets so Weird and Abstract

As the dictionary definition suggests, when a regress looms, there seems to be no end in sight. Out of politeness to the audience, Louis leaves the intermediate stages of the explanatory regress unstated, and we re-join the dialogue at a later stage when the why?-questions have become significantly more abstract—so much so, that Louis describes the whole process as an "insane deconstruction." We might certainly regard it as a deconstruction—I will return to this point in a moment—but it's far from insane; in fact, the increasingly abstract *answers* sound remarkably like some of the classics of Ancient Greek philosophy. Here's the continuing dialogue:

DAUGHTER: Why?

LOUIS: Well, because some things are and some things are not.

DAUGHTER: Why?

LOUIS: Well, because things that are not can't be!

DAUGHTER: Why?

LOUIS: Because then nothing wouldn't be! You can't have fucking nothing isn't . . . everything is.

DAUGHTER: Why?

Again, Louis captures something philosophically significant here. We can compare this to Aristotle's definition of *truth* in Book IV, Chapter 7 of his *Metaphysics* (written around 350 B.C.):

> To say of what is that it is not, or of what is not that it is, is false, while to say of what is that it is, and of what is not that it is not, is true.

You can find very similar claims in Plato's dialogues (such as *Sophist* and *Cratylus*, where Socrates says: "Speech which says things as they are is true, and that which says them as they are not is false."). The routine would almost work as well if Louis were to quote Aristotle or Socrates verbatim!

So, these snippets embody two major theories with which philosophers have wrestled over the millennia. The first is sometimes known as the "correspondence theory of truth"—it claims that statements are *true* when they describe the way things actually *are* (they correspond to the facts). Thus, a good explanation is an answer to a why?-question that describes, as Louis puts it, what *is*.

The second is sometimes known as the "Principle of Bivalence" or the "Law of excluded middle"; it's the idea that every sentence has exactly one truth-value—true or false— with nothing in between. Thus, when Louis tells his daughter that some things *are* and some things are *not*, that explanation is supposed to exhaust all the possibilities; it shouldn't leave any room for further questioning about the factual status of the answers.

So the regress of why?-questions is not *insane*; it's at least as sensible as Aristotle and Socrates, and most would agree that's well within the bounds of sanity. But it's certainly a deconstruction; as philosophers know (and Louis's daughter seems to sense), even though the correspondence theory of truth and the law of excluded middle are widely accepted, these general principles might *still* require some justification, no matter how abstract. Given the ever-present possibility of regress, we might still seek explanations of (or justifications *for*) what seem to be the most basic and abstract answers one could possibly give.

The conception of explanations as "answers-to-why?-questions" is thus subject to a deep problem; we can never finish answering all of the (legitimate) follow-up questions to what started out as a seemingly straightforward request for information. So we might ask: if explanations *just are* "answers-to-why?-questions" then does that mean that one can never, fully, explain *anything* in an ultimate way? In one sense, on this conception of explanation, we can never be "done"; or worse, we can never really provide a *full* or *complete* explanation (even if we also discuss the nature of truth or of logic itself). This is why, as Louis points out in his opening remarks to the routine, the parent who says "When I have a child I will answer all of their questions" is sadly mistaken. And although we might think that this impossibility is because children—and philosophers—are particularly mischievous in their continued questioning, it's actually a much more general feature of explanations themselves.

But in fact—and fortunately—despite demonstrating the problem of regress for the conception of explanations as "answers-to-why?-questions," Louis also gives us the resources to identify two ways of *stopping* that regress. That's what I want to talk about next. In some cases, given explanation's practical goal, "Because I said so"—or a more profanity-laden analogue—will suffice to end the onslaught of why?-questions. In other cases, it would be a mistake to think that we're restricted to "because"-answers; sometimes, "Why not?" is the best we can hope for.

Shut Up and Eat Your French Fries!

There are two ways that parents can standardly stop an explanatory regress and end a child's questioning. Louis identifies these, and so we might apply his insights to their equivalents in (philosophy of) science.

In the dialogue, Louis finally 'snaps'; his ultimate, regress-ending answer goes:

DAUGHTER: Why?

LOUIS: Oh fuck you; eat your French fries you little shit, godammit!

Philosophers and scientists don't often express their sentiments in such terms (at least, not out loud), but something analogous may often happen. At some point, we simply *run out* of both specific facts and general regularities to cite in answer to a why?-question; we have to end an explanatory regress with an either "That's just the way it is" or what the philosopher Samuel Alexander describes as a "brute empirical fact . . . to be accepted with the 'natural piety' of the investigator."

Consider an explanatory regress whose penultimate answer is "Because the speed of light is 186,000 miles per second." When the (inevitable?) follow-up "why?"-question comes, the answer is simply "That's just the way the universe is." In other words, although the why?-question can still be *asked*, there is no further answer—the speed of light, in this instance, admits of no further explanation; it is a brute fact that must be accepted with "natural piety" while you shut up and eat your French fries.

The reference to "brute facts" may, of course, be somewhat unsatisfactory—it ends the regress, but not with the kind of answer that the explanation-seeker was anticipating. But it is nonetheless *an* answer—*an* explanation—that, in a sense, generates understanding. The questioner (child or philosopher) has arrived at the point at which they must accept (and understand) that this is just *how things are* and that they must therefore cease questioning. So given the pragmatic goal that I mentioned above, it's this kind of answer that means an explanation can be ultimately "finished." A brute fact (or even a "because I said so") may be enough to end the regress and complete the explanation for all practical purposes.

Why Not?

There is one final way of ending an explanatory regress—one that Louis hints at in the "Why?" routine, and develops elsewhere in the same special—that, in effect, stems from a more subtle consideration of how to answer why?-questions. It's tempting to think that why?-questions always deserve because-answers; indeed that's the route Louis takes in the snippets of the dialogue I quoted above. But that's not the only option. I am reminded here of Christopher Hitchens's moving account of his receipt of a cancer diagnosis in his book *Mortality*. He writes: "To the dumb question 'Why me?' the cosmos barely bothers to return the reply: Why not?" In some cases, there *is* no because-answer to a why?-question; the best we can do is "Why not?"

Earlier on in the "Why?" routine, Louis hints at this kind of answer, albeit with a slightly more nihilistic flavor. When addressing the fact that his ignorance and defective moral compass stem from the lack of guidance he received from his parents, the dialogue goes:

DAUGHTER: Why?

LOUIS: . . . Because *they* had shitty parents. It just keeps going like that.

DAUGHTER: Why?

LOUIS: 'Cause, fuck it, we're alone in the universe and nobody gives a shit about us . . .

Elsewhere in the same *One Night Stand* special, Louis indicates a similar, regress-blocking, strategy for answering why?-questions. He tells a story—as part of the general theme of how much his wife hates him—concerning an incident when he loaded the dishwasher, filled it with detergent, but then forgot to switch it on. His wife demands an explanation: "Well *why* didn't you turn it on?" Louis's response is revealing. He says "Like I have a *reason* for not turning it on . . . Can't I just be stupid . . .?"

These two cases suggest the following conclusion: if we think that explanation-seeking why?-questions always deserve because-answers, we will inevitably be disappointed, for some facts just *don't have* a further reason that explains them.

Many of the most striking scientific results of the twentieth—the Heisenberg uncertainty principle, quantum indeterminacy, chaos theory, Gödel's incompleteness theorem and so on—suggest that there are fundamental limits to what we can know and what we can explain. And these limits are not merely there because of our ignorance; they're basic features of the universe itself. When we ask why?-questions about the phenomena that are constrained by these limits, the *best* we can do is to answer with a "Why not?" And that's the kind of answer that blocks an explanatory regress because it simply doesn't permit yet another comeback.

Thank You Very Much Everybody, Goodnight

It's a kind of irony that I would devote more than three thousand words to discussing a small segment of a stand-up special, one of whose overarching themes concerns the intolerance of verbosity. But it's striking that a three minute "bit" as the closer of a half-hour standup special can simultaneously formulate a philosophical theory, anticipate a major objection to it, and then suggest two ways of overcoming those objections.

But that's testimony both to the genuine philosophical richness of Louis C.K.'s comedy, and to his daughters' exemplification of the philosopher's relentless questioning. At least, that's the explanation that satisfies me; that's just the way things are, and why wouldn't they be? If you don't think it's good enough, you can shut up and eat your French fries.

14
Louis C.K.'s God

SILAS MORGAN AND ROBERTO SIRVENT

I think if there is a God, I don't know if it's the one in the Bible because that's a weird story: he's our father, and we're his children. That's it. "Our Father who art in heaven." Where's our mother? What happened to our mom? What did he do to our mom? Something happened. Somewhere in Heaven there's a porch with a dead lady under it, and I want the story. Somebody's gotta check the trunk of God's car for bleach and rope and fibers.

—LOUIS C.K.

Louis C.K. talks *a lot* about God. But why? Maybe because so many other comedians avoid it. Or maybe because other comedians are so bad at it.

Whatever his reasons, we know a few things about Louie's faith. Although he was raised Catholic, he no longer believes in God. At the same time, he doesn't like referring to himself as an atheist. When he talks about God or religion he treats it like any other subject: he mocks it perversely. But he's also refreshingly sincere and humble. When asked by Terry Gross during an NPR interview about taking up topics like religion, Louis C.K. admits:

The areas I'm going into are touchy. Maybe there's a God; maybe there isn't. Is God divorced? Did God kill his wife? You feel a little sweat on the back of your neck when you get there, but if you stay there for a second, you can find something joyful and funny in it. And it's such a great thing to go to a scary place and laugh. I mean, what's better than that?

Not only is it scary, it gets pretty damn uncomfortable. But so is Louis's comedy. After all, he always finds a way to shame, comfort, and make us laugh at the same time. In that sense, he's a lot like God.

Louis thinks God is hilarious. Well, not quite God exactly, but rather how people think about God. How they talk, what they believe about him, and what they're willing to do in his name. Louis is constantly challenging us to be more honest, more thoughtful, more introspective, and more critical of ourselves. His comedic strategy, if he has one, is to focus on the banal, mundane, and ordinary patterns of life. His comedy is also about pulling the curtain back on modern urban life, all in an effort to expose what he finds to be the dangerous presumptions, beliefs, and practices that often get concealed by good manners and polite tropes. If comedy at its best uncovers the inhumane and broken aspects of our culture, then it's no wonder that Louis finds religion so funny.

Louis is not interested in the typical philosophical arguments against religion. He's not interested in disproving God in five easy steps. Rather, he tries to show that religion leads to what Theodor Adorno (1903–1969) called "damaged human life." It causes people to focus on the wrong things and to treat other people poorly. It misses the key points of its own teaching.

To use philosophical terms, we could say that Louis's critique of religion is both *negativistic* and *immanent*. It is *negativistic* because it addresses the question of how not to believe in God. And it is *immanent* because it critiques faith from a place of faith. That is, despite his apparently anti-faith stance, we find Louis's take on God and religion to be a riff on faith, not a strict departure or disavowal of it.

Overall, Louis's comedic take on God is a complex analysis of vulnerability, shame, and taboo. It is also a case study on deep, penetrating honesty and self-criticism. Louis thinks comedy is one of those places where you can be honest, unfiltered, and truthful about the world—and get away with it. This allows him to take up the question of religion with a transparency and openness unavailable to most public commentators (or priests for that matter). When he talks about God, he does so with almost psychoanalytic interest. Yes, he is bringing to the surface our guilt, trauma, repression, and so on. But he helps us look through the shame towards something more honest and ultimately more human.

God Is Like a Shitty Girlfriend

The first season of *Louie* takes up the question of belief in the episode titled "God." In a flashback to his early childhood years growing up in a Catholic school, Louie takes on the decidedly not-funny subject of Jesus Christ's crucifixion. Christianity teaches that Jesus Christ, the incarnation of God in human form, was tortured and crucified by the Roman imperial forces, a divine act of sacrificial suffering that contributes to human redemption—in this life and the next. Classically known as the doctrine of atonement, it is often thought that human sin made Christ's suffering and death necessary.

The episode picks up with Louie and a friend making light of this story during a theology class. Leaving the Catholic sisters no choice, they bring in a medical expert to impress upon Louie not just the physical nature of Jesus's suffering, but also his responsibility for it as a human sinner. The doctor goes into excruciating detail of the crucifixion. At the end, he settles the point of the whole drama, "Why'd you drive in Jesus's nails with your sins? *You* let him die with your careless, faithless sins." Little Louie is wracked with guilt, shame, and fear. And understandably so. Mission accomplished for the Catholic sisters: Louie is tormented, feeling completely responsible for Jesus's death. It's as if he was the one who ripped the skin off Jesus's back "into ribbons" and nailed him to the cross. It wasn't the Jews or Romans who crucified our Lord. It was Louie!

Louie's mother becomes the story's theological hero. "I did that to him, Mom," Louie cries. In response, Louie's mom insists that not only was her dear son not responsible for Christ's suffering and death, but that she really doesn't believe in this whole atonement thing to begin with. Her Catholicism is of the skeptical variety. She prefers to do away with that stuff about Jesus being God, dying for our sins, and offering eternal life. But she has no problem with Jesus as a moral exemplar. "Jesus was a really, really nice guy, who lived a long time ago," she says. "And he told everyone to love each other, and boy did he get his for that, but you had nothing to do with it!" The conversation continues:

MOM: The whole thing is a bunch of . . . [sigh] malarkey.

LOUIE: Why do you make me go there?

MOM: I thought it was selfish, just because I don't have religion, not to give it to you. It's a big deal, religion, maybe you might want it some day, but if I knew it was going to stress you out so much I would never have done it.

Then, Louie's mom does what any good mom in this situation would do: she takes him to get donuts. Business as usual in Louie's comedic universe. The existential threat raised by religion can easily be neutralized by food. Sunday brunch, anybody?

In relating to the common experience of many children raised in the Catholic church, Louie critiques the practice of using theology to instill fear and guilt in children, all in the name of teaching moral formation. What brought Louie peace and freedom was not the Catholic sisters' certainty, but his mom's honesty. The honesty of faithlessness and skepticism. Louie's point is clear: religion is harmful. It has destructive effects on people. It breaks them down, takes their innocence, and overwhelms them with fear, guilt, and shame.

Or, in the ever-so-honest words of Louis C.K., "God is like a shitty girlfriend." Through an unusually profane reading of the Abraham and Isaac narrative, Louis pictures God drunk-dialing Abraham, daring him to sacrifice Isaac "just for the hell of it." Sure, it is irreverent, but only because it is also funny. After all, who can't relate to the experience of feeling that God acts in pointless, random, and crazy ways? "If there is a God," Louis says, "then that dude is an asshole." Religious or not, who among us has *not* felt this way before?

Aren't these statements about God just a tad bit offensive? Probably, but Louis doesn't care. It's not that he's an asshole, heretic, or the anti-Christ. It's not that he thinks Christians believe in fairy tales. And it's certainly not because he's being disrespectful. In fact, Louis shows a tremendous amount of respect for Christians because he actually tries to *understand* them:

Something I've learned over the years is that when you talk about religion, you want to talk to religious people. Even if you're talking about something that's contrary religiously or provocative, a religious audience is a better audience for that. If you talk to a bunch of cool atheists in leather and suede, you know, sucking on their vape sticks or whatever they're doing, they're not going to get it because they don't even think about God. It's not even on their radar, you know? So they're—but if you tell religious people, I don't know if there's a God, I don't think there's a heaven, where's God's ex-wife, these things, they have a connection to it that means something. (NPR interview, 2014)

This "connection to it" cannot be reduced to some abstract philosophical system. Faith is a way of life, a way of being in the world. This is why Louis says we must talk to religious people if we're going to understand them. If faith were a mere intellectual exercise or checklist of beliefs, then we would only need to read a book or two. But if faith is more than that—if it's a way of living, existing, struggling, and breathing—then it's going to take a bit more work. And it's going to be way messier than going to the library.

Did You Look in the Downstairs Bathroom?

Louie has a complicated take on the relation between atheism and religious belief. In a recent Reddit chat, Louis says that while he is "not an atheist," he "does not believe in God." Louis has been repeatedly critical of atheists, raising important questions about the relationship of faith and doubt in religious thought. During his infamous SNL monologue, he slammed atheists for their arrogant denials of God's existence:

I'm not religious. I don't know if there's a God. That's all I can say, honestly, is "I don't know." Some people think that they know that there isn't. That's a weird thing to think you can know. "Yeah, there's no God." Are you sure? "Yeah, no, there's no God." How do you know? "'Cause I didn't see Him." There's a vast universe! You can see for about a hundred yards—when there's not a building in the way. How could you possibly . . . Did you look *everywhere*? Did you look in the downstairs bathroom? Where did you look so far? "No, I didn't see Him yet." I haven't seen *12 Years a Slave* yet; it doesn't mean it doesn't exist. I'm just waiting until it comes on cable. (*Saturday Night Live*, 2014)

At first glance, Louis's critical understanding of atheism seems to be a bit crude and unfair here. In its most basic sense, atheism rejects the tenets of traditional theism where God is viewed as the *absolute and ultimate being*. This means that God is all-knowing, all-powerful, and all good. He is also completely transcendent, indivisible, independent, immutable (cannot change), impassible (cannot suffer), and timeless (eternal, not subject to the transition of time). According to Louis, though, "atheism" is something else. For him, to claim that "there is no God" is to say "I'll only believe it when I see it!" Louis should know better, since he doesn't represent the atheist argument fairly. After all, there are a lot of things that we haven't seen or experienced directly that we can reasonably say don't exist, like unicorns and flying spaghetti monsters. Plus, not all atheists would say they're one hundred percent certain that God doesn't exist. They only claim that it's more likely than not that he doesn't.

But let's give Louis the benefit of the doubt. *If* atheism is about being absolutely certain that God is not out there somewhere, Louis cannot call himself an atheist. If atheism requires the same level of certainty claimed by some religious believers, then Louis wants nothing to do with it. An atheism that is too sure of itself, too confident in its own lack of belief, is just as problematic as a theism that is equally closed-minded.

Here, Louis charts out what might be called an "ethics of belief." This term originates from discussions in philosophy of knowledge, or epistemology, from the eighteenth century. A predominant position in this debate is called *evidentialism*. The central principle is that one should only *firmly* believe on the basis of "sufficient" evidence. What is considered "sufficient"? We're glad you asked. It means that the evidence you have for believing something is strong enough for the belief to be *justified as knowledge*, if and when deemed to be true. We are therefore ethically obligated to believe or not believe something based on the level or degree of evidence that we have for that belief.

As an evidentialist, Louis says he doesn't believe in God because that is the strongest belief he has *here*, *now*, and *so far*. It's the strongest belief he can have based on the evidence he currently possesses. But Louis can't say for sure. After all, "There's a vast universe! You can see for about a hundred yards—when there's not a building in the way. How could you possibly. . . . Did you look *everywhere*? Did you look in the downstairs bathroom? Where did you look so far?"

God or Gods?

So far, we have focused on how Louis criticizes religion as a system of belief. But if we're going to probe deeper, we have to look at another way that philosophers study religion. A substantivist account of religion examines what we *believe* about God. A functionalist account, on the other hand, examines what we *treat* as God. In other words, we should be less interested in our beliefs than on the objects of our absolute devotion. What are those things that we, in the words of Paul Tillich (1886–1965), treat with "ultimate concern"? Religion, then, is not really about what we *believe* with our *minds*, but with what we *do* with our *bodies*.

Using the example of patriotism, the Roman Catholic theologian William Cavanaugh describes the functionalist account perfectly: "If it walks like a duck and quacks like a duck, it is a duck. If it acts like a religion, it is a religion. If people pledge allegiance to a flag, salute it, ritually raise and lower it and are willing to kill and die for it, it does not much matter if they acknowledge it is only a piece of cloth and not a god."

Louis's comedy consistently reveals our lives' many gods, those things that are not just objects of our devotion but of our worship. This is when he's at his most offensive. After all, we're only offended when someone makes fun of what we consider sacred. Everything is fair game for Louis. Some of us worship our self-image by spending an enormous amount of time and money trying to get that perfect body. Of course, perfection is always beyond our grasp. But that doesn't stop us. Louis offers a perfect antidote to this obsession: "I finally have the body I want. It's easy, actually. You just have to want a really shitty body." Others of us—philosophers included—treat knowledge and wisdom as our ultimate source of meaning. "I wish I could know everything ever," Louis says. "Like that would be my wish." Many philosophers share that wish. But if we're going to be honest, that exhausting pursuit usually leaves us feeling just like Louis: "I'm stupid. I really am stupid," he says. "And it bothers me."

The rest of us just worship *stuff*. This includes the stuff we put into our bodies: "I don't stop eating when I'm full," Louis says. "The meal isn't over when I'm full. It's over when I hate myself." No matter how much we get, it's never enough. The same is true of America's obsession with money, markets, and supermalls. What, you don't believe us? Take Louis's observation about how far our politicians go to promote this gospel. "Even after 9/11, during the darkest moment of our recent history, the President told us, 'Go shopping' . . . That's how we were told to uphold American values," Louis continues. "Go out and fucking buy more shit."

Sure, "God" might be dangerous. But so are our "gods." What's most dangerous is not a God that we might absolutely *believe* in. Rather, it's the thing or things in life that we're absolutely *devoted* to. It's the same point made by one of the greatest philosopher-novelists of our time: David Foster Wallace. In a speech given at Kenyon College, Wallace puts into words what Louis C.K. knows only deep down:

> Because here's something else that's weird but true: in the day-to-day trenches of adult life, there is actually no such thing as atheism. There is no such thing as not worshipping. Everybody worships. The only choice we get is what to worship. And the compelling reason for maybe choosing some sort of god or spiritual-type thing to worship— be it JC or Allah, be it YHWH or the Wiccan Mother Goddess, or the Four Noble Truths, or some inviolable set of ethical principles—is that pretty much anything else you worship will eat you alive. If you worship money and things, if they are where you tap real meaning in life, then you will never have enough, never feel you have enough. It's the truth. Worship your body and beauty and sexual allure and you will always feel ugly . . . Worship power, you will end up feeling weak and afraid, and you will need ever more power over others to numb you to your own fear. Worship your intellect, being seen as smart, you will end up feeling stupid, a fraud, always on the verge of being found out. But the insidious thing about these forms of worship is not that they're evil or sinful, it's that they're unconscious. They are default settings . . . They're the kind of worship you just gradually slip into, day after day, getting more and more selective about what you see and how you measure value without ever being fully aware that that's what you're doing.

If David Foster Wallace is right, it wouldn't be a stretch to say that Louis is involved in a theological project of his own. By pointing out all the pursuits and passions that "eat us alive," we are exposed to both our false hopes and our false gods.

Maybe There's Something There

It feels good to laugh at yourself, doesn't it? Louis's take on religion is philosophically interesting not just because it mocks and critiques, but because it is deeply cathartic. It gives us the opportunity to release fear, trauma, and disappointment. It provides relief from the anxiety we sometimes feel from never being able to talk about these topics openly in the public space of cultural life (or at the dinner table for that matter).

But there's also something deeply cathartic about Catholicism itself. Its commitment to grace, virtue, and hope. Its belief in human freedom, responsibility, and redemption in God's good future. These are only matched by the faith's stubborn refusal to give in to darkness, and its persistent call to live in solidarity with what Ignacio Ellacuría called the "crucified peoples" of history.

Although reflections on faith can easily devolve into simplistic moralism or naïve sentimentality, there is a certain resilience, grit, and, yes, *Catholicism* present in Louis's comedy. In one of his most candid moments, he admits that it's hard to stay away from the "scary" area of religion:

> I just couldn't help straying into these areas. It's a little [mischievous]. I just want to go over there and see if there's anything there. That's just always been my nature. . . . I'm also not afraid of it. I'm not afraid if I go somewhere and I upset everybody. I've been there. I guess I was in trouble a lot when I was a kid, so I got used to it. When you're never in trouble, you can never go to places like that. . . . I know I can survive everybody being pissed off at me. So when I started going onstage, I realized if I talk about this stuff I might upset people in the room, but it's worth it because maybe there's something there. (NPR Interview, 2014)

Here, Louis shows us a distinctly Catholic way of looking at comedy—and philosophy. The Catholic pattern of reflection, judgment, and action derives from the teachings of the founder of the Jesuit order, Ignatius of Loyola (1491–1556). It is meant to do away with any distinction between *private* faith and *public* life. It's meant to help individuals live in the tensions between faith and doubt, belief and skepticism, fear and courage. It's meant to expose us to the challenges, contradictions, and opportunities that come with being human. Even when faced with ugly, uncomfortable, painful realities, the individual is empowered to pay attention—to see what's *really* going on.

This method is instructive for those of us who want desperately to find, see, and touch what is real. A world that is bigger than our philosophical categories and boxes. A world that is neither as beautiful or as grotesque, as clear or as opaque, as straightforward or as confusing as we might think. At its best, Catholic philosophy joins Louis by reminding us that faith is impossible without doubt. Belief requires skepticism.

And religion? Well, religion needs a bit of comedy to make it through the day.

15
God Started in 1983

Matt DeStefano

In late 2014, Louis delivered the opening monologue for *Saturday Night Live*. He began with some innocent banter, but quickly moved on to discussing God and the afterlife with his usual blunt approach. "I think there's no Heaven," Louis said to the audience. "I think there is maybe a God, but no Heaven." While many people think the concepts are nearly interchangeable, it is certainly within the realm of possibility that God could exist without having also created Heaven. Louis continues by imagining a conversation between God and a man who has just arrived in Heaven:

DEAD GUY: Where is Heaven?

GOD: I don't know who is telling people [about] that. I'm supposed to make a universe and then another separate awesome place for afterwards?!

DEAD GUY: Well, where do I go?

GOD: Just stand here in this room with me.

DEAD GUY: This sucks. I don't like it.

GOD: Tell me about it, I've been here since 1983.

This bit marries Louis's absurd comic style with his apathetic views towards God. Imagining God standing in a room for the better part of three decades paints a terrific picture, and even more absurd is imagining that God began punching a timecard in 1983. God as a sort of break room gadfly is not an image that has been popular among philosophers. The questions that have preoccupied philosophers historically are quite different.

Should We Care whether God Exists?

Many people are first drawn to philosophical investigation by thinking about the "Big Questions," such as the meaning of life, God's existence, and the difference between good and evil. Religious practices all over the world reflect the importance that people place on not only believing whether God exists, but trying to discern what this God might be like and what He may want from us.

Belief in God can be life-changing. People will rearrange their diet, make significant sacrifices in their personal lives and for their family, devote hours in prayer and meditation, and dutifully alter their behavior to follow what they believe God's plan for their lives is. This importance placed on God's existence and role in our lives is—to put it mildly—slightly different from imagining God sitting in a room for a few decades.

Louis does not have much to say about whether God actually exists. His honest answer is that he does not know. However, I think his relative silence on the question of whether God exists can be understood by thinking about whether Louis thinks the question matters at all. My interpretation of the joke about God being in a room, and his general lack of sympathy with well-developed theology is that Louis does not think it matters much to our individual lives. As we will see, he doesn't seem to believe we can know whether God exists, and he doesn't think that belief in God is necessary for living a moral life. However, being apathetic about whether God exists might strike some of us as rather odd.

Many philosophers have argued that the impact of God's existence upon our lives is so great that *the practical importance* of God's existence might give us reason to believe. When we normally consider whether something exists, we carefully weigh the evidence in favor and against, then make a determination. We generally don't take our desire for it to exist into question, nor do we weigh the consequences of its existing as evidence for or against the fact of its existence.

For instance, imagine a young child is reasoning about the existence of Santa Claus. They have the following evidence against Santa's existence: they saw their parents sneaking around on Christmas Eve with large bags, their friends at school told them Santa did not exist, and considered arguments about how a sleigh flies or how it manages to visit all of the houses it needs to in one night. When it comes to their deliberation, however, the child is worried that if Santa Claus does not exist—they will no longer get presents! This consideration should *not* come into play for the child's reasoning about Santa's existence. The negative consequences of Santa's non-existence are not reasons to believe that Santa does exist. However, not all philosophers are convinced that pragmatic consequences should not help us decide what to believe.

Pragmatic arguments for God's existence are arguments that rely on practical advantages we might get from belief in God. One of the most famous pragmatic arguments is called Pascal's Wager. This argument says that there are four possible conditions of the world, given that we can either believe that God exists or not, and that God can either exist or not exist. For illustrative purposes, consider this chart below:

Pascal's Wager Options:	If God exists...	If God does not exist...
Believe in God	Go to Heaven	Nothing.
Don't believe in God	Go to Hell.	Nothing.

Consider the world in which God exists. Pascal thinks that in this world, it would be better to believe that God exists. If you believe that God exists, you gain everything. In the Christian tradition (which Pascal is operating under, although many other traditions have similar doctrines), you get to spend eternity in bliss. If you do not believe in God, however, it's likely that you spend eternity in Hell. In the world where God exists, then, it seems like it's far better for the individual to believe in God. After all, Heaven seems a hell of a lot better than Hell! (Sorry, I couldn't resist the pun.)

Now consider the alternative state of the world in which God does not exist. If you don't believe in God in this world, you happen to be correct. However, there aren't a ton of positive consequences for being right about the non-existence of God.

According to most atheists, we probably don't even get to have any post-death bragging rights. In this same world, if you do believe in God, you happen to be wrong. It seems like your biggest loss is spending a few hours in Church that you could have spent sleeping in.

Now imagine that you have no idea which state of the world we are in—the one where God exists or God does not. The evidence and arguments don't push you in either direction necessarily—that is, the evidence isn't *decisive*. It seems like the options from "Believe in God" (Heaven, nothing) are much preferred to "Don't believe in God" (Hell, nothing). Therefore, Pascal says, you ought to believe in God. Pascal is aware that you can't simply will yourself to believe in God, but argues that you should develop practices (involving yourself in the spiritual community, studying religious texts, and so forth) that might push you toward believing in God.

Not all philosophers have considered God's existence to be very important to our lives as human beings. Louis would find a worthwhile companion in an ancient Greek philosopher named Epicurus. Epicurus thought that the lives of the gods mattered very little to human beings. He was an early advocate of hedonism, a doctrine that says that to live a good life is to enjoy the pleasure and happiness in your life while minimizing the pain. Epicurus was adamant that philosophy could help guide us to realize how this sort of life was possible. The culmination of his philosophy was expressed by his four-part cure: "Don't fear god, don't worry about death; what is good is easy to get, and what is terrible is easy to endure."

The fact that Epicurus's four-part remedy begins with a warning against fearing God is telling. We might think that this offers an argument against Pascal's wager. Perhaps by believing in God, we might have more reason to fear God's wrath, or His disapproval of our actions, or disappointing Him in some other way. If fearing the gods amplifies the stress we feel in our everyday lives, it might be a strike against the pragmatic value of god-belief.

Epicurus expands on this in his *Principal Doctrines*, saying "A happy and eternal being has no trouble himself and brings no trouble upon any other being; hence he is exempt from movements of anger and partiality, for every such movement implies weakness." Epicurus was talking specifically about the

Greek gods. He thought that the Greek gods, being already content and immortal, would not have any interest in human affairs. Any interaction they had with human beings was likely to introduce suffering, tragedy, or petty human grievances into their lives. While we might eagerly point Epicurus to the corpus of Greek mythology to show how they had plenty of suffering to go around, I think the point can still stand on its own. It does not seem in any supernatural being's best interest to enter into the affairs of mere mortals.

Another consideration that Louis brings up quite brilliantly is that we might not find God worthy of worship. If the God described by many traditional religions is a God we find morally reprehensible, even if we thought God existed, we might be hesitant to praise or worship Him. In a bit of standup, Louis compares God to a "shitty girlfriend." He brings up the story of Abraham, where God instructs Abraham to kill his own son. God goes about and pesters him ("There's only like eight people back then, and God would just go and bother one of them"), telling him that he needs to kill his son Isaac. Abraham has no idea why God wants him to do it ("Dude, you're so insecure!"), but eventually agrees to murder his son. When Abraham is about to do it, God comes and stops him. Louis compares this to a shitty girlfriend:

GOD: You won't do it because you don't love me!

ABRAHAM: Okay, I'll do it.

GOD: Wait, why are you doing it?

ABRAHAM: WHAT THE FUCK DO YOU WANT FROM ME?

Did You Look in the Downstairs Bathroom?

The popular usage of "agnostic" has come to mean something close to "I don't know whether God exists." However, there is another meaning of the term which I think closely describes Louis's own views. T.H. Huxley, an English biologist, famously coined the term "agnosticism" at a party in London that founded the Metaphysical Society. It is taken from a description of Acts 17:23 which describes an altar which was inscribed to an unknown God. For Huxley, agnosticism represented the view that we would never be able to know about the ultimate origins of the universe. In other words, it is not possible for one to know whether God exists because that sort of knowledge is off-limits to us. The type of evidence that we would need to deliberate about God's existence is simply not available to us given our limits as human beings.

Louis seems to register as an agnostic in *both* senses of the term. In the *Saturday Night Live* monologue we mentioned earlier, Louis delivers this bit:

> "I'm not religious. I don't know if there's a God. That's all I can say, honestly, is 'I don't know.' Some people think that they know that there isn't. That's a weird thing to think you can know. 'Yeah, there's no God.' Are you sure? 'Yeah, no, there's no God.' How do you know? 'Cause I didn't see Him.' There's a vast universe! You can see for about one hundred yards when there's not a building in the way. How could you possibly . . . did you look everywhere? Did you look in the downstairs bathroom? Where did you look so far? 'No, I didn't see Him yet.' I haven't seen *12 Years a Slave* yet; it does not mean it does not exist.

See how strong of a burden Louis puts on the atheist here. Imagine that this same argument was raised against someone who claims to know that unicorns do not exist. I'm confident in claiming that I know that unicorns do not exist. But I don't need to scour the entire Earth to be sure of it.

Louis has the burden of proof backwards. We ought to withhold belief about the existence of things until we have some evidence in their favor. If someone told me that the Loch Ness monster existed, I would push her to provide me with evidence. It would be unreasonable for me to assume the Loch Ness monster existed until we had searched every body of water that it could possibly live in. Instead, a reasonable person ought to withhold her belief until she is shown good evidence to the contrary.

Given that Louis admits the most he can say is "I don't know," I think it's safe to assume that Louis thinks the evidence for God's existence is scant. At the very least, the strength of the available evidence has failed to convince him that God does exist.

One way that many religious traditions have dealt with inadequate evidence is by introducing the concept of faith.

Faith is a notoriously difficult concept to define. One of the most popular ways of conceiving of faith is belief without sufficient (or demonstrable) proof, or believing despite uncertainty. This popular conception of faith could be based on a straightforward reading of Hebrews 11:1 "Now faith is the substance of things hoped for, the evidence of things not seen." Many people see faith as a virtue to be praised. They think that having belief in the face of uncertainty is something to be admired.

Louis's take on the value of faith is less favorable. An aptly titled episode of his television show, "God" (Season One, Episode 11), opens in a dingy restroom in which Louis sees a hole in the bathroom wall with "HEAVEN" scrawled above it. He laughs to himself and goes about his business, but is shocked when a well-dressed and pleasant man begins to undress suggesting he is going to partake. Louis asks him if he's seriously considering it, and the man responds that of course he is, "It says Heaven, right there!" In absolute bafflement, Louis asks him how he knows that something terrible isn't going to happen if he sticks his appendage in. The man replies "I don't know, you gotta have faith." The next few seconds Louis is simply staring in disbelief.

The sketch comes down hard on the virtues of faith. The bewilderment on Louis's face at the end of the clip seems to indicate that he finds the man's actions utterly ridiculous. The sketch is obviously a parody and taking 'faith' at its most extreme, but it's telling as to how Louis thinks of faith as a general concept. Given the lack of evidence that any sort of "Heaven"-like experience will come out of using the glory hole, Louis thinks the man is mad for trying to do it anyway.

Philosophers have historically argued that believing without sufficient evidence is irrational. Others have gone a step further and said that not only is believing without sufficient evidence irrational, but it is immoral. The most extreme position on this issue comes from a philosopher W.K. Clifford in his paper "The Ethics of Belief." Clifford argues that not only is it *irrational* to believe something without sufficient evidence, but it is also morally wrong to do so.

To illustrate this, Clifford gives an example of a ship owner who makes his money by transporting emigrants in old ships that aren't fit to sail. One particular voyage, the ship owner debates with himself about whether he ought to let the ship go without doing the proper maintenance to ensure that it is sea-worthy. In order to not lose the profit, he attempts to convince himself to believe that it is seaworthy. He reminds himself that it has sailed many times before and gotten to its destination without difficulty. He reminds himself how hard the contractors and shipbuilders worked on it, and persuades himself that he should not doubt their abilities. He ultimately persuades himself that it will be safe, and sends the ship with passengers to its destination.

After he sends the ship on its voyage, it sinks halfway there and everyone on board perishes. Clifford thinks that the ship owner is morally responsible for the deaths of those on board. A reasonable objection is that the ship owner isn't wrong for holding the belief, only for acting on it. However, Clifford thinks that if the belief was gotten through improper evaluation of the evidence, then the person has failed in his moral duty. This is because belief is importantly connected to action, and holding a certain belief will give us a tendency to act in a certain way. The ship owner is going to have a tendency to send the ship to sail if he thinks that it will reach its destination safely. Therefore, Clifford concludes with a remarkably strong commitment: "it is wrong always, everywhere, and for anyone, to believe anything upon insufficient evidence."

The consequences of Clifford's view for religious believers is that if there is insufficient evidence for believing in God, it becomes immoral to believe in God as a matter of faith. This is a rather extreme thesis, but it seems that Louis is quite conscious about people believing off of insufficient evidence—though his most vocal criticism is actually aimed at the non-believers who claim to know there is no God.

You Did This to Him with Your Sins!

The fear of God can be a powerful tool for motivating people to act according to their moral duty. As Luke 12:5 says, "But I will show you whom you should fear: Fear him who, after the killing of the body, has power to throw you into hell. Yes, I tell you, fear him." As a parent might hold the fear of punishment over a child to teach him the right path, God's punishment looms over us when nobody else can hold us accountable.

One worry we might have is that the fear of God is so great that it could cripple our ability to act freely. If people are afraid that acting immorally might result in their being punished for eternity, it would significantly curb their motivation for acting however they wanted. This fear cripples our ability to lead meaningful lives which we author, and instead might make us appear to be fearful servants that carry out God's bidding. Theist philosophers have often argued that this is why God does not make his existence immediately apparent: to keep us from being forced to follow God and act the way we think we are required to. Given that we cannot be certain about God's existence, we need not live in perpetual fear.

Louis does not seem persuaded by the idea that we need fear of punishment to act morally, and he seems even less convinced that God necessarily holds us accountable. "God" (Season One, Episode 11) begins in a Catholic church, where young Louie and others are being improperly pious about the suffering of Christ on the cross. The nun in charge gets angry at their insolence, and brings in reinforcements: an intense doctor who laments the biological and physiological sufferings of Christ on the cross in a detailed and harsh manner—ending in the Doctor ushering a young Louie to drive a nail through a fellow student's arm. When Louie refuses, the Doctor asks why Louis could do this to Christ but not to one of his classmates: "You did this to him with your sins!"

At the end of the episode, a young Louie goes back to the church and tries to save Jesus and ends up in trouble. His mom asks him what's wrong, and Louie goes into a diatribe about how his sins are hurting Jesus. The response is incredulity: "You are not bad! You're a good kid. You make mistakes. You do bad things sometimes. I'm not done raising you . . . but you're a good person."

His mom describes Jesus as a "really good person" who lived a long time ago. She calls the idea that Jesus rose from the dead "malarkey" and implores Louie that Christ was a really good person who taught people to love each other ("and boy did he get his for that!"), but that it didn't matter one iota to Louie now. The most telling line comes near the end of the conversation, where his mom says "All I know is that you have to be good to people where there is or isn't (a God) . . . nobody's going to watch whether or not you are good to people, you have to take that on yourself." Louis's mother is making the common argument that we don't need to be religious or believe in God in order to live moral lives. The fear of God is not mandatory for treating others with respect and kindness. We're the only ones who can "take on" our responsibility to be good to people.

An Apathetic Agnostic

The parts of Louis's television show and standup that we've looked at paint a vibrant picture of Louis on the topic of God. We are presented with someone who thinks the best he can say with regard to God's existence is "I don't know," who lambasts atheists for being sure there is no God, and who ultimately denies that the question matters very much. It also appears that Louis is quite certain that we can live good lives without God, and that moral instruction from theism does not necessarily make us better people. This is why I suggest we think of Louis as an "apathetic agnostic," a person who doesn't think we can know there is a God and also thinks maybe we shouldn't care.

VI

Having a Lot of Beliefs and Living by None of Them

16
You're Not Starving

PHIL SMOLENSKI

"I have a lot of beliefs, and I live by none of 'em," is for many of us, an all too accurate description of how we go about our daily lives. They're our beliefs. We like believing in them. We like believing that things like letting children starve in Africa is evil. We live in a highly unequal world where many of us enjoy a pretty comfortable life, while the World Bank estimates that just over two billion people live on less than two dollars a day.

And we like to believe that it's wrong that there are people who are starving to death while we have so much ice cream in our freezers that our children would break down into tears if they knew it existed. We like believing that something should be done about kids starving in Africa. We like that part—having these beliefs. They're our little "believies." They make us feel good about who we are. But if donating some of our money to charity gets in the way of something we want, like a sixty-inch flatscreen, we usually don't let our beliefs stand in the way.

There seems to be something seriously wrong in this way of thinking, and Louis calls us out for thinking that we're really good people, when we're actually living a really evil life without thinking about it (*Louie*, Season One, Episode 1). Just think of those times when you're out with friends shopping, and you say, "I'm starving. I haven't eaten for *hours*, and now I'm *starving*." Louis responds that that's just offensive, "Because some people are starving, and they don't say it. You never see a little kid in Africa with his ribs showing and he's like, 'I'm starving right now. I'm like starving to death. It's, like, annoying'" (*Saturday Night Live*, 2014). If we're really concerned with

189

being good people, we need to find out what our obligations to the Global Poor are, even though they're distant strangers. And we need to recognize that we're actually living morally questionable lives. Most of the time, we just want a doughnut.

Third World poverty *is* a real thing, and it's a serious moral wrong. One of the reasons why Third World poverty is so wrong, and why our lives are evil for not doing anything about it, is that we can significantly reduce the amount of suffering in the world at little cost to ourselves.

We Make Them Die with Our Cars

I'm not suggesting that we start mowing down our neighbors with our cars, but Peter Singer, a famous contemporary moral philosopher, is suggesting that we forgo buying that new car and instead put the money towards famine relief. In "Famine, Affluence, and Morality," Singer argues that if we're capable of preventing something bad from happening, without too great of a sacrifice, we're morally obligated to do it.

To get us to see what he means, Singer uses the analogy of a child drowning in a pond. Imagine you're Louis and you're walking through Central Park on your way to the Comedy Cellar for a set, when you come across a child who fell into the Turtle Pond. You're the only one around to help, and since the child is in a shallow part of the pond, you're not in any danger if you decide to wade into the pond to save the child. At worst your shoes will get ruined and your pants will get wet, so you'll have to go home to change, which means that you'll miss your set. Compared to the inevitable death of a child if you decide to do nothing, getting your clothes a little wet and missing a set doesn't seem like much of a sacrifice. Singer thinks it would be grotesque to allow for such minor considerations to prevent us from saving the child, so we're morally obligated to wade into the pond.

One reason why we might not want to wade into the pool is that it's not our child. Seeing the child drowning in the pond, Louis would probably respond, "You're not mine, I don't love you . . . I don't even have any instinct to protect you. I don't care if you die. Seriously, I won't feel anything if you die. I'll have to pretend if you're dead" (*Shameless*). Even though it's not our child, why might we feel morally obligated to save the drowning child? Singer argues that morality needs to be impartial, and so it is a mistake to think that we only have special obligations to our own kind. The kind of obligations we have to other people, including strangers, will vary by degrees. So it seems uncontroversial to conclude that one of our obligations to others is to prevent bad, life-threatening things from happening when it's in our power to do so at little cost to ourselves.

Fortunately, for drowning children everywhere, most of us aren't as evil as Louis pretends to be on stage, and we'd probably agree that we should go in to save the drowning child. No matter how punctual it would make us, or how good our set would be, it is always a serious moral wrong to continue walking past the drowning child.

Singer thinks that if we have a moral obligation to save the drowning child, we should feel the same way about making sizable donations to alleviate Third World poverty. In both cases we're faced with children who are in imminent danger, and it is well within our power to save them at little cost to ourselves. In the drowning child case, we'd have to miss our set at the Comedy Cellar, our pants would be soaked, and our shoes may never recover. While in the case of starving children in the Third World, it would only cost us some of our disposable income. If the principle applies in the case of the drowning child, it applies here as well.

Singer questions how we can justify spending so much on luxuries when people are in danger of dying from starvation. Louis readily admits he doesn't have a justification:

> My life is evil. There are people who are starving in the world and I drive an Infiniti. That's really evil. There are people who just starve to death; that's all they ever did. There's people who are born and are like 'Oh, I'm hungry," and they just die; that's all they ever get to do. (*Louie*, Season One, Episode 1)

And it's not just Louis's life that's evil. Most of us aren't making sizable donations to organizations like OXFAM or UNICEF, apart from a couple of bucks during the holidays, and yet we all sleep like babies!

We can distinguish between two kinds of acts: acts of duty, and acts of charity. Acts of duty are things that we're required to do, and failing to do what is required of you would be a moral wrong. In the case of the drowning child, it would be a serious moral wrong not to save the child. But it doesn't seem like the starving children in Africa are like drowning children. Sending money to a charitable organization is usually considered to be an act of charity. Charitable actions are "supererogatory," which means they go above and beyond what is required by duty. They are done out of a sense of generosity. These are acts which it would be good to do, but it would not be wrong to fail to do. And so we praise those people who donate to good causes, without generally condemning those who spend that money on a new smartphone.

If one day we were so moved by one of those UNICEF commercials that we decided to trade-in our Infiniti for a cheaper car, like a Ford Focus with no miles on it, and we could get back something like $20,000, we could take that money and save hundreds or thousands of people dying of starvation. Just think about how good we'd feel about ourselves, and how much people would praise us for our generosity; that is, except for Peter Singer. Even though most people would think it's amazing if we donated all that money, Singer says it's a mistake to think of it as an act of generosity. Expensive cars are luxuries, and Singer maintains that we're not entitled to such extravagancies when there are people starving to death. We had no right to have the luxury car in the first place, so Singer doesn't think we should be praised for simply doing the right thing.

It's My Stuff, and I've Earned It

Singer wants to challenge the way we traditionally draw the line between acts of duty and acts of charity. Giving to organizations that work to help feed hungry children in poor countries has always been seen as something that it'd be nice to do, but hardly required of us. Singer argues that we have a *duty* to help alleviate Third World poverty. In order to fulfill that duty we're going to have to make sizable donations to charitable organizations. Giving to charitable organizations is no longer left up to us to decide. According to Singer it is morally wrong not to donate to charitable organizations.

The size of the donation that Singer has in mind for people to contribute would be, on average, ten percent of their annual income. Personally, Singer donates upwards of twenty percent of his annual income, and he believes that the ideal scenario would have everyone donating even more. However, even ten percent of everyone's income could have a significant impact on Third World Poverty, and in a relative sense, we wouldn't even lose that much. Reflecting on the state of consumerism in America, Louis remarks, "Most Americans have so much crap, you could lose most of it and still have more shit than the average Canadian" (*Hilarious*).

Most of us may want to respond as Louis does: "I've got a nice apartment and a nice car. I earned it and you can kiss my ass" ("Starvation Can Be Character Building"). This kind of response distorts the reason why we're morally obligated to make these donations. It's true that most of us have earned the things that we have, and Singer isn't telling us that we can't have any nice things. The reason we're obligated to donate is not just because we have so much in relation to those who have so little. We're morally obligated to donate because while our children attempt to choke down candy-flavored medicine,

> most kids in the world don't have medicine. They just don't have it. When they get sick they just die on a rock with a bear eating their face. That's how most of the world handles that. 'Nah, he's got a sniffle, ring the bear bell, and put him outside. *(Louie,* Season Two, Episode 10)

We're morally obligated to donate, not because we have *so much*, but because others simply don't have *enough*. Wherever we draw the line for how much we should donate to charitable organizations, Singer wants us to stop thinking of these donations as something that would be nice for us to do, and instead to start thinking of them as something that is required of us.

The Key to Human Greatness

If we really care about not living an evil life, donating money to charities may not be enough. We need to take into account how we're inflicting harm on the Global Poor. We may want to respond that perhaps that was true back in the days of slavery, but those days are behind us. Reflecting on how we've been able to achieve so much, Louis suggests, "maybe every incredible human achievement in history was done with slaves. Every single thing where you go, "'How did you build those pyramids?' 'We just threw human death and suffering at them until they were finished.'" (*Oh My God*) But, someone might argue, Louis is talking about things that happened long ago, and have long since stopped. We've made substantial moral progress in response to these and other forms of harmful conduct.

In *World Poverty and Human Rights*, Thomas Pogge writes that we need to pay attention to the way the global institutional order actively harms the Global Poor. The global institutional order is the whole system of international organizations, like the World Trade Organization (WTO) and the International Monetary Fund (IMF), international laws that govern things like copyrights and trade, and the global marketplace as a whole. The global institutional order is basically the framework or set of rules that structure the global competition between countries. Pogge's assessment is that we've stacked the deck so badly against the Global Poor that we're actively causing them harm.

Louis thinks that: "There's no end to what you can do when you don't give a fuck about particular people. You can do anything. That's where human greatness comes from, is that we're shitty people, that we fuck others over" (*Oh My God*). And if we look at how the WTO is currently structured, it seems that Louis is right! The WTO is an intergovernmental organization that regulates international trade, and its aim is to promote free trade and a fair competition between countries.

Whereas most opponents of the WTO are typically opponents of open markets, free trade, or globalization, Pogge's criticism is that the WTO has opened up *our* markets too *little*. Rich countries insist upon asymmetrical protections of their markets through quotas, duties, export credits, and subsidies to domestic producers. The result is that we've managed to gain all the benefits of free trade while withholding these benefits from the Global Poor. The problem is not that the global institutional order is an adversarial system that prioritizes the needs of our co-nationals and other group interests. The problem is that the framework that structures the competition is not even minimally fair with regards to the Global Poor.

Maybe we're not persuaded that we're evil people because of how international organizations like the WTO are structured since we're not responsible for negotiating those terms. However, Pogge would remind us that we're also responsible for a certain amount of harm imposed on the Global Poor through our consumer practices. Our insatiable desire for cheap consumer goods has created factories in the Third World that are effectively run like prison camps. Many people work twelve- to eighteen-hour days, and some are forced to work standing up, with limited opportunities to use the restrooms.

Pointing to his latest smartphone, Louis says, "Even today, how do we have this amazing micro-technology? Because the factory where they're making these, they jump off the fucking roof because it's a nightmare in there." (*Oh My God*). Workers slave away in dehumanizing conditions so we can leave a comment like "Suck a bag of dicks" on someone's cat video on YouTube. Conditions are similar, if not worse, in other kinds of factories, but especially in the clothing and shoe industries. As long as we continue to demand rock bottom prices for our consumer products, nightmarish factory conditions are likely to persist. And so long as they do persist, we'll need to recognize that we're actively responsible for this catastrophe.

Louis thinks that we have a choice, and Pogge would probably agree: "You can have candles and horses, and be a little kinder to each other; or, let someone suffer immeasurably, far away, just so you can leave a mean comment on YouTube while taking a shit" (*Oh My God*). The suggestion here isn't as radical as it may seem at first. Neither Louis, nor Pogge, is calling for the death of capitalism and a triumphant return to the days of rotary phones, manual credit card machines, and donkeys as the primary source of transportation.

A lot of progress could be made in terms of justice and fairness if rich countries dropped these protectionist barriers against exports from poor countries. In real-world terms, Pogge suggests that if these barriers could be dropped, wage levels would rise substantially, and hundreds of millions of people would be able to escape poverty and unemployment. And, as consumers of goods that are produced by the Global Poor, we should avoid products made in factories that resemble prison camps. Instead, we should opt for fair-trade alternatives to encourage manufacturers to change working conditions. It'll mean that our consumer products will probably cost a little more, but that seems like a small price to pay for justice. So maybe we should listen to Louis here and just try to be a little kinder to each other.

The Banality of Evil

Behind all the jokes about masturbation and the joys of divorce is a man who's deeply concerned about discovering what's the right thing to do. "There are people that really live by doing the right thing, but I don't know what that is, I'm really curious about that. I'm really curious about what people think they're doing when they're doing something evil, casually" (Weiner interview).

Reporting on the trial of Adolf Eichmann, in *Eichmann in Jerusalem* (1964), Hannah Arendt uses the phrase the "banality of evil" to characterize Eichmann and his role as a chief architect of the Nazis' "Final Solution," the Nazi plan to exterminate the Jewish people. Most of us tend to think that the greatest evils of humankind arise from selfishness and other sinful or base motives. So when Eichmann was finally captured and put on trial, what struck Arendt most was that the man on trial was neither perverted nor sadistic. What was most troubling about Eichmann was that he was "terribly and terrifyingly normal." Eichmann was responsible for helping to organize local Jewish populations, and to make arrangements for them to be transported to the concentration camps, where the majority of them were sent to their deaths. Despite the obscene nature of his actions, Eichmann was never motivated by a malevolent desire to do evil, which is why Arendt describes this as the banality of evil.

The person responsible for one of the greatest crimes against humanity was not an abnormal monster, but an "utterly innocuous human being." Arendt portrays Eichmann as operating unthinkingly, following orders, efficiently carrying them out with no initiative and no intentions, good or bad. Arendt is not looking to excuse Eichmann's behavior. She is looking to demonstrate that one of the greatest human evils did not require the presence of hatred; all that was needed was the absence of imaginative capacities. Eichmann, and all the people like him who supported the Nazi regime, were unable to contemplate the nature of their deeds from the perspective of the victims.

Even though we're not responsible for the Holocaust, Louis thinks "it's really interesting that we benefit from so much suffering, and we excuse ourselves from it. I think it's really interesting, I think it's a profound human question" (Weiner interview). If we're looking for an answer to this question, we should turn to Arendt's concept of the banality of evil. Our behavior as consumers within the global system does not exhibit a malevolent hatred towards the Global Poor. As consumers, we feel like utterly innocuous individuals, and we operate unthinkingly, with no consideration for the impact that our consumer decisions have on the Global Poor. Most of us don't have malicious intentions or beliefs, but our participation in the global economic order makes us complicit in the harms it produces among the Global Poor.

We don't tend to think about how the clothes our children wear are made by children their age, professionally. As Louie jokes ironically, "Americans only buy things that come from suffering. They just enjoy it more when they know someone is getting hurt" (*Louie*, Season Two, Episode 10). Arendt would respond that it's not a delight in the suffering of others that motivates our behavior. It's an absence of the imaginative capacity or sound thinking and judgment that would have made the human and moral dimensions of these harms more tangible to us. Most of us don't think about where our clothing comes from. We don't think about the prison camp-like conditions in the factories that make our smartphones. Louis seems to agree because he doesn't think we face the hard moral questions about our actions, and instead "everyone sheepishly goes, 'Oh, I'm just not doing it, I'm not doing the right thing.'" It's a willingness to let evil things happen—even when we think it's wrong—that is captured by Arendt's concept of the banality of evil.

What's disturbing about Eichmann is that he insisted that he had done nothing wrong. Contrary to the prosecution's assertions, Eichmann argued that he had no intentions, good or bad, and that he was only obeying orders. If we're asked about our own consumer habits, it seems that we'd respond that we too don't have any bad intentions towards the Global Poor, and we're just following the rules set up by the global market. As Louis says, "I think a lot of people think they're good people . . . living a really evil life without thinking about it" (*Louie*, Season One, Episode 1).

While we're not responsible for the deaths of millions of Jews, our collaboration in the global market is, according to Thomas Pogge, partially responsible for an estimated death toll of thirteen million people annually. And it's not just Americans who should be held partially responsible. It's everyone in the Developed World who shops unthinkingly—without giving a second's thought about how those goods were produced, or what kind of effect our consumer habits have on the Global Poor.

Given the magnitude of the suffering, Arendt is right to conclude that the greatest evil in the world is created by nobodies. It's committed by men and women without motives, convictions, wicked hearts, or demonic wills. We allow for the banality of evil in the world by acting unthinkingly.

Maybe We Don't Really Deserve the Best?

It's pretty safe to say that starvation is not a big concern for most Americans. Each of us tends to go to bed with a full stomach, and most of us aren't really concerned about where our next meal is going to come from. As we lie in bed, thinking about that Cinnabon we're going to get on the way to work, we like to believe we're good people. We like the idea of being good people, when in fact many of us are morally suspect at best. Louis would probably say we're pretty shitty. So if we're actually concerned about being good people, Louis suggests we need to stop thinking in terms of "I need to do this because I fucking deserve the best," and more in terms of whether, "I need to do this so I don't freeze to death in the winter" ("Starvation Can Be Character Building").

17
Louis's Little Believies

RYAN JAWETZ

Louis C.K. is a failure. This is a strange thing to say about the most successful comedian in America, but it's true—at least if you take his word for it. In his stand-up specials and TV shows, Louis portrays a character who spends every day being defeated by the vagaries of modern life. His relationships are disastrous; his parenting is suspect; his career is floundering.

Worst of all, this version of Louis is a hypocrite. He knows what he should do, and does the opposite anyway. The genius of Louis is that he makes us complicit in his hypocrisy, because he presents us with a person whose moral flaws mirror our own. Every moment of painful recognition bring us closer to realizing that we too have a vast gulf between our beliefs and our actions. Through his art, Louis forces us to confront our own moral failures.

We all want to be good people. At the same time, we make decisions that we know to be wrong. Like Louie, we are guilty of treating our deeply held values as nothing more than what he calls "little believies," to be discarded as soon as they are no longer convenient. Why do we ignore our beliefs about right and wrong? How can we make choices every day that we know to be unethical? What is going through our heads when we decide to be immoral?

What Is Moral Failure?

In the series premiere of *Louie*, Louie does a stand-up comedy segment with an excellent example of moral failure:

199

There are people who are starving in the world, and I drive an Infiniti. That's really evil. There are people who just starve to death. That's all they ever did. . . . It's totally my fault, 'cause I could trade my Infiniti for like a really good car, like a nice Ford Focus with no miles on it, and I'd get back like $20,000. And I could save hundreds of people from dying of starvation with that money, and every day I don't do it. Every day I make them die with my car. (*Louie*, Season One, Episode 1)

Louie's bit gives us a blueprint for moral failure. First, there must be a particular action that has moral worth. In other words, the activity that Louie describes can be evaluated as good or evil. In this case, the activity is an inaction—Louie's refusal to trade in his car for a cheaper model. Taken in a vacuum, this inaction might not seem to have moral value. Think about the last time you bought a car. When you considered the cost of various models, did you wonder whether purchasing a cheaper car made you a good person? Or were you simply concerned with getting the best possible deal for the car you wanted? Most of us would agree that our goal would be to get the best deal, and that paying $30,000 instead of $25,000 would have no bearing on whether we are good people. However, this activity does not take place in isolation.

By spending more money on a car, we pay what economists call an opportunity cost: the inability to spend that money on something else. As Louie points out, he could have paid less money for a car and used that money to prevent people from starving. Let us agree that, all things being equal, preventing starvation is morally good. Since the goal of preventing starvation has moral value, it stands to reason that actions that advance or hinder this goal can be moral or immoral as well. Since owning a more expensive car hinders Louie's ability to prevent starvation, his refusal to trade in his car is a morally significant action.

Another quality of moral failure is that the person who is acting in a morally significant way—the moral agent—is aware that their actions are immoral. Louie begins the bit by claiming that driving a nice car in a world where people are starving is "evil." We could say that Louie *knows* that his behavior is immoral. But now we have a problem: philosophers disagree whether knowledge about morality is even possible. Some philosophers think that it is impossible to know anything about good and evil, and that when we say something like, "Murder is evil," all we are really expressing is our personal feeling that we don't like murder. Fortunately, we don't need to settle this centuries-old argument at this very moment. For our purposes of learning about moral failure the important part is not whether the moral agent knows that their action is moral or immoral, but whether they *believe* that it is.

For example, if you believe that consuming alcohol is morally wrong but you have a drink anyways, we can say that you have suffered a moral failure regardless of whether we agree with you that drinking alcohol is immoral. Your *hypocrisy* is the key ingredient, not whether your belief corresponds to any objective moral truth. Even if nobody else thinks your action had moral worth, your belief that it is morally significant is self-fulfilling: if you believe that drinking is wrong, any action you take based on that belief is morally significant. Because of your own beliefs about drinking, we can consider your abstaining from alcohol to be a moral success, and any instances of your drinking alcohol to be a moral failure. Whether we agree with your moral principles is irrelevant, what matters is your ability to stick to them.

Now we face the difficulty that some people have beliefs about right and wrong that seem to the rest of us to be terribly mistaken. You might believe that it is morally correct to assassinate a politician who disagrees with your views, but you lack the courage to carry out the assassination. Do we really want to call your inaction a moral failure, given that this failure results in someone *not* being murdered? And we would be forced to say that if you did act on your beliefs by killing the politician, then it would be a moral success.

However, we can treat the morality of the action as separate from our capacity to act on our beliefs about the action. It's possible to condemn moral agents both for the wrongness of their beliefs (if we think that being right or wrong about morality is possible) and also for their hypocrisy in failing to live up to those beliefs. To return to the example of the alcohol-drinking goody-goody, we can both rebuke that person for their prudish insistence on temperance and blame them for being a hypocrite when they drink, even if we believe that their decision to drink should not have moral worth. Making this distinction protects the moral belief criterion from logical absurdity.

There is a final component to moral failure, which is that the hypocritical action (or inaction) must be freely chosen. Louie has the option of continuing to drive his expensive car or trading it in for a cheaper model, and he chooses to ignore his better judgment and keep driving the Infiniti. Since nothing agitates philosophers more than talking about free will, we need to keep our definitions narrow. When we say that you act freely, we just mean that you are not under any sort of duress, and you have the ability to act either with or against your beliefs. There is nobody holding a gun to Louie's head telling him that he is not allowed to trade in his car, and he does not live someplace where only expensive cars are available. Unlike Laurie forcing Louie to go down on her in her truck (*Louie*, Season Three, Episode 2), no one will smash Louie's head into a window or threaten to break his finger if he decides to get a less expensive car and donates the profit to charity.

Louie believes that owning an expensive car is morally wrong, but he chooses to do so anyways, even though he could easily do the right thing. You may recognize this dilemma from your own life, since most of us have at some point spent money on a luxury item rather than giving the money to charity. You might have felt some guilt about your choice. Louis will not let you brush that feeling away. After all, if Louie driving an Infiniti is "evil," what does that say about you?

Why Does Louie Experience Moral Failure?

We now have the three components of a moral failure: an action or inaction that violates the moral beliefs of the agent and is freely chosen. Since Louie believes that being a good person requires him to get rid of his unnecessarily expensive car, and he has the ability to do so, why doesn't he do it? Louis's body of work conveys many different kinds of motivation for the behavior of his character Louie. Discerning the reasons behind Louie's actions—some morally significant, some not—will shed light on the possible reasons for his moral failures, and ours as well.

So, why doesn't Louie do what he thinks is right and trade in his car? The simplest possibility is that he is lazy. After all, the moral failure in this case is a lack of action, so we could blame this failure on ordinary inertia. Louie would need to go out of his way to switch cars, and it is easier for him to continue using the car he already owns. This account is plausible, given Louie's frequent depictions of himself as an indolent, passive person wedded to creature comforts. Yet the laziness hypothesis is not enough because we have seen him be more active on other occasions. Earlier in the premiere episode, Louie helps supervise a field trip for his daughter's class, even coming to the rescue when the school bus breaks down by calling a fleet of limousines to take the children home. Clearly, situations exist where Louie can take more of an initiative, so there must be some motivational factor present here that is missing from the case of his starvation-causing Infiniti.

When the bus breaks down, Louie is motivated to help because he needs to act on behalf of himself and his daughter. If Louie and Lilly were not directly affected by the bus accident, he would have had no incentive to do anything about it. It is true that Louie helps all of the children on the bus, but that is a tangential result of his self-serving action. We can't prove that Louie is thinking mostly of himself and his daughter, but consider the counterfactual: Louie orders a car just for him and Lilly. Louie would then be forced to confront his own guilt at having abandoned the other children, Lilly might protest at having to leave her friends, and the teacher could call him out for his inconsiderate behavior. Instead, Louie gets to be the hero to his daughter and her classmates.

The only downside for Louie is the presumed financial sacrifice of ordering the limos. But the show immediately cuts to Louie's bit about owning a luxury car, indicating that (in this episode) money is not an issue for him. It is hard to argue that Louie was at all concerned about helping others when doing so apparently cost him nothing. The connection between these two segments suggests that his motivation to act in this situation is the very same selfishness that causes him *not* to act when it comes to trading in his luxury car. Louie is primarily interested in himself, and since trading in his Infiniti for a Ford Focus would require him to be minutely less indulgent, he refuses, even though he believes that the exchange would prevent people from starving. His moral failure is thus a function of both laziness and selfishness.

Those factors are still only part of the answer, however, since Louie does show the capacity to care about people outside of himself and his children. The fact that he volunteered to chaperone the field trip in the first place suggests that he is not entirely selfish, although it is possible that he had ulterior motives for attending, such as wanting to watch over his daughter or get out of a more annoying obligation. A clearer example of Louie looking beyond his immediate circle of interest is when the southern sheriff asks for a kiss on the lips and Louie obliges him (*Louie*, Season One, Episode 5). Kissing the man does not benefit Louie in any tangible way, since Louie no longer needs his help. Although the man is a law-enforcement officer, he does not threaten Louie, and in fact comes across as very polite and unimposing, so duress does not seem to be a factor. In Louie's own words, he decides to kiss the sheriff because he "can't think of a compelling reason not to" (*Louie*, Season One, Episode 5).

Of course, Louie only has that realization after he initially refuses to kiss the sheriff. After Louie's refusal the man implies that Louie is being ungrateful. So besides the absence of a reason not to kiss the sheriff, Louie actually does have a reason *to* kiss him: he wants to convince the sheriff that he is a good person—the kind of person who shows gratitude to others. Louie's discomfort at kissing a male stranger is overpowered by his fear of being judged negatively. This aversion to negative judgments must go beyond a merely selfish desire to be liked, because we know that Louie is sometimes willing to take a stand when he believes he is in the right, regardless of the consequences. For example, Louie sabotages his sitcom because he doesn't want to compromise his comedy (*Louie*, Season Two, Episode 7).

Even though Louie could stay well-liked by his collaborators and advance his career by saying nothing, he is not motivated enough by the fear of their negative reactions (or by his self-interest) to remain silent— their judgments do not compromise his positive self-image as someone with artistic integrity, so Louie does not worry about them. In contrast, Louie pays attention to the judgments of other characters when their opinions of him could cut against his belief that he is a good person. The smooching sheriff confronts Louie with the possibility that he is actually ungrateful and rude. Since Louie is invested in his idealized view of himself, this stranger's judgment against his character prompts him to overcome his natural hesitance and accede to the kiss.

Kissing the sheriff is an extreme example, but there are many instances of Louie reluctantly doing things to satisfy other people, from agreeing to an unsuitable movie role to pacify his dead agent's daughter (Season One, Episode 6) to going to a nightclub because the babysitter thinks he's a loser (Season One, Episode 3) to helping his one-night stand shop at Ikea (Season Three, Episode 7). Louie does these things out of a sense of duty, to avoid conflict, or maybe because he, like all of us, has moments of altruism. In general though, these sorts of reasons only move Louie to behave unselfishly when they carry the implied possibility of being judged and found wanting (say, for refusing a social obligation). He needs to convince himself that he's a good person just as much as he needs to convince everyone else. Thus, Louie's deep-seated insecurity can be a powerful impulse to action. Yet insecurity is only a motivating force when there are other people around to provoke or exploit it.

Aspiring to be a good person is laudable, but for Louie that incentive alone, without the threat of potential judgment, is not an effective motivator. In *Live at the Beacon Theater*, Louie declares his belief that donating one's cadaver to science is the right thing to do. He instantly follows up by stating that he is not actually going to donate his body, because the thought grosses him out. In the context of his stand-up performance there is nobody else to judge him for this contradiction, so he has no reason to act differently. Louie argues in *Oh My God* that our innate moral sense that murder is bad is far less important to preventing murder than the severe consequences of being caught. Wanting to do the right thing, especially when it means acting against his own interests or desires, is not enough by itself to affect Louie's behavior. There must be negative consequences to acting selfishly for Louie to make different choices, and in his life the most prevalent and potent possible consequence is the judgment of his character by the people around him. When that possibility is absent, Louie reverts to his self-interested norm.

As Louie is choosing every day to keep his luxury car, there is nobody there to judge him for his decision, as far as we know. No one in his life is bringing up his choice of car to try to shame him into trading down. And since Louie seems to have lost his religious beliefs at a young age (Season One, Episode 11), the possibility of divine judgment holds no sway. So without the fear of negative judgments from other people, Louie has no incentive to act unselfishly. If anything, we would think it odd if there *were* a person in Louie's life whom he worried might judge him for driving a nice car. Do our friends try to shame us for our unnecessary consumption? Are our colleagues and peers actively concerned about our charitable donations or lack thereof? It's far easier to ignore each other's moral failures, so that we do not have to reckon with our own.

What Happens When We Experience Moral Failure?

In another stand-up segment from the first season, Louie details an encounter between his friend's country-bumpkin cousin and a homeless man:

> We pass this homeless guy and she sees him—I mean, we all passed him, but she saw him. She's the only one who actually *saw* him. We didn't—me and her cousin were like, "So? He's supposed to be there. So what? There's a perfectly good reason why that's not me and it's him. The right people always win, I'm sure of it . . ." My friend's cousin immediately just gets down on one knee and says, "Oh, my God! Sir, are you okay? What happened?" What happened? *America* happened. What do you mean, "What happened?" So she's down there, "Sir, can we call someone?" And me and my friend, we're from New York, this is the crazy part, we immediately go to her: "Oh no, no, honey, don't." We start correcting her behavior like she's doing something wrong. "Why, is he okay?" "No, no, he needs you desperately, that's not the point. We just don't do that here. You silly country girl." (Season One, Episode 3)

Based on our three criteria, we can call this incident a moral failure on Louie's part. First, the morally significant action that Louie takes is to prevent his friend's cousin from helping a homeless man, and to refuse to help the man himself. Second, even if we don't believe that helping or failing to help the homeless is morally significant, Louie clearly believes that it is: he notes that his inclination to change the country girl's behavior is "crazy," and that the man needs their help "desperately." Third, Louie chooses to prevent the country girl from helping the homeless man, even though he could let her help or try to help the man himself.

Louie and his friend's cousin react to the homeless man in completely different ways, reflecting their differing histories and expectations. The country girl has never witnessed urban homelessness before, and the man's abject state horrifies her. Rather than seeing the homeless man as grotesque or repulsive, she recognizes him as a human being in distress. Her instinct is to help him return to a state of normalcy. To Louie, an urbanite who sees homeless people every day, the man already is in his normal state. He is less a human being than a natural phenomenon.

Louie recognizes that the homeless man needs help, but not only is he not moved to act, he impedes another person's attempt to act. The reasons for this moral failure are apparent. Helping the homeless man would be inconvenient and require him to change his usual pattern of behavior, so it is easier to let the man be. Perhaps self-interest could overcome this inertia, but providing help could be time-consuming and would not offer Louie any tangible benefits.

Louie's fear of negative judgments could overcome the lack of a self-interested motive, but because Louie's friend shares his city-dweller standards of conduct and the cousin is so naive, Louie is not worried about being judged by either of them. He certainly isn't concerned about the judgment of the homeless man, whom he can barely see as human. In the absence of these factors, Louie has no motivation to reconcile the conflict between his belief that the homeless man needs help and his hypocritical unwillingness to provide that help or even allow it to be offered.

Louis uses this bit to call attention to a moral phenomenon that any person who has ever walked around in a city has experienced. We are able to help homeless people at little cost to ourselves, yet we consistently refrain from doing so. We would prefer to believe, like Louie, that homeless people "are supposed to be there," and that we bear no responsibility for easing their suffering. This might be true, but the pang of guilt that we might feel when we turn away from a panhandler suggests otherwise.

Louis is too smart and may be too morally ambivalent to preach to us about helping the homeless. Instead, his story reminds us of our own encounters with homeless people, and while he exaggerates the language for comedic effect, his rhetoric is similar to the typically unvoiced justifications of social position that the people in his audience might contemplate. Louis makes clear the absurdity of believing that our status is entirely deserved and that therefore we have no obligations to the less fortunate. The experience that Louie describes is common enough that we don't need to imagine what we would have done in Louie's place, because we already know the answer, and that knowledge makes ignoring our own moral failures impossible.

Leading his audience to acknowledge the casual hypocrisies of our daily lives is important to Louis's comedy, but he is interested in more than that. In *Live at the Beacon Theater*, Louis talks about having had many opportunities on various flights to give up his first-class seat to a soldier sitting in coach, but never actually making the offer. Louis believes that it would be morally good to give his seat to a soldier, but repeatedly decides against acting on this belief. Then Louis continues:

> And here's the worst part: I still just enjoyed the fantasy for myself. . . . I was actually proud of myself for having thought of it. I was proud! "I am such a sweet man. That is so nice of me to think of doing that and then totally never do it."

Louis gets to have his ice cream and eat it too: he congratulates himself for even imagining the possibility of giving up his seat to a soldier, even though he never does it. The incongruity of this attitude is obvious when taken to its logical extreme. If all of your actions are moral failures, you can't be a moral person. Otherwise, we would be forced to say that people whose actions are always morally wrong can still be considered moral people as long as they hold the correct beliefs, even though they never act on those beliefs.

A murderer who believes murder to be wrong is not a moral person based on his moral beliefs being correct—he is still a murderer! Holding praiseworthy beliefs does not make you a good person if you do not act accordingly. Louis's bit illustrates that the danger of moral failure is not just that we might act wrongly, but that we will treat the gap between our beliefs and our actions as having no moral significance at all. This outcome would be disastrous for our entire system of ethics.

When we no longer consider our moral hypocrisies to be worth condemnation, we lose the capacity to be persuaded by moral judgments. Severing the connection between moral belief and moral action would mean being unable to reprimand people for acting against their beliefs or to praise people for acting in accord with them. Then Louis's unwarranted self-satisfaction with his moral beliefs would not be ridiculous; it would be the norm. Most of us already do find some satisfaction in our moral beliefs, but the fact that others can point out the places where our beliefs and actions diverge remains a powerful check on our tendency toward sanctimony.

Hypocrisy is fundamentally a logical contradiction, and in a society that prides itself (correctly or not) on reasoning, being called irrational is a weighty charge. When moral contradictions are no longer relevant, that argument will not be possible.

As a result, we would be able to deflect any moral criticism of our actions by appealing to the correctness of our beliefs, because the gap between them would not be subject to moral scrutiny. Louie reliably demonstrates that having praiseworthy moral beliefs is far easier than consistently acting on those beliefs. So in a world where moral failures go unnoticed, we would all be satisfied in our delusions of unerring morality, cheerfully ignoring all moral judgments, convinced of the rightness of our conduct by the effortless perfection of our moral beliefs.

There can be no moral debate without persuasive moral criticism. A society without substantive moral debate is a society without politics, without ethics, and without art. At the heart of the comedy of Louis C.K. is the conviction that even though none of us truly lives up to our moral beliefs, we have to struggle to make those beliefs a reality. Our moral failures, like Louie's, are reminders that our "little believies" are meaningless unless we are willing to fight for them.

18
Believies Are Not Motivaties

JASON DOCKSTADER

I have a lot of beliefs, and I live by none of 'em. That's just the way I am. They're just my beliefs. I just like believing them. I like that part. They're my little believies. They make me feel good about who I am. But if they get in the way of a thing I want or I want to jackoff or something, I fuckin' do that.

—LOUIS C.K.

There are many very funny and quite incisive observations about morality in Louis C.K.'s comedy. Louis often addresses moral issues by emphasizing the stark contrast between what morality seems to require and what people are actually like. He plays on the fact that many of his own moral intuitions and beliefs do not correspond all that well with his behavior.

Louis does not seem to be all that motivated by his own moral beliefs and judgments. For a philosopher, this is a very interesting phenomenon. In fact, Louis often sounds like he holds certain positions in debates on the relationship between morality and motivation. These debates on moral motivation take place within a field of philosophy called meta-ethics.

Meta-ethics is a branch of philosophy that asks questions about various aspects of moral judgments. For example, it asks questions like, which sort of mental state do moral judgments express? Is it beliefs, desires, or emotions? Or is it perhaps some combination of these? Are moral judgments assertions? Or are they perhaps some other type of speech-act? If moral judgments are assertions are they true or false? If they are true, does that mean there are moral facts to which they correspond? If there are moral facts, are they merely in the mind or are they in the world, or perhaps even outside it? There's a great variety of possible answers to these questions.

Moral motivation is an issue of interest to meta-ethicists. There are two key debates that define the study of moral motivation today. Both debates deal with how moral judgments might move us. On the one hand, there is the debate between Humeans and anti-Humeans. While it is not clear whether David Hume himself was a Humean, contemporary Humeans claim that merely holding a certain moral belief—say, that one ought never to harm the innocent—is not sufficient for being motivated. In other words, holding a moral belief alone could not move us. We need something else, namely a desire. Anti-Humeans disagree. They claim that holding a certain moral belief is sufficient for being motivated. In other words, moral beliefs do move us. They *are* our moral motivations.

Now, on the other hand, there is also the debate between motivational internalists and motivational externalists. This debate is concerned with the nature of the connection between moral judgment and moral motivation. Internalists claim that the connection is a necessary one. This means that if you make a moral judgment you're thereby necessarily motivated by it. Externalists disagree and claim the nature of the connection is merely contingent, meaning that you're not necessarily motivated by a moral judgment. Where you stand in one debate doesn't necessarily determine where you stand in the other. Also, where you stand in either debate can be determined by your prior meta-ethical commitments. For example, your view of moral motivation will probably be affected by whether you regard moral judgments as primarily expressions of beliefs, emotions, or desires.

Before we look at where Louis stands in these debates, we should note that he seems to hold a couple of other basic meta-ethical positions. For starters, Louis appears to be a moral cognitivist of some sort. Moral cognitivism is the position that holds that moral judgments express beliefs. Louis seems to think that moral judgments are not (only or merely) a means of emoting or projecting feelings. Instead, moral judgments aim to describe the morally pertinent qualities of actions or persons.

Louis also at times seems to be a moral success theorist. This means that he often claims that certain moral judgments are in fact true and so moral judgments succeed in corresponding with some moral fact of the matter. Now, I am not claiming that Louis has some worked-out meta-ethical theory that he offers in his comedy. It could be that the way he uses moral discourse is merely another example of how we all use it in an everyday sense. What we can say for sure is that Louis plays up the cognitive aspect of everyday moral speech and announces the apparent truth of certain moral propositions. It could be that he does this for comedic effect, emphasizing the contrast between what has to be morally true and how that truth is somehow open to serious doubt or ineffectuality.

So, for example, Louis concludes his most recent stand-up special, *Oh My God*, with the now famous 'of course, but maybe' bit. Here he asserts three moral propositions that he says are of course true, but which seem at the same time to be open to serious doubt. Louis arrives at this bit by discussing the conflict between good and bad thoughts we have in our heads everyday. He says:

> You know, you have your bad thoughts. Hopefully, you do good things. Everybody has a competition in their brain of good thoughts and bad thoughts. Hopefully, the good thoughts win. For me, I always have both. I have the thing I believe—the good thing, that's the thing I believe—and then there is this thing . . . and I don't believe it, but it is there. It's always this thing . . . and then *this thing*. It's become a category in my brain that I call "Of course, but maybe."

Louis then gives three examples of moral claims that he believes and knows to be true, but which he still cannot help but see as open to doubt. These are the moral judgments that, of course, children with nut allergies should be protected, that it is a terrible tragedy when soldiers die in combat, and that slavery is the worst thing that has ever happened.

Louis treats these beliefs as true. They are not mere expressions of his desires or emotions. This is an example of his moral cognitivism. However, he still has trouble with their being completely true because he finds there to be something clearly empirically questionable about each belief. There is thus something lacking to each moral truth. Perhaps, then, we could say that Louis is, at least based on this bit, a partial moral success theorist, that is, that true moral beliefs are only partially true for him.

This bit echoes a theme found throughout most of his comedy. This theme is that, for Louis, no matter their truth, moral beliefs do not quite have the power we may think they have. They can fail to move us when they are believed and known to be true. There is something about a moral belief, according to Louis, that is fundamentally lacking. I think that Louis's sense that moral beliefs have this defect contributes to his holding certain positions in the debates over moral motivation, namely Humeanism and externalism.

Why Not Kill and Eat a Dolphin? Louis's Humeanism

Recall that the debate between Humeans and anti-Humeans is concerned with whether a moral belief is sufficient for moral motivation. The anti-Humean says that a moral belief is sufficient in some way. Some anti-Humeans claim that just by holding a moral belief we would be moved to act in accordance with it. Other anti-Humeans claim that a moral belief is sufficient for causing the desire that would motivate us to act. Others still claim that not one belief alone but rather a bunch of moral beliefs composes an ideal of how a truly virtuous and rational agent would behave and thus by believing in this ideal one would be motivated to act morally.

For the anti-Humean of all stripes, the sufficiency of belief for motivation entails that a failure to be motivated is a *cognitive* failure. In other words, to be morally demotivated is to be ignorant of what one ought to do. After all, the anti-Humean would say, if you truly believed you ought to perform a moral act, you would not fail to be moved to act. Moral demotivation thus amounts to either lacking a moral belief or having a deficient moral belief.

The Humean counters the anti-Humean by claiming that moral beliefs are insufficient for moral motivation. There just needs to be something else, something more than belief, in order for us to be morally motivated. What is needed is desire. A belief in itself does not move us to act, but a desire to act in accordance with a belief might. Believing that some act is the right thing to do is not enough. We need to also want to do the right thing. So, we need more than just the belief. The main reason the Humean says this is that beliefs in themselves are causally inert. A belief is the attitude we have when we take something to be true. A belief is like a description or reflection of the world, the mental approximation of what is going on out there.

In themselves, beliefs are not aiming to change the world in any way. Instead, they are trying to report the facts. They are trying to fit to the world. Even the belief that, say, we ought to keep promises does nothing in itself to get anyone to keep their promises. What is needed is the desire to keep promises. Desires, unlike beliefs, do not want to fit to the world. Rather, they want the world to fit to them. Desires want to change the world, not describe it as it is. This is called the 'direction of fit' problem. For the Humean, this problem shows that beliefs are insufficient for motivation. However, that beliefs are insufficient does not mean they are irrelevant. They are still needed for motivation.

To be morally motivated, you need not only believe the world is or ought to be a certain way. You also need to desire it to be a certain way. That is the only way you'll really be motivated to act. When it comes to being morally motivated, the Humean says that while beliefs might be necessary, they are never sufficient. Desires are needed as well. And not just any desires. The desire must be appropriately related to the belief.

This is true even though there is no necessary connection between beliefs and desires. As two distinct mental states, the Humean regards it as possible you could either have a certain moral belief without an appropriately corresponding desire to act on that belief, or have a certain desire without an appropriately corresponding belief to guide that desire into a proper motivation to act. This is why it appears many can have the same moral beliefs while acting in quite distinct ways, or have roughly the same desires and yet believe radically distinct things.

What then seems to explain moral demotivation, for the Humean, is either some disconnect between your beliefs and desires or a wholesale lacking of a belief or desire. Since it is more common to have some idea of what you should do, it's likely the lack of desire that explains moral demotivation. Notice, however, that the Humean is not saying that you fail to be morally motivated because your moral belief is somehow incoherent or false, as the anti-Humean would say, but rather because your beliefs and desires do not effectively correspond or because you simply lack the desire to do anything about your belief.

So, is Louis an anti-Humean or Humean about moral motivation? Does he think merely holding moral beliefs is enough to be motivated? Or does he doubt that beliefs are sufficient for motivation? Based on a few bits in his comedy, he appears to be a thorough Humean.

One bit from a 2004 show deals with Louis's views on eating meat. He has no problem admitting that eating meat is wrong. Just as he knows that enslaving people, one's own soldiers dying in combat, and leaving children with nut allergies unprotected are all wrong, he knows it is wrong to eat meat. He is a cognitive vegetarian. The problem is that he does not care that he believes that. He does not see the moral wrongness of eating meat as a reason not to eat meat. The belief is not enough to get him to change his behavior. He simply does not care that it's wrong. He knows it is terrible to eat meat, but that it is terrible is not important to him. Louis says:

Here's the thing, why not kill and eat a dolphin? Why not? 'Oh because . . .' Why not? I don't fucking get it. If you are a tuna, fuck you, we're eating you. So, I don't really see the difference. And I think it is wrong to eat tuna, and dolphin, and cows and everything, but I eat them, I eat them all, because I don't care that it's wrong. I totally think it's terrible, but that's not important to me that it's terrible. So what if it's wrong? It tastes good, and I like the way it feels when I eat it, so fuck it. But I'm not going to pretend that I'm doing something that is okay . . .

In another show around the same time, before again addressing the morality of meat-eating, Louis abstracts out to the basic point he is making: merely believing that something is morally wrong is not sufficient to motivate one to do anything about it. Believing and caring are two different things, two different levels or mental states. One needs to "give a fuck" that something is morally wrong in order for its wrongness to motivate one to do something about it. Louis says:

I guess that would be wrong, to fuck a dead kid. I guess. I was trying to think—I was going through my head—what things are wrong and what things are right. And I guess that's what makes you a good person, or a good citizen, is knowing what is right from wrong, but I don't think that is all of it because you have to give a shit that something's wrong. You know what I mean, because that's another level, because you could know something's wrong and just not give a fuck. Like, I eat meat all the time, every day. I don't think it's right. I think it's wrong to eat meat. I really do.

This seems clearly Humean. Later, in his 2011 Beacon Theatre special, Louis takes a further step in his thinking about the nature of moral beliefs. In this bit, we find him admitting to holding many moral beliefs, but living in accordance with none of them. The topic this time, instead of eating meat, is donating your organs or whole body to science after death. Louis says he agrees with this practice and thinks it is the morally appropriate thing to do. The problem, again, is that he simply will not or cannot do it. He doesn't care that it's the right thing to do. He then goes on to address the status of his moral beliefs: they are just inert mental events he enjoys having and feeling, but which exert close to no causal influence over his behavior. Moral beliefs are mental events to feel good about having, not mental events that inherently move us to do anything.

> Some people try to do something noble with their bodies. They try to have their bodies have some use after they are dead, which I think is a good thought. You are only borrowing your body. You are only borrowing everything. If your body is worth anything when you're done with it, you should pass it on. That's something I really believe. I mean, I'm not going to do it because I don't want to. . . . I have a lot of beliefs and I live by none of them. That's just the way I am. They're just my beliefs. I just like believing them. I like that part. They're my little *believies*. They make me feel good about who I am, but if they get in the way of a thing I want or I want to jack-off or something, I fucking do that.

If Louis were not a Humean, he couldn't possibly confess the causal impotence of his moral beliefs. While Louis's moral beliefs appear to have a clear affective impact on his mental life, apart from the subtle shot of self-congratulation they offer, they don't seem to motivate him to act in any morally correspondent way. In other words, *believies* are not *motivaties*. Again, there needs to be desire.

I Guess That Would Be Wrong, to Fuck a Dead Kid

Recall the other key debate in the study of moral motivation: internalism versus externalism. This debate is concerned not with the possible sufficiency of belief for motivation, but with the nature of the connection between judgment and motivation. Are we *necessarily* motivated by a moral judgment? Or is moral motivation only *contingently* connected to a moral judgment?

The internalist says there is a necessary connection between judgment and motivation, while the externalist says there is only a contingent connection. In other words, for the internalist, to sincerely utter a moral judgment is to necessarily be motivated to act in accordance with it, while for the externalist one could sincerely utter a moral judgment and either not be motivated by it or find that one's motivation to act in accordance with it is rooted in something besides the judgment itself. There are degrees to motivational internalism. Strong internalism says you're motivated no matter what by a judgment, while weak internalism will admit that there may be other factors—like weakness of will, depression, and overall irrationality—that could contravene the necessary connection between judgment and motivation. Even still, the weak internalist will emphasize that any 'normal' or 'rational' or 'good' person will necessarily be motivated by their moral judgments. Most internalists favor weak over strong internalism.

For the externalist, the connection between judgment and motivation is merely contingent, meaning that there is nothing to a judgment that makes it necessarily motivating. If you're morally motivated it will most likely be an expression of a deeper feature of your nature like a general disposition to do the right thing in certain circumstances. That the judgment itself does not necessarily motivate does not mean it does not contribute in some way to your motivation. It's just that it does not *have* to. Your motivation to do the morally appropriate thing could have little to do with the moral judgments you make.

A main difference between the internalist and externalist is that it is impossible, according to the internalist, for you to sincerely make a moral judgment and not be thereby motivated, while for the externalist, because of the contingency of the connection, you could easily make a judgment and not thereby be motivated. Also, for the externalist, you need not manifest any symptoms of depression, weakness of will, or irrationality if you're not moved by your judgments. It could just be you made a moral judgment and yet felt no reason to act in accordance with it. There is nothing incoherent about that.

There does not seem to be anything pathological about externalism, as the internalist might claim. In fact, it's internalism that seems to fail to reflect our common experience. We make many moral judgments we find ourselves feeling no or only very little motivation to do anything about. The actual impact people's moral judgments have on their motivations varies wildly. While some may be moved by their judgments, many others are not, and it would be ridiculous if all those who are not moved by their judgments were revealing some kind of abnormality. Perhaps internalism holding true for some people—people necessarily motivated by their judgments—might itself be abnormal and even pathological.

So, do Louis's observations about moral beliefs make him more of an internalist or externalist? It appears he is much more of an externalist. If he finds beliefs insufficient for motivation, and yet holds a kind of moral cognitivism (where moral judgments do express beliefs that are occasionally true), then externalism would more likely reflect his comments on moral motivation than internalism. The general emphasis Louis places on the causal inertness of beliefs would be very difficult to square with him holding an internalist position.

After all, if beliefs do nothing in themselves to motivate us, how could Louis then seriously propose a necessary connection between moral judgment and motivation? In the bits we looked at, he makes explicit moral judgments and right away admits to the impotence of the beliefs expressed in those judgments. If the judgments were necessarily connected to motivations, he would find it difficult, if not impossible, to confess his lack of motivation. An impotent belief expressed in a judgment cannot necessarily motivate. It may not even contingently motivate. Louis thus has to be an externalist. This is good news for Louis because it makes his position coherent. His Humeanism naturally segues into a latent externalism, and philosophers often note the natural affinity between these positions. Philosophers often support externalism if they also support Humeanism. The great variety in the motivational force of moral judgments implies that they only move us contingently and usually require some accompanying desire.

What's interesting about Louis's position is the role his cognitivism plays in his understanding of moral motivation. If Louis were a cognitivist, Humean, and internalist, then we would have a problem on our hands. Indeed, we would encounter what some meta-ethicists call 'the moral problem:' the irreconcilability of cognitivism, Humeanism, and internalism. Cognitivism says that moral judgments express beliefs, which, as we've seen, Louis agrees with.

There's nothing wrong with claiming that moral judgments express beliefs, but if it were further claimed that those beliefs were insufficient for motivation and yet their expression in a judgment necessarily motivated us, then we would be holding an inconsistent position. Luckily, Louis does not appear to be an internalist and so we do not encounter the 'moral problem'.

A final point about Louis's Humean externalism is that it allows for the conceptual possibility of the amoralist. The amoralist is a key figure in debates about moral motivation. The amoralist is someone who makes sincere moral judgments and yet is not motivated by them. For the internalist, the amoralist is a conceptual impossibility. If you made a sincere moral judgment, you would necessarily be motivated. If you were not morally motivated, you did not make a sincere moral judgment. You could not get away with sincerely judging and not necessarily being moved.

The weak internalist would not deny that your sincere moral judgment could be defeated by weakness of will, depression, or other irrationalities or pathologies, but these are external conditions that would not affect a rational, normal and competent moral judge. Now, if the only way to preserve internalism against Louis's claims would be to speculate about his mental health, then I think that would smack of desperation. For, unless we were comfortable with a kind of arrogant armchair psychoanalyzing, who are we to determine whether Louis is depressed, weak, or mentally ill?

Instead of resorting to such nonsense, let's grant that the amoralist is conceivable and thus possible, and so externalism is more likely to hold. Externalism has no problem explaining the very common experience of making genuine and sincere moral judgments and yet not being moved to do much about them. The nature of the connection between judgment and motivation is contingent and requires a prior affective or conative push or pull to activate your moral beliefs.

To claim that amoralism is possible and that Louis is probably an amoralist himself is neither to speak falsely nor cast accusations. Not to let it go unsaid, that Louis's position allows for amoralism does not entail it allows for immoralism, or that Louis's observations make him immoral. Rather, he is amoral, just like many of us.

Being amoral may not be desirable, but it is certainly real. It can also be very funny, which may be a greater kind of justification.

VII

Take Some
Responsibility
for the
Shitty Words
You Want
to Say

19
The Playful Thought Experiments of Louis C.K.

CHRIS A. KRAMER

If you don't think it's great being white you're an asshole!

—LOUIS C.K.

In what world is it possible that the assholes Louis C.K. is addressing would not only continue listening to and *enjoying* his apparent verbal violence directed at them, but also accept his accusation as true? In what world could this lead to attitude change among the "assholes" in the audience?

That world is this one—the real world. In much of Louis's humor, he creates a fictional *joke*-world, but one in which he intends to convey something as actually being true in the real world. So, what he's saying is, in one sense, *serious*. As a comedian, he is of course being playful in his performance, because he truly intends to get people to laugh, but he also wants them to follow him to his punchline or "conclusion."

Louis is using a persuasive device that is a ready-to-hand weapon in the philosopher's arsenal (and the scientist's too): the thought experiment. This is a tool for testing ideas in the workshop of our minds, sometimes to bring to our attention an important concept, or to convince us that something is true. Usually, a thought experiment is a fantastic account that "hooks" us in a way that straightforward arguments rarely do, and induces us to shift perspectives and see what has always been right beneath our noses but we have failed to notice, often because we wished not to.

Philosophers Playing with Thought

Philosophers like to use make-believe worlds—"possible worlds"—to help readers wrap their minds around otherwise complex and controversial issues that cannot be examined in a real physical laboratory, especially when doing so might require harming another person. For instance, if we're pondering what would have to be extracted from someone so as to remove her personal identity, we can't just start poking around in her prefrontal cortex to see what happens. But we can do this in imagination—in a thought experiment.

With thought experiments, a philosopher can construct little stories from which we can easily draw a mental picture to aid in understanding. We imagine brain transplants to tackle identity dilemmas, or chasing a beam of light to unravel the puzzles of special relativity, or, as Louis muses in *Shameless*, we can visualize how World War II could have been avoided if Louis had a time machine to go back and *rape* Hitler.

One of the most influential of all philosophical thought experiments comes from Plato who gets us to envision what it would be like to confuse shadows for reality and how we might even threaten to kill those who dare to point out our flawed worldview. We don't mistake Plato's famous "Allegory of the Cave" for a true historical account, but when we picture prisoners chained to a cave wall whose entire world consists of the shadows of puppets cast upon the back wall by the light of a fire, we learn something that might be true about human minds in the real world. Two connected insights from this story are also found in Louis's comedy: the awareness of our deep-seated tendency to hold onto our feelings of certainty, and our willingness to remain closed to alternative accounts of the world and ourselves that disturb that complacency.

When one of the escaped prisoners returns to the darkened cave after being illuminated by the genuine light of the sun, Plato proposes that the others would violently oppose him just for suggesting a new way of seeing, contrary to their habituated outlook. Reading this thought experiment, we have no illusions about who is closer to the truth within the story. But Plato's literary description invites us to consider how the fictional characters are similar to us (*Republic*, line 515a).

We might call this a Socratic form of "education" in which he "draws out," *educes*, frames of reference already within his readers. Plato is stoking our imaginations triggering the appropriate emotions and our *own* ideas. As Ernst Mach, the philosopher of science who popularized the phrase "thought experiment" puts it; these ideas "are more easily and readily at our disposal than physical facts. We experiment with thought, so to say, at little expense."

We see the world and ourselves through frames or expectations that have formed over time through experience. These lenses are also constructed through cultural stereotypes that can contaminate our perception of other people, frequently without our conscious awareness. Since these frames can be implicit, we need some means of drawing our attention to them. Philosopher Tamar Gendler argues that thought experiments elicit "a reconfiguration of internal conceptual space." The experiment in thought extracts what we already (should) know about a question. It allows us to compare our assumptions that were not initially formed through argument, with specific details in an imaginative scenario. Gendler is mostly concerned with scientific thought experiments, but a similar case can be made for ethical or social observations of the sort Louis addresses in his performances and TV shows.

In one example, Gendler equates the Biblical parable of King David with a successful thought experiment. This is the tale of the King of Israel who takes advantage of and impregnates the beautiful woman Bathsheba and has her husband killed. David comes to see his actions for what they are when he gets swept up in a fictional story about the unjust actions of the central figure.

The moment of conversion is when it clicks for David that the imaginative scenario mirrors his own, and he cannot avoid the conclusion that he is guilty. He finally "gets" the "punch line" but by way of an indirect, imaginative construction. David is *encouraged* to recall his own ideal principles and apply them to a fictional case. But the moment he does this, it strikes him that he is violating his own imperatives in the *real world*. This facilitates an attitude change in David in a way straightforward argument likely would not have.

Gendler claims that this example shows how to overcome the closed-mindedness common to hubris or pride "by framing

the story so that David is not in a position to exhibit first-person bias with respect to what turns out to be his own actions.
. . . The story he has been told is fully effective; it reshapes his cognitive frame, and brings him to view his own previous actions in its light."

The focus here is on the reshaping of frames of reference and the openness to being persuaded through imaginative creations. This requires the inclination to shift perspectives even if doing so might otherwise be unpleasant, as is usually the case when an inconsistency has been spotted between your professed values and your behavior. But the thought experiment brings readers into the story which, as Gendler claims, makes them (willing) contributors in the *"constructive participation
. . .* of the *experiment-in-thought."*

When we get the point of a thought experiment there is often a flash of recognition or feeling of "Aha, I get it." This is the "Huh!" or "That's funny" response that is often the beginning of genuine philosophical thinking. What distinguishes comedians like Louis is his expertise in pushing the "Huh!" and "Aha!" mental states of understanding common in thought experiments, with the emotional, *motivating* feelings of mirthful "Ha-ha's" in humorous laughter.

Comedians Playing with Thought

Some philosophers, such as John Morreall and David Gooding, have commented on the connection between thought experiments and jokes. Gooding points out that "thought experiments have much in common with jokes . . . There is a punch-line requiring an insight which changes our understanding of the story. In both cases we see the point without its being articulated as an argument." These elements are found in Louis's humor, most of which *could* be backed up by direct argument, but this is not necessary when he presents it in a way that tunes us into something that is just obvious to us *now*, after our frames of reference have been adjusted.

Louis explores many situations where our ideals conflict with other dogmas that we tenaciously hold onto because they validate our nation or us, like the slogans "My country right or wrong" or "The US is the single greatest and best country God has given man on the face of the planet," or being constantly told "You are amazing" (*Live at the Comedy Store*). Most of us believe that there are no morally relevant differences between men and women, or between whites and blacks, or that the ideals of the US should generate a genuine meritocracy in which the individual is solely responsible for all of her successes *and failures*.

But Louis confronts us with these ideals and reveals how they are inconsistent with actuality. Here are two of these unpleasant realities that we all know to be true but conflict with our professed principles: the fact that our country was built primarily by slave labor, and the fact that eighty percent of US history has been one of categorical exclusion for most of the world's population. Louis's humorous thought experiments make it extremely difficult to continue ignoring these sorts of incongruous or contradictory beliefs. He employs the same approach when he confronts the everyday inconsistencies of our beliefs and actions as he does when he exposes the absurdities of racism, sexism, or classism.

Louis's Serious Play

As with well-constructed thought experiments, Louis's social commentary is methodically fashioned. He meticulously tests words to get just the right language to humorously remind us of truths such as the fact that women were only *granted* the right to vote in 1920. That byte of information has much more bite with the way Louis presents it: "American democracy is ninety-four years old! There are three people in my building older than American democracy" (*Saturday Night Live*, 2014).

Louis thrives in the spaces of tension created by smashing together ideas that we didn't think (or wish) to compare. Relating the age of individual apartment dwellers with our majestic democracy gives us more than a simple fact. We *see* this fact in a different and compelling context.

In order for us to get a joke, much less enjoy it, shifting perspectives is essential, and Louis is quite good at encouraging a broadening of views in a critical fashion. His jokes are constructed in the way philosophical thought experiments are, which (as Tamar Gendler puts it) "allow us to make use of information about the world which was, in some sense, there all along, if only we had known how to systematize it into patterns of which we were able to make sense."

To frame the facts in his performances in the form of logical arguments would look as ludicrous as reasoning to the conclusion that we take technology for granted today; something Louis reminds us about with his anecdote on the incongruity of the "miracle of flight" and our complaints about having to wait a little on the runway: "Did you fly through the air like a bird, incredibly? Did you soar into the clouds, impossibly? Did you partake in the miracle of human flight and then land softly on giant tires that you couldn't even conceive how they fucking put air in them? . . . You're sitting in a chair in the sky. You're like a Greek myth right now" (*Hilarious*).

The exaggerated comparison stresses one of his points. Really, he seems to be saying that it is not hyperbole at all to compare our capacity to make giant metal ships fly through the air to acts of Gods. In one way, this is an observation about flying that is so obvious it need not be stated. But the humorous framing of the issue cleverly opens his audiences to an insight about something that is transparently true, and yet we don't have the urge to respond sarcastically with "Oh thanks, Captain Obvious!" because we see now that these things *do* need to be stated.

But Louis goes further with this bit, appealing, as he does very often, to time travel, a staple of so many thought experiments: "If you could go back in time to Orville Wright and go, 'Hey, dude, I had to sit on the runway for *forty* minutes.' And he'd be like, 'Oh, shit. Well, let's not even bother then. Hey, Wilbur, shut it down. They make you wait for a bit'" (*Hilarious*).

We need not respond to this piece with "That is so true" and certainly not with "Yeah, time travel really *is* possible." But only the most closed-minded prideful person would not recognize in this thought experiment at least a glimpse of his own unwarranted impatience and ridiculous behavior.

Louis's Really Serious Play

Louis also attends to social and moral concerns that have significant consequences if they remain buried. He shows us how we have become habituated into complacency and comfort, whether it is through the gadgetry of technology or the subtle bigotry that is more than a mere residue from an explicitly racist and sexist past. And we need the reminder that this was not all that long ago: "Every year white people add one hundred years to how long ago slavery was . . . and its not like it ended and everything was *amazing* for black people . . . and it just ended like a clean shit where you don't have to wipe" (*Live at Carnegie Hall*).

In one performance, he envisions an early encounter between indigenous people in the "new world" and white European "settlers." In this made-up scenario, he invites his audience to recognize an absurdity in our past, but also one that continues to have consequences today:

> I really think that white people are from another planet because when we came to America, it was so nice. It was just Indians. And they weren't even Indians. We called them that by accident. And we still call them that. We knew in a month that it wasn't Indians but we just don't give a shit. We never correct it. We came here. They're like, "Hi." And we're like, "Hey, you're Indians, right?" And they're like, "No." "No, this is India, right?" "No, it's not. It's a totally other place." "You're not Indians?" "No." "Ahh, you're Indians." "You're Indians for hundreds of years after." (*Live at the Beacon Theater*)

Now, this is not a historical account that, say, Columbus jotted down in his diary: "Day 1—India. Inconceivably, the Indians refuse to be called 'Indians.'" It is an imagined situation invented by Louis. The audience gets the playfulness here, but Louis is not playing *frivolously*. He is serious about the claim that white people generally "just don't give a shit," and, as he has said many times, this is because they usually don't have to.

To return briefly to the opening quotation of this chapter, here is the context of the thought experiment in which that accusation is levied: "Here's how great it is to be white. I could get in a time machine and go to any time, and it would be fucking awesome when I get there. That is exclusively a white privilege. Black people can't fuck with time machines!" (*Chewed Up*). Louis makes a direct claim but in a fictionalized setting that is contoured with witty humor. The humor is not merely sugar-coating on an otherwise distasteful subject; it is the driving force used to jar us out of our arrogance.

Louis disrupts our smugness related to class as well: "'White trash' is the only racial expression you can use and nobody gets offended...'I saw this guy who was white trash' . . . 'fuck that guy . . . let's laugh at him because he is poor and he's starving to death, fucking loser . . . let's go shit right in his face right now'" (Vancouver, 2004). We're not likely to ever go to the extremes Louis imagines in this scenario, but the hyperbole shifts our frames to make us aware of the harmful words we unthinkingly use.

Louis, like many philosophical thought-experimenters, "exaggerates or distorts his observations as a participant-observer talking to people in his own society about the familiar cultural rules and behavior patterns in *their* and *his* own society", and highlights information that they knew "all along but no one ever said it like that to them before" (Stephanie Koziski, "The Standup Comedian as Anthropologist").

He's not saying something that is astonishing or that requires a great burden of proof to logically defend. We know what he says is true in the way we know we are "sitting in a chair in the sky" when in an airplane. We get what he intends in the way David gets what Nathan reveals to him through fiction, not argument: "I'm not saying that white people are better. I'm saying that *being* white is *clearly* better. Who could even argue with that?" (*Chewed Up*).

When in the hands of a capable comedian like Louis, we have even more incentive to follow the story and comprehend what it says, for we get the pleasure of mirth or the "Ha-ha" experience of humor in addition to the "Aha!" experience of discovery. The cognitive "Aha!" can be stimulated by the emotion of mirth.

Tweaking Our Mirth Addiction

By "tweaking" I have in mind two distinct senses: twisting or cajoling us in order to get us to recognize the unjustified beliefs we possess; and adjusting or fine-tuning our sets of beliefs that have just been tweaked. The phonetic similarity to "meth addiction" is not accidental. In the spirit of thought experimentation and humor, I am exaggerating the connection, but only a bit.

Louis is an experienced comedian, which means he knows his audience and he knows how to construct a joke or humorous story with the right language, content, and tone to achieve the response he wants. He knows how to exploit our addiction to humor. The term "addiction" is quite strong, but it expresses the penchant we have to get our fix of funniness. Hurley, Dennett, and Adams point out that our compulsion to laugh at humor is as powerful as our desire for candy, music, drugs, and sex (*Inside Jokes*).

With each of these examples and with humor, similar regions in the reward centers of our brains light up upon receiving the fix. Ward Jones tell us that "As the mesolimbic area contains dopamine-releasing 'reward centers', these correlations provide support for the claim that *finding funny* is a physiologically pleasurable state." We feed this habit through movies, cartoons, TV series, YouTube videos of cats behaving like furry humans, and comedy clubs, or "Mirth Labs." Louis uses at least three of these modes to hook us on his humor, and like a benevolent drug dealer, he has legions of uninhibited "users" who are prepared to trail him almost wherever he dares to go—and there aren't many bounds to Louis's humorous visions.

"Humor is a modern human addiction", or at least a "near addiction" (*Inside Jokes*) but there are benefits that come with our humor habit—side effects may include: raised consciousness, exposed fallacy, baring of erroneous presuppositions, onset of a playful and open disposition, and well-defined cheek muscles. These are each positive side effects; it is good to recognize when we have reasoned poorly by committing a fallacy, and when hidden assumptions or presuppositions are brought to light.

Louis's jokes expose the gaps between our ideals and our habitual behaviors. Current cognitive science supports this positive role of humor as an error-detection device for our complex system of beliefs, much of which is unconscious: "So there has to be a policy of double-checking these candidate beliefs and surmisings, and the discovery and resolution of these at breakneck speed is maintained by a powerful reward system— the feeling of humor; mirth" (*Inside Jokes*).

Louis's humor is especially rewarding because it is exceptionally *hilarious*, and we are given an opportunity to see the world differently without the discomfort that accompanies direct attempts to force a shift in perspectives. We can see our flaws through Louis's experiments in thought that at times seem removed from reality: "It doesn't matter 'cuz I'm gonna lie to you" (*Shameless*). But in other instances he fabricates a funny fable that is "not true, but it is as true as anything that does happen" (*Oh My God*).

The Fruits of Louis's Mental Masturbation

Self-love is a good thing, but self-awareness is more important.

—LOUIS C.K., *Comedy Store*

In *Hilarious*, Louis claims he is stupid, but not stupid enough. He thinks about his own thinking enough to recognize when he is being ridiculous, and his humor allows him to construct playful, but *real*, stories to help with analysis. Here he differs from many comedians and philosophical thought experimenters, and I think his comedy is better for it.

Louis engages in what I would call a positive form of mental masturbation—sometimes actually about his own addiction to masturbation—where he plays with himself in the *laboratory of his mind*. But this form of "self-love" includes deep "self-awareness," and also an audience. It has a practical purpose.

It is uninhibited play that lures audiences to mentally play with themselves outside of the constraining rules of logic, language, and society. Louis uses self-deprecation to expose his own ignorance to let us into his mind, which is really an indirect method to get us into our own. He's not telling us how unique he is; he's uniquely showing us how similar we are to him, and in doing so, he makes self-reflection alluring. In his latest standup special, he indicates what he thinks is important. Here is the end of the quotation that opens this section: "You need to once in a while go 'Ugh I'm kind of an asshole'" (*Comedy Store*). But this recognition is the beginning of critical introspection, a movement away from self-absorption.

By invoking playfulness, Louis is also eliciting curiosity and creativity in his audience. He opens spaces for others to creatively connect notions in a benign but *not* tensionless environment. We can entertain the ideas Louis presents without responding combatively or defensively. Through tweaking our mirth addiction, Louis breaks us out of our seriousness, or attitude in which we seek certainty and stubbornly avoid ambiguity, incongruity, novelty, complexity, tension, and doubt—the stuff of humor and life.

Louis is serious in the same way that philosophers are serious even though they are "making shit up" (*Oh My God*) in thought experiments. Louis employs a similar device with his humor, and in many ways is more effective than philosophers in raising consciousness for his much larger and more diverse audiences who then spread his word.

It's best to end with Louis's own words regarding the aims of his humor: While "I am playing with the audience . . . I don't believe in just upsetting people. I believe in taking people to upsetting territory and making them glad they went there. . . . If you just make people happy, you're a fucking whore. If you just hurt them, you're a murderer. But if you take them to a scary place and make them laugh, that's worth doing" (Sundance 2010, *Hilarious*, Intro and Q&A).[1]

---

[1] The idea for this chapter arose out of a couple of sections from my dissertation, *Subversive Humor*, Marquette University, 2015.

20
Feminists *Can* Take a Joke

JENNIFER MARRA

I don't think women are better than men, but I do think that men are worse than women.

—LOUIS C.K.

Comedians and feminists are natural enemies, says Louis C.K. in a 2012 interview with Jon Stewart. A lot of people would agree. Comedians make their living poking fun at others, and feminists think that some jokes are harmful and contribute to larger societal problems.

But Louis has somehow been hailed as a hero by both groups; feminists such as Madeleine Davies have cited the 2014 episode of *Louie* titled "So Did the Fat Lady" as proof that Louis is "one of the greatest comic minds of our generation," while comics like Ian Goldstein point to his willingness to talk about any topic, no matter how offensive, and constantly write new material.

How is this possible? On the one hand we have a comic who points out double standards of beauty between men and women, and at the same time we have the same comic calling women words like "cunt" and "bitch." How do we reconcile this? Is Louis a feminist spokesperson or part of the problem?

Natural Enemies?

What does "feminist" even mean? There are a lot of definitions, but let's clear up the most common misconception right away:

"feminist" does not mean "man hating lesbian who thinks women should rule the world." Feminism is the idea that women and men are both human beings, and thus ought to have the same rights and be held to the same standards. To be a feminist is to fight against oppression in all forms against any group. That is, fighting for equal pay for women or equal rights for the LGBTQ community are both feminist actions. What this means is that anyone, of any gender, can be a feminist. You don't have to be a woman. You don't have to be sexually attracted to women. You don't have to have a lot of female friends. You just have to hold the view that women are people. That's really all there is to it. So there really is nothing inherent in feminism that makes it necessarily an enemy of comedy.

Feminist *philosophy*, as explained by Jennifer Mather Saul, "begins from a critique of more traditional philosophy." "Traditional philosophy" is one way of saying "the ideas of powerful white men." Because these men had the time to devote to thinking, the money and connections to publish, and the privilege of having their ideas taken seriously by virtue of the fact that they were men, a great deal of the history of philosophy is the voices of rich white guys.

This isn't a problem in itself; these thinkers made extremely important contributions and their work should be read. The problem comes, feminists believe, when philosophy focuses *only* on these voices. So feminist philosophy seeks to balance out these voices with others, focusing a great deal on minority perspectives in order to get a better understanding of humanity as a whole.

Without these perspectives, we don't have a complete picture. You can't solve problems if you don't know about them, and it's impossible to solve the problems of human experience, morality, and truth if you only hear the voices of the powerful. So when Louis lets his female characters speak, and when he listens to women and tries to put himself in a position of understanding, Louis is performing feminist philosophy. He does this as well when he talks about white privilege, and the experiences of Black and Native American communities, and first world problems. And he certainly does this when talking about rape culture on *The Daily Show*.

Why Don't You Shut Up and Learn Something?

Just as feminist philosophers begin from critiquing traditional views, so too does Louis's standup begin by exposing common assumptions about society, children, parenting, race, women, and more. Louis looks at the ideas and morals that we take for granted and asks us to stop and think about them, if only for a little bit. He often does this by crafting his jokes from a perspective that never gets attention. Take this bit about Christians opposing environmentalism in *Live at the Beacon Theater* for example: "If you believe that God gave you the Earth, . . . why would you not have to look after it? Why would you not think that when he came back he wouldn't go, 'What the fuck did you do?! I gave this to you, motherfucker, are you crazy?!'" (*Live at the Beacon Theater*, 2011). In this bit Louis lets God speak, and in doing so he exposes the underlying and often ignored presumptions of Christian understandings of God and the world. Or this bit from *Chewed Up*:

> I'm not saying that white people are better. I'm saying that *being* white is *clearly* better. . . . Here's how great it is to be white. I can get in a time machine and go to any time and it would be fuckin' awesome when I get there. That is exclusively a white privilege. Black people can't fuck with time machines. A black guy in a time machine is like, "Hey anything before 1980, no thank you, I don't want to go." But I can go to any time. The year two. I don't even know what was happening then. But I know when I get there, "Welcome, we have a table right here for you, sir." (*Chewed Up*)

Louis not only gives voice to African Americans when he says "No thank you" on their behalf, he also allows us to see from a white perspective things white people take for granted. Most white people are spectacularly unaware of the privileges their whiteness affords them because, to them, it's just *normal.* Because it's considered normal, it's assumed that the world works this way for everyone. It takes Louis calling attention to this assumption for a white audience member to even be aware of the fact that these things *aren't* actually normal, they are luxuries afforded only to some.

In the second episode of the first season of *Louie*, Louie and some comic friends are playing poker. In the course of some good-natured banter, the word "faggot" gets thrown around as an insult like it's going out of style, something pretty typical among the straight male crowd. Like a good feminist philosopher, Louis writes this episode so that the use of the word itself becomes part of the conversation. As an audience, we may presume that the word is harmless and just something people say. But this presumption is challenged head on when Rick, a gay comedian, articulates the perspective of a gay man upon hearing the word. He says:

> You might want to know that every gay man in America has probably had that word shouted at them while they're being beaten up, sometimes many times, sometimes by a lot of people all at once. So, when you say it, it kind of brings that all back up. But, you know, by all means use it. Get your laughs. But, you know, now you know what it means. (*Louie*, Season One, Episode 2)

Here again we have a great example of giving the minority a voice. Louis's not the one giving the speech, but he does have full creative control over his show just as he has full creative control over his standup performances. In choosing to include these marginalized voices, Louis is acting as a feminist philosopher.

At one point, Louie asks Rick about an event called City Jerks. When another comedian protests, clearly very uncomfortable with a conversation about gay sex, Louie snaps at him: "Hey, why don't you shut up and learn something?" That is what feminist philosophy is all about. Don't disregard something because it makes you uncomfortable, Louie is saying; don't refuse to believe something because you can't relate to it, and don't assume that everyone experiences life the same way that you do. Our situations are different, and in order to understand each other we have to listen to each other.

So Did the Fat Lady

The 2014 episode of *Louie* titled "So Did the Fat Lady" (Season Three, Episode 4) made a huge splash within the feminist community. In it, Louie begrudgingly accepts a date with a charming, overweight waitress named Vanessa (played by Sarah

Baker). The two end up genuinely enjoying each others' company, though Louie seems hesitant about pursuing a relationship. While reporting on how awkward dating is in itself, Vanessa explains that it's particularly hard given that she is "a fat girl," a point which Louie automatically counters by saying that she's not fat. And Vanessa is having none of it. What follows is a tense, brutally honest, unapologetic seven-minute confrontation of societal beauty standards and the way that men treat women who don't fit those standards.

Throughout, Louie remains relatively silent, allowing Vanessa to explain her frustrations with being lied to about the romantic relevance of her weight ("You know what the meanest thing is you can say to a fat girl? 'You're not fat.'"). It's not that Vanessa has a skewed body image and thinks she's fat when really she's a Size 4; it's that she's so much more than just a fat girl, and her fatness shouldn't be the only thing that determines whether or not she deserves love or respect. She calls out the fact that it's both socially acceptable and charming when men acknowledge that they are fat, "but if I say it, they call a suicide hotline on me." Being fat, Vanessa explains, should not be the end of the world for a woman, just as it's not the end of the world for men, and yet men make fat women feel as though they are hated and undeserving of romantic attention.

The fact that Louis as writer silences Louie the character and allows Vanessa to hold him responsible for perpetuating the double standard was hailed by feminist blog Jezebel as "absolutely magnificent," finally—*finally*—giving voice to a stigmatized community that society is still unwilling to acknowledge it has a problem with. Making fun of the fat girl is still widely acceptable in American culture, and comedians in particular take cheap shots at them all the time. To confront this, to write himself in as the character who is performing the very behavior that is being condemned, and to refrain from allowing Louie to try and make excuses or justify himself, is huge. Louie knows he's wrong, realizes that he's been a part of the problem, and doesn't try to wiggle out of it. And Vanessa is a strong, cute, funny, charming person who is also fat, knows she's fat, and won't let him get away with pretending she's not. Why can't she be all these things and a fat girl at the same time? This is a question that she not only asks Louie, but asks the audience as well. If men can be all of those things at once, why can't women?

For Louis to write this episode, to cast an actual overweight actress, and to give her control over the scene is indisputable evidence of his desire to do and perform feminist philosophy. Is it uncomfortable? Yeah. Yeah, it really is. And good, because it should be. To be otherwise would be disingenuous to Vanessa's experience and the experience of every other fat girl who has lived her reality. For Louis to go for it despite the discomfort of acknowledging his personal responsibility in perpetuating the problem is an incredible example of feminist philosophy in action.

The Tosh Rape Joke Debate

In the summer of 2012, Louis got a lot of heat for tweeting what many people assumed was a statement in support of comedian Daniel Tosh, who had found himself at the center of a debate involving rape jokes. Louis explains in this interview that he had been on vacation and wasn't aware of the controversy at all; he simply tweeted Tosh because he had seen an episode of his show, *Tosh.0*, and wanted to say that he enjoyed it. In the course of the interview, Louis says that he doesn't think it was a bad thing for Tosh to have told the rape joke and sparked the debate. He says, "All dialogue is positive . . . I think you should listen. If someone has the opposite feeling from me, I want to hear it so I can add to mine. I don't want to obliterate theirs with mine—that's how I feel . . ." He goes on, "I've read some blogs during this whole thing that have made me enlightened to things I didn't know. This woman said how rape is something that polices women's lives. They have a narrow corridor; they can't go out late; they can't go to certain neighborhoods; they can't dress a certain way. That's part of me now, that it wasn't before" (*The Daily Show*, 2012).

The acknowledgement of the role that rape plays in women's lives is crucial. Many people aren't willing to take this step, which is only one of many first steps that feminist philosophers believe is crucial to understanding the way human beings live and how to go about making those lives better for everyone. The first step is educating yourself about the lived experiences of other people. It is to take their experiences seriously and understand, as much as you can, what it is like to live in their shoes. It is to listen to them and hear what they have to say, and not to dismiss it outright because your gut reaction tells you that it's not worth your time. By educating himself, and in turn educating us about the realities of what feminist philosophers like Claudia Card call "rape culture," Louis is doing good work for women.

"Cunt," "Faggot," and "Nigger"

But hang on, you may be thinking, what about all the jokes making fun of women? When he says that the difference between men and women is that men will break your shit but women are fucked up and "will take a shit inside your heart" (*Chewed Up*), he's playing into what feminists would consider very damaging gender stereotypes. In *Hilarious* he refers to a woman he has never met or even seen as a "cunt." He uses the word "faggot," and not always as a means to make a point like in the poker scene. Louis says "nigger," and in *Chewed Up* he gets mad when other people self-censor by saying, "n-word." How can we say that Louis is like a feminist philosopher, doing good work by giving voice to the marginalized, when he uses slurs for those very groups?

Now, I'm not going to argue that Louis is off the hook here, or that he shouldn't be held accountable for using those words. What I will say is that sometimes he uses the words to take power away from them or to make us rethink our use of them. For example, when he's pissed off about people saying "the n-word," he's not pissed off because he thinks they should say "nigger" instead; he's pissed off because he thinks "When you say 'the n-word,' you put the word 'nigger' in the listener's head. . . . You're making me say it in my head! Why don't you say it? Take responsibility for the shitty words you want to use!" Here he's not encouraging people to go around saying "nigger." He's encouraging people who *want* to say it to acknowledge their responsibility in doing so instead of "hid[ing] behind the first letter."

Okay, sure, you may say, but he follows that up with saying "faggot": "Don't hide behind the first letter like a faggot." What about that? What about when he's saying these words and it isn't in some kind of virtuous context? To that I say, you're right. He's not a poster child for feminism or feminist philoso-

phy, but that doesn't mean he isn't a feminist or doesn't perform feminist philosophy. In fact, I would argue that part of the
reason why Louis's feminist comedy is so powerful and important is precisely because he's not the perfect poster boy. Louis
fucks up, just like we do. He's just like the rest of us in that he
falls into stereotyping and bias despite himself. Even when we
are so well intentioned, we make mistakes. Sometimes we
make those mistakes and only realize years later that it was a
mistake. But he's trying. And that's the key.

Louis speaks to large and diverse audiences about controversial issues, and he can do it without making them defensive
precisely because he's trying to figure it out himself. He fucks
up. And he *knows* that he fucks up. He's not afraid to admit
that he's wrong, to self-deprecate, to point out how he has stupid impulses that the intelligent part of his brain has to deal
with. At the end of the day, Louis is doing good work. He's not
perfect, but neither are any of us. We listen to him because we
can relate, and it is because we can relate to him that we are
more able to relate to the alternative perspectives he offers.

If Louis were the type of comic who was *always* politically
correct, *always* sensitive to the words he used, *always* using
comedy to educate audiences on the experiences of the
oppressed, he would have a much smaller group of like-minded
fans. Only people who already agreed with him would listen
and he would just be reinforcing things that they all already
knew and agreed with. But he's not that guy. And being "not
that guy" has given him a much bigger audience, with a complex demographic and a variety of opinions and beliefs, who
can all relate to him on some level or another.

While I may be well aware of rape culture as a woman in
America, the guy next to me has probably never thought about
it. Yet we're both there, listening to Louis, because he can speak
to both of us. Now this guy who came to hear about jerking off
while the kids are away hears Louis talking about rape culture,
maybe for the first time. And it's coming from the mouth of a
guy like him acknowledging that, hey, it's a thing. He might go
home and think about that or he might not, but now he's been
exposed to the idea, which is better than never hearing about
it at all or assuming women are just being dramatic or over-
sensitive. Would this guy have intentionally gone out to see
someone speak about rape culture? Likely not. But he did

intentionally go out to see Louis talk about masturbating and in the course of the evening he ended up learning something he didn't know before. And he got to laugh along with some "shame glaze" jokes at the same time. Everyone wins.

So, yeah, Louis shouldn't call anyone a cunt, but the fact that he does doesn't automatically mean that he's not, or cannot be, a feminist. Louis's a feminist because he doesn't want his daughters to grow up to be "the hot chick at the bar," because he tells rape jokes that aren't at the expense of the victim or making light of the act itself. He's a feminist because he writes stories about what it's like to be the fat girl in the dating world, and he gives the fat girl a voice, he lets her speak, he doesn't interrupt her. He is attracted to women, not girls, even though, yeah, he'd still fuck them, if they would let him. He wants us to know that women are sexual beings ("fuck a woman well and she'll leave you alone"), that rape controls their lives, that we can learn from offense, and that learning others' perspectives and educating oneself on why people take offense can bring something positive out of an otherwise negative situation.

Try, Fail, Repeat

Louis an especially powerful and important feminist voice in contemporary culture precisely because, like the rest of us, he too can fall into gender stereotyping. The self-conscious, reflective style with which he delivers his jokes and produces his show are crucial to educating his audience on very real, and very dangerous, inequalities that exist in American culture. Louis makes the crucial point that feminism isn't just a chick thing. Feminists do have a sense of humor, and Louis himself is irrefutable evidence.

21

If You're Not White, You're Missing Out

MYISHA CHERRY

Louis C.K. is not afraid to talk about . . . well, anything really. Donned regularly in a black T-shirt on stage, he opines about his daughters, his sex life as a fat guy, social media and how we have ruined the environment. But the one thing that's rare for a white comedian to discuss in his act is the topic of race and his experiences with racial privilege. Louis talks about it and seemingly feels comfortable with it. He's the satirical Tim Wise, brilliantly revealing to us the reality of race, racism, and privilege—from a white male perspective, under the genius of comedic rhetoric, perfect timing, and societal truth.

Instead of sounding like he is trying too hard to be an ally to blacks, or an anti-racist whose mission is to transfer white guilt to his white audience, Louis's comedy instead makes us laugh and think and see at the same time. Louis is a "comedic philosopher of race" whose racial content in his act helps us understand a current social buzzword known as privilege.

The Joys of Being White

Louis admits in *Chewed Up*,

> I'm a lucky guy. I got a lot going on for me. I'm healthy, relatively young . . . I'm white. Thank God for that . . . that's a huge leg up. Are you kidding me? I love being white . . . Seriously, if you're not white you are missing out . . . it's thoroughly good! . . . And I'm a man. How many advantages can one person have?"

247

These advantages that Louis speaks of are called "identity privilege." Privilege is a systematic structure that grants unearned
advantages to a select few based on their identity. Peggy
McIntosh describes privilege as an "invisible package . . . of special provisions." These provisions are based on our identity.
Louis explains that by thanking God that he is white. He is not
implying that white people *are* better. Instead, he is suggesting
that white people *have it* better. There is a difference. The idea
that white people are better is a scientific claim that has been
debunked. The idea that white people have it better is a cultural
claim that social science continues to show is true. For Louis,
privilege is unearned and has nothing to do with merit.

A comedic philosopher of race, Louis explains that just as
our identities vary, so too do our privileges. This is emphasized
when he states, "And I'm a man." In an interview with Opie and
Anthony in which Louis reveals he was born in Mexico, black
comedian Patrice O'Neal says, "I'm more American than Louis
C.K. and he gets to live the American Dream." Louis responds,
"That's right, because I look white." Louis knows that privilege
comes with being a man, but greater privileges come with
being a white man. Just as oppressed people can experience
various kinds of oppression based on the intersection of their
identities, so too can people experience privilege based on certain intersections of their identity. There can exist white privilege and heterosexual privilege, but also white American
privilege and white male privilege. Louis recognizes that he
benefits from being at the intersection of white and male. He
makes us aware that this intersection comes with benefits that
other intersections such as black and male or white and female
may not experience.

For Louis, white privilege can create what he calls "white
people problems." White people problems are not really problems at all. It's when your life is so amazing you make up
things to be upset about. While other identity groups experience inequity in the job market, heightened racial targeting,
brutalization and arrests for crimes they didn't commit, Louis
jokes that white people complain about having to choose a language at the ATM machine. What Louis hints at is the ability
to distinguish people who have white privilege or male privilege from non-privileged people by the "troubles" they complain
about. If they are complaining about a lack of job opportunities,

they are probably black or a woman. If the biggest complaint at hand is about how slow the ATM machine is, the person living this experience is most likely white or male.

If they are complaining about the former, perhaps we should give them the time and freedom to complain because they actually have something worth complaining about. Louis explains this idea further in a *Tonight Show* interview, telling Jay Leno of a time when he informed his daughter that she had no room to complain. For him, she was doing well because, "She looks good on paper. She's a white girl in America . . . she has more clothes made by children her age professionally," so she doesn't get to complain. For him, he wasn't saying that if you are white you don't get to complain. His intention in telling the story was, "if you're black you get to complain more."

Why is this so? Well 'privilege' is not meant to refer to the special advantage you receive in elementary school when you get unlimited recess because you scored high on tests or earned five stars for the week while those other fifth-grade slackers clowned around all day. The real world application of the notion of privilege means there are other groups of people who are locked out of the social advantages and opportunities you have. These people are locked out, not because they're slackers, but because of their skin color, gender, sexual identity, social class, or their disability.

This is why some people have a problem with the concept of "privilege." For them, it obscures our understanding of oppression. They believe that the concept of privilege pertains to an excess of social goods. As a result, "privilege" refers to advantages and fails to capture the denial of human rights and the exclusion of certain groups. But Louis uses the term to refer to the unfairness, disadvantage, and rights restrictions carried out by political and economic systems. For him, it is also a social system that individuals benefit from. Unfortunately, individuals can be in denial about the privilege this social system grants them.

Why Won't We Admit Our Privilege?

Some people are privileged but unaware of it and deny it; others are aware of their privilege but deny it anyway. Louis acknowledges his white male privilege and shuns those who refuse to admit the same. He explains in an interview with Jay Leno on the *Tonight Show*, "If you are white and you don't admit that it's great, then you are an asshole."

"Asshole" is Louis's term for privileged folks in denial; I will call them "privileged deniers." Given the history of America, it's a historical fact that white Americans have had certain social and economic advantages over other groups because they are white. White Americans were never slaves, never held in internment camps, and never subjected to Separate But Equal laws. That's why Louis jokes about time machines being "exclusively a white privilege." A white man can go into a time machine and go to any time and be welcomed. However, a black man may not want to go anywhere before 1980 because of the systematic oppression blacks as a group have experienced throughout American history.

Although times are not as bad as they once were in the United States, the idea that this is a post-racial society is wishful thinking. As Louis explains to Jay Leno, "It's not as if slavery ended and everything has been amazing . . . like it ended like a clean shit where you don't have to wipe." In another interview with Opie and Anthony he continues by stating that it's not as if slavery just ended "and we've been showering them with gifts since then."

There's empirical evidence that can be invoked to support Louis's point. One example is the wealth gap between whites and blacks, which remains very wide (Pew Research Center, 2011). Additionally, black crime is seen as pathological while white crime is rarely mentioned at all (Michael Jackson, 2013). When it is mentioned, mental illness is invoked to justify it. Black and brown criminals are disproportionally incarcerated for drug crimes. White felons are more likely to be called back for interviews than black applicants with no criminal record. Although racism is not as systemic and explicit as it once was, there is clear evidence that many people still hold biased and racist views. You only have to go on twitter, check the recordings and emails of a former NBA owner and current NBA executives, the comment sections of blogs, and the testimonies of countless minorities who have experienced hate crimes, harassment, and discrimination to witness the mayhem.

The privileged deniers may deny their identity privilege for several reasons: 1. they may have a utopian idea of society and thus be unaware or refuse to believe society's ills; 2. they may like to think that their own efforts allow for their advantage, or 3. they may be so focused on their disadvantage that they refuse to recognize their social advantages. In any case, Louis thinks that anyone who doesn't admit his or her privilege is still an "asshole."

A "But for Now, Weeeeeeeeee!" Mentality

Is admitting one's privilege enough? In *Oh My God*, Louis notes that we can admit our privilege and still be complicit in it. To be complicit is to comply with or go along with a racist, classist, sexist, ablest, transphobic, homophobic, or any type of oppressive practice.

Louis claims that human greatness comes from the fact that we are shitty people. He notes that we have smartphones because the people who are creating them are making the technology under horrible conditions. We choose to text people and in doing so we let people suffer. We could be content with candles and horses and in turn be a little kinder to others but we are not.

Louis doesn't put all the blame on Apple or Samsung. It's the consumers who are aware of what they are doing and are therefore complicit in the suffering of others as a result of using the technology. Their complicity is blameworthy. They are aware that the benefits of technology come at the cost of other people's suffering. Likewise, a person can acknowledge that they have privilege and still be complicit in it. Someone can sustain an unjust system even when he or she does not intend to oppress others.

Louis is trying to highlight how complicity works. We may not directly oppress others, but if we are complicit within a system that does, then we are not all that innocent. When we have identity privilege and do not speak out against the unjust system that creates it or attempt to extend that privilege to others who do not have it, we are complicit in their suffering.

Although someone may be forthright in acknowledging their privilege, as Louis is about his own privilege, acknowledgment is not enough to fix the problem. Notice in his phone example that Louis suggests acknowledgement *as well as* an attitude of kindness in order to change things. We can admit we have identity privilege, but that will not improve the social conditions that create the privilege. We will need more than acknowledgement. Acknowledgment alone will still have us complicit but an attitude change such as kindness may be a way to open up new possibilities to others who otherwise feel locked out of basic rights and opportunities.

For Barbara Applebaum, complicity is much more complex than Louis thinks. For instance, in *Being White, Being Good,* Applebaum quotes an example where she tells of a well-intentioned white person who decides to move out of her all white neighborhood. But the very fact that the white person has a choice to move, based on her race and economic status, is an example of her being complicit in privilege. Applebaum notes that with all good intentions, it may be difficult if not impossible for people with privileged identities to escape their privilege and become one hundred percent non-complicit. A White person, a cisman, a straight person, or an abled woman may find that they cannot escape their privilege.

Moreover, Applebaum believes we should move away from fault discourse and focus more on the mobilization of resources to disrupt unjust social systems. Instead of being obsessed with policing one's complicity in privilege, one should spend that time challenging unjust systems. If we focus too much on the individual and their guilt, we will forget that privilege and oppression are systematic and must therefore be fixed systematically.

Applebaum and Louis C.K. seem to be in disagreement with each other. In Louis's show *Chewed Up,* he admits that being white gives a person a leg up. He doesn't want to go to the future because white people are going to pay for what they have done. For Louis, they deserve it. Louis's white guilt is on display. He also challenges us to be kind. However, instead of going beyond the individual and saying "lets challenge the system that creates the privilege," he says, "I don't want to go to the future to find out what happens to white people; we are gonna pay hard for this shit . . . but for now, Weeeeeeeee!" In Louis's statement, the guilt is present but the social criticism and social action are not. The idea of an inevitable karma is present, but not a current suggestion on how to change things now. An acknowledgement that privilege exists is present but it seems as if Louis is endorsing complicity and inaction.

Tell Us What to Do, Louis!

Before we get on Louis for not offering us solutions, perhaps we should view Louis as a comedic philosopher of race whose job is more descriptive than prescriptive. Maybe his job is to show us what privilege looks like and leave it up to others to give us a theory on how to change things. Louis has noted that he once went into a store, walked around a bit, and upon getting into his car, he realized he didn't pay for his bottled water. He assumed the cashiers didn't say anything because they believed he was a white man who would pay one day. That is some great privilege! That is one leg up! On the other hand, in many communities in America, people are being killed because their skin color, clothing, or where they decide to walk, make them *appear* as if they will steal something. Louis acknowledges his privilege and tries to get us to see the world as we all have created or contributed to it. Perhaps getting us to see our privilege and the social system that creates it is his only job as a "comedic philosopher of race." What to do and how to do it, is left up to us.

VIII

Of Course
but Maybe . . .

22
Sometimes Cartesian

ERIC SCHOLL

Louie is not your typical sitcom. It breaks every rule of the comedy genre, including the biggest one: there have to be jokes. Season Four played more as a situation tragedy in places, dealing with some very dark, existential themes and often foregoing laughs entirely. And for a show that is at times brutally realistic, it contains many moments that are flat out strange. People do strange things, like putting their penis into a hole in the wall of a filthy restroom. They witness strange events, like a man's head popping off and rolling under a garbage truck. They have strange names, like "Pissshitfart" (hippies!), or Tape Recorder.

Or Never. Never Cartesian.

Never Say Never

What are we to think of Never Cartesian, the eccentrically dressed, curiously destructive ten-year-old schoolmate of Louie's daughter? Never is not exactly a main character in the *Louie* universe. He's mentioned in the episode "So Old/Playdate" (Season One, Episode 4), but all we really know about him is that he has a hyper-concerned mother and is, according to Pamela, "...a piece of shit." We don't actually see him until Season Three, when he gets his own storyline—he's the Never in "Barney/Never" (Season Three, Episode 6). His first physical appearance raises lots of questions: why doesn't Lilly like him? Why the red bow tie? Why can't he eat carbon? And what's with that name? Never Cartesian?

If you majored in math or philosophy (full disclosure: I didn't —I was a film major) you will recognize that "Cartesian" refers to noted seventeenth-century philosopher and mathematician René Descartes. Descartes does not get many references on television. The only other one I can think of is in the infamous Monty Python philosophers' song (". . . And René Descartes was a drunken fart, I drink therefore I am") so when he *is* referenced, it must be for a reason.

So what does it mean? And if Never is, well, never Cartesian, what does that make Louie? Always Cartesian? Sometimes Cartesian? Louis C.K. is well versed in philosophical concepts, so it's unlikely this is a throwaway gag—a philosophical name drop. No, I believe Never Cartesian is a clue to interpreting the somewhat murky distinctions between reality and unreality in *Louie*.

Louie is steeped in dreams and dream imagery, drug- and food-induced hallucinations, and scenarios that don't feel like they are of the waking world. Garbage men burst through windows, a helicopter whisks Louie's date away, and a speedboat is available when he needs to escape from his father, to name a few examples. Louis C.K. borrows heavily from surrealism, a movement fascinated by the psychological and sexual power of dreams. He confirms this influence when he casts Hollywood's quintessential surrealist David Lynch as Jack Doll in Season Three's *Late Show* arc. The flashback sequences in Season One's *God* could easily be lifted from a Luis Buñuel movie, with its focus on the sensual nature of religious guilt.

Never's episode has its surreal moments as well. Louie has to take Never for the day because his mother is having her vagina removed. Yep, that should be a warning sign. So should the fact that Never's mom tells Louie she doesn't say no to him. Within seconds of his mom's departure, Never shoves a baby carriage into traffic, leading to an explosive chain of events. At the apartment, Never eats raw meat, shoves a rug out the window and has an accident that leaves him soaking in a pool of diarrhea. These are all classic *Louie* scenarios—funny, disturbing, and bearing little resemblance to the workings of the world as we know it. What's that got to do with a philosopher who lived more than four hundred years ago?

"Method" Acting

Descartes was mostly concerned with developing a master method that would link all forms of science and mathematics. His two most famous contributions were the development of Cartesian coordinates, and the coining of the phrase "Cogito, ergo sum," "I think, therefore I am." (Or more to the point, "I am thinking; therefore I exist.") Before Descartes could develop a new method of science, he had to remove all doubt from philosophy. In two of his masterworks, *Discourse on the Method* and *Meditations on First Philosophy*, Descartes lays out a series of steps for eliminating any idea that cannot be proven clearly, distinctly, and beyond doubt. Anything that remained would be incontrovertible truth.

Descartes was a rationalist. He believed that all truth—anything that could be clearly and distinctly known—could be discerned through the mind alone, without input from the senses. Why? Because we can't necessarily trust our senses—if we could, it would mean objects get smaller as they get farther away, which is pretty clearly impossible. In his *Meditations*, Descartes's first step was to detail all the ways our perceptions can be deceived. We think we understand the reality of our surroundings, but our senses lie. There's also the possibility we are mad, or deceived by a malevolent demon. Unlikely, I know . . . but hard to disprove. In the end, Descartes was able to cast doubt on pretty much everything he knew, or thought he knew, unless it could be proved beyond all doubt. One thing he *could* believe: if there is doubt, there must be a doubter. If there is thought, there must be a thinker. If I think, I must exist. That, he knew for sure.

What do we know for sure in Louie? What is concrete, beyond doubt? Not a lot . . . he is a comedian, and he has two daughters, whom he loves very much. Other than that, pretty much everything is up for grabs. Characters come and go, sometimes being played by entirely different actors. The size of his family varies: just how many sisters does he have, and why don't they appear in his childhood flashbacks? His mother and one of his dates are played by the same person. (I'll leave that for the Freudian chapter). African American actress Susan Kelechi Watson plays his ex-wife Janet in Seasons 3 and 4 (despite the fact that his kids couldn't be whiter), but a younger Janet is played in a flashback by Caucasian actress Brooke Bloom. And what's with that recurring rabbit head? Louis C.K. has very little interest in continuity, or logic, or the rules of the world as we know them. If there is one constant, it's a sort of dream logic, where the absurd happens without comment and we are never entirely sure if what we see is really happening.

Which brings us back to Descartes. One of the main reasons for Cartesian doubt is that, in addition to the possibility that we are mad, misinterpreting our senses, or deceived by a demon, there is the possibility that we are, simply, asleep. Dreaming. Isn't it true, Descartes asks in his first meditation, that dreams can seem an awful lot like reality?

> How often, asleep at night, am I convinced of just such familiar events—that I am here in my dressing-gown, sitting by the fire—when in fact I am lying undressed in bed! Yet at the moment my eyes are certainly wide awake when I look at this piece of paper; I shake my head and it is not asleep; as I stretch out and feel my hand I do so deliberately, and I know what I am doing. All this would not happen with such distinctness to someone asleep. Indeed! As if I did not remember other occasions when I have been tricked by exactly the same thoughts while asleep! As I think about this more carefully, I see plainly that there are never any sure signs by means of which being awake can be distinguished from being asleep. (*Meditations on First Philosophy*, p. 13)

This passage suggests two things. First, Descartes had tremendously boring dreams. And second, anything that occurs in reality may also be represented in a dream state. If you can perceive it, you can also dream it, and there is no real reliable test to know whether or not you are dreaming.

And let's face it, Louie's Manhattan is a pretty dreamlike place. On the subway, for instance, Louie slips into a daydream in which he is given a hero's reward for sopping up a pool of bubbling liquid with his shirt. Absurd, yes, but not all that far removed from the scene that preceded it, in which a classical violinist plays a beautiful solo while a homeless man strips down to his pants and washes himself with a water bottle. Louie's waking moments are really no stranger than his dreams. In many episodes, the dream world seems to seep into

Louie's reality. How else to explain the scene in which a homeless man is dragged into a town car by men in black suits, only to be replaced—by an identical homeless man?

Perchance to Dream?

Try to prove you are not dreaming. Go ahead. I'll wait. Can't do it? I didn't think so. Neither can Louie's younger daughter, Jane. In Season Four's, "Elevator, Part One," Jane wakes screaming and terrified. Louie calms her down, but Jane thinks she's still dreaming—it's just "a nice dream now." The next morning, as they approach the subway, Jane announces that they are all still in her dream. "It's really cool! Almost like real life," she says. That's fine, until she decides to test her theory, stepping off the train as it pulls away from the platform. At this point, Jane's "nice dream" turns into very real terror for Louie and Lily as they frantically make their way back to Jane on the platform. "No, this is not a dream!" Louie shouts. "This is real! People get hurt! It's a dangerous world! Kids get stolen. They disappear forever, Jane! This is real, bad things happen!" Does Jane accept this? Not really. She cries and declares, "This is a horrible dream."

Jane is on the path to Cartesian understanding. She has come to doubt her senses, as did Descartes in the first *Meditation*. He would use the later *Meditations* to reaffirm the world, piece by piece, but Jane is not there yet. She knows she exists, but doubts the reality of everything else and tries to test it. Louie knows clearly and distinctly that the world is big, dangerous and that bad things happen.

Louie features many scenes that are specifically and concretely labeled as dreams, but others are more slippery. Dream logic abounds in *Louie*, and it is often extremely difficult to tell what we should take at face value.

Let's start with a scene that is clearly a dream. Louie is eating a bowl of ice cream in bed watching the news when the beautiful news anchor starts saying inappropriate, unprintably sexual things. Probably a dream, based on our experience of the world, right? A news anchor would *probably* not say, "The mayor's mom drinks pee." Then, Louie himself pops into the newscast; the woman slaps him and he wakes up. Aha! It's an ice cream-induced nightmare. Confirmed. Never mind that

Louie prefers the dream, going back to sleep in hopes of having sex with the anchor.

Similarly, the dream sequence in "God" (Season One, Episode 11) follows standard TV dream conventions: it starts with a young version of Louie asleep, rolling in bed; it adds grating music, illogical edits, anxiety-producing shots of a gory Jesus, running nuns and Louie driving nails into his classmate's hands. It ends, as do all good TV dreams, with Louie waking with a terrified shout. Again, clearly a dream, but again, not *all* that different, in tone or disturbing content, from the previous flashback scenes. The dream and the flashback share certain visual assets, but the dream is obviously a dream.

But what if it's not so obvious? The "Elevator" series in Season Four has many moments of unexplained dream logic.

> **Exhibit A:** Louie is seeing a therapist with his ex-wife Janet. As the conversation becomes uncomfortable, Louie calmly walks to the window, sticks his head out, and releases a long and cathartic scream that echoes through Manhattan. He calmly sits back down and continues the conversation. No one else in the scene has noticed or commented. Did it happen?

> **Exhibit B:** A hurricane bears down on New York, submerging Cuba and killing LeBron James. And the rest of the Miami Heat. Oh, and twelve million other people in Florida. (A small bird also dies, but of sadness, says the TV reporter). Absurd, yes, even nightmarish. Yet in neither of these examples is there a waking moment; no point at which it's revealed that it's just the ice cream or a fever-induced fantasy; nothing but the sheer strangeness of the moment that separates these plot elements from the much more realistic six-part "Elevator" arc.

You May Say I'm a Dreamer

Sometimes it's unclear if Louie himself is sure of his waking-or-dreaming state. In Season Four's "Model," Louie finds himself in an unexpected (and of course sexual) scenario. After bombing, publicly and spectacularly, in front of a wealthy audience at a benefit, he ends up in the car of Blake, a beautiful and wealthy model (and astronaut's daughter). The scene is filled with things that just don't add up, from their mismatched physical appearance to the awkward first conversation across a vast mansion courtyard to the too-perfect dreamy light as they drive to her father's house on the shore.

After a swim and some initial sexually charged dialogue and groping, we cut to Louie and Blake in bed, post sex.

> BLAKE: Are you okay?
>
> LOUIE: Yeah, yeah, no I, yes. Yes, very okay, this is . . . okay . . . Yes. I just don't, you know the thing is, I don't generally . . . do the whole . . . I mean it's not . . . It's just like a very beautiful astronaut's daughter . . .
>
> BLAKE: Model.
>
> LOUIE: Model, okay throw that in there—model kind of people—type of person doesn't usually take me home and have sex with me. It's not my usual . . . It's not how I roll.
>
> BLAKE: Well maybe it is not really happening.

Aha! Maybe it isn't, which would certainly explain a lot about what we have just seen, and are about to see. If this *is* a dream, it's about to become a very bad one. Louie accidentally punches the model in the eye and is sued by her wealthy family. In the end, Louie is saddled with a crippling financial burden—paying the family $5,000 a month, probably forever.

Does this actually happen? It certainly seems rife with Freudian dream elements, starting as anxiety dream (Louie bombing), moving to wish fulfillment (sex with a model) and ending in punishment (crippling financial burden). But despite this switch to nightmare mode, the harsh punishment is never mentioned again, in any other episode. Is this simply a self-contained storyline, or could it be a lucid dream?

Of all of the fuzzy lines between dream and reality, the Liz storyline is probably the fuzziest. Much has been written about the Season Three finale—"New Year's Eve" (Episode 13). Midway through this episode, after a hilariously horrific series of Christmas preparations, Louie runs into Liz, the quirky bookstore clerk he dated in "Daddy's Girlfriend" (Season Three, Episodes 4 and 5). Louie has been pining for Liz and now, despite all logic, here she is on the bus. But just as he reaches her, she faints—blood pours out of her nose, and she is rushed to the hospital, where she dies.

When I show this scene in class, I always ask my students,

"Did Liz die?"

Invariably, the answer is, "Um . . . yeah . . . ?"

"How do you know?" I ask.

"Because we saw her die! The doctor called it! She sure seemed dead."

They know she's dead because they *see* it. Their senses tell them it's true. *But*—as we know from Descartes's *Meditations*, the senses are not necessarily to be trusted. There are a number of dream indicators besides the extended dream sequence in which Louie's grown daughters discuss their "career-y things." There's the TV news program that *seems* to be recommending suicide to Louie personally, the outrageous coincidence of reuniting with Liz just at the moment of her death, and, for lack of a better word, the general "dreaminess" of it all.

If we look even further back, Louie's first interactions with Liz are pretty dreamy as well, full of black and white fantasy segments, bizarre reality TV shows in which contestants get stabbed, and a walking date through a luminous Manhattan filled with mood swings, poignancy, joy and terror. The episode ends with a series of wordless, mostly black and white close-ups of Liz, her face a mix of shadow, raw emotion, and loss. A couple of episodes later, these same images come to Louie in a dream, along with a mouthed message from Liz: "I love you." At this point, my students go from absolute certainty that Liz is dead to an uncertainty that she ever existed!

Louie doesn't necessarily give us the answer to that question. But what about our original question: is Louie (the character) Cartesian? Not particularly. He floats between a gritty, realistic Manhattan and a dream space where dogs change shape, people occasionally talk in gibberish and cars are smashed to smithereens for no reason. Louie takes it all in, never questioning the reality of any of it.

So why is *Louie* (and Louie) so dream-obsessed? Season Five offers a clue. In the episode "Untitled" (Episode 5), Louie gets trapped in a nightmare cycle that contains many familiar

Louie themes (sex, failure, anxiety, rabbit heads) and one new one: horror, in the form of a bald man with distorted features who is intent on sinking his teeth into Louie's neck. It's a deeply creepy image, but one that feels like it's from another show, or *ten* other shows. It's odd because it's so familiar; so much like what we expect out of a nightmare. Most *Louie* dream images are strange and deeply personal to his experience. This one is more primal—the thing that lurks in the darkness—and therefore less personal. I was tempted to write this off as Louis C.K. simply playing to an audience that now *expects* dreams—essentially creating the ultimate TV dream sequence, using every trope in the book.

But if you look at the content of the dreams, it's not that simple. Each dream arises from some form of short- or long-term angst: stolen comedy bits, fear of castration, fear of failure, and most important, the simple fear of nightmares. These dreams continue until Louie discovers the cause: his refusal to help a distraught woman move a heavy fish tank. The nightmares stop when he returns to help her. (It probably doesn't hurt that he also has sex with her. This is *Louie*, after all). Is it progress that, in this episode at least, Louie is able to (mostly) separate dream from reality? Hard to say. But he is able to put his dreams to good use for once. He uses them to processes his anxieties and failures, much as through *Louie,* Louis C.K. seems to process his.

So what about Louis C.K., *Louie's* creator? Could he be considered Cartesian? Sometimes . . . Descartes's method did not simply end by declaring the world an illusion born of a fever dream. He used the dream argument as one method of doubt to purge his thinking of anything that could not be proven clearly and distinctly. The process left him with one sure fact—that he exists. But he didn't leave it there—he used that grounding as the basis to establish irrefutable (in his mind) proof of the existence of a true, perfect God, and with these two solid facts—an "I" and a God—was able to reaffirm the existence of the world, at least in mathematical terms. Here is where Louis C.K. and Descartes diverge—in *Louie's* world, there *is* no god. He's made it very clear, in many episodes, that he's more of an empty void kind of guy. And with no God, we never make it to Descartes's next step. Louis C.K., the all-powerful creator of Louie's world, leaves us in a world of doubt, somewhere between waking and dreams.

But is that such a bad thing? Not as far as Louie is concerned. If Louie is dreaming, of having sex with a beautiful
model, or finding love (even for a day) on a New York rooftop,
or spending New Year's Eve with a welcoming Chinese family,
is that any worse than spending New Year's alone, wracked by
suicidal thoughts? Would Descartes think so? He probably
wouldn't even accept the terms of the equation, being beyond
the scope of mathematics. But Louie is only sometimes
Cartesian. He has an idea that things may not be as they seem,
but he can live with the doubt.

23

Louis C.K. Meets the Unconscious

Duncan Reyburn

In "So Old/Playdate" (Season One, Episode 4), we find Louis C.K. sitting down to tell his therapist that he finds sex to be "like, such a confusing thing." Somewhat distractedly the therapist tells him that sex is really quite simple because it's really just a mechanical act involving the meeting of certain body parts and a climax that results in the death of the woman. "She dies?" Louis asks, utterly horrified by what his therapist has just said. "Oh no," says the therapist quickly, "I was thinking of something else."

Here, the therapist, apart from proving his utter incompetence, exposes a strange aspect of human communication. As many of us often do, he says one thing while he really means another. Or, to use the old Freudian joke, he says one thing, but means his mother. Most of us think of ourselves as rational, self-determined beings. We are, or so we think, the gods who rule over our own lives and masters of our own fates. But then occasionally something else speaks through us: through dreams, screw-ups, general clumsiness, slips of the tongue and even jokes. Through these accidents, we suddenly find ourselves wondering what else might be going on beneath the surface, especially when we hear people ask questions like 'Why do I make such silly mistakes?' or 'Why do I get so unreasonably angry at my kids when I really love them?' or 'Why do I choose friends who treat me so badly?'

Enter Louis C.K., who tells us that what we suspect is really true; there really is something else going on beneath the surface. "Everybody has a competition in their brain of good thoughts and bad thoughts. We hope," he suggests, that "the good thoughts win" but to some degree we have to accept that we "always have both" things in our minds, and they're both vying for attention and expression. There's "the thing I believe, the good thing—that's the thing I believe. And then there's *this thing*, and I don't believe it, but it is there. It's always this thing—and then *this thing*." Louis calls this the of-course-but-maybe category, but it may also be called the of-course-but-maybe contradiction. Aristotle said that logic cannot abide contradictions, but life isn't always logical. In any case, it turns out that this contradiction is a very helpful way to understand what at least some of psychoanalysis is all about. Of-course-but-maybe identifies, among other things, the quintessential struggle between what we want to think and what we actually think, as well as what we want to do and what we actually do.

Louis continues to explain his of-course-but-maybe category by suggesting that, *of course*, we need to go out of our way to protect a kid who has a severe nut allergy. We have to include warnings on those labels for those who risk their lives every time they eat chocolate. We all believe this thing because it's so patently obvious. But if a kid touches a nut and dies, Louis suggests, then *maybe* it was meant to be. Maybe evolution was just doing its job, making the fit survive and the weak kick the proverbial bucket. *Of course*, we don't think for a minute that this should happen and Louis admits that if anything happened to his nephew, who really does have a nut allergy, he'd be absolutely devastated. But he also recognizes the hypocrisy that's in all of us. *Maybe* it should happen after all, because it's the kind of thing that does happen from time to time. So there's this thing—the thing we believe—and then there's *this thing*. We don't believe it, but it's there, annoying the hell out of us (*Oh My God*).

When we really think about it, Louis's nut allergy death example is highly alarming. Who would dare think such an atrocious thing? But then maybe we think things like this all the time. Like, of course, everyone should be equally well off. This horrific gap between the rich and the poor is utterly unjust! But maybe, we may find ourselves thinking from time to time, that beggar on the street corner should have worked a little harder. Maybe karma kicked his ass because that's what that lazy bastard deserves. Maybe he's just a run-of-the-mill sluggard, rather than some guy who was born into difficult and demeaning circumstances. *Of course*, no one believes that. But then again *maybe* everyone thinks that. I could go on, and so I shall.

Of course, I know that pigging out on too much chocolate is unhealthy, but I can keep doing it anyway. And you know that smoking is a bad idea, but knowing it isn't enough to keep you from indulging. And, of course, if you're religiously inclined you should protect the earth because you believe that God made all of life and everything good, but maybe it doesn't really matter to you so you keep using fossil fuel and even drive to places within walking distance because it's sometimes just more convenient to ignore what you believe.

Louis notices that a lot of anti-environmentalists are Christians, and he asks, "if you believe that God gave you the Earth" then "why would you not look after it?" Well, Louis has actually already answered his question: Because there's this battle between the thing we believe and this (other) thing. He even admits that he's got the same problem; that his own hypocrisy is just as much of a problem as the hypocrisy of others: "I have a lot of beliefs and I live by none of 'em. That's just the way I am. They're just my beliefs. I just like believing them. I like that part. They're my little believies; they make me feel good about who I am" (*Live at the Beacon Theater*).

So this of-course-but-maybe contradiction doesn't only identify the primal struggle between what we want to think and what we actually do think, but also points out the gap between what we believe and how we actually speak or act. This is known in psychoanalysis as disavowal. I know very well, *but . . .* Hey, wait a minute! Who put that *but* there? There's this thing (my very own collection of little believies) and then there's *this thing* (the thing that I do but don't want to do or think but don't want to think). Wherever this thing goes, *this thing* is right there waiting in the shadows, ready to pounce.

But what is this this-thing-*this-thing* thing anyway? (I hope that sentence made you smile. Have you ever seen a sentence with this many *thises* and *things* in a row before?). Well, perhaps psychoanalysis can help us to figure this one out. To me, this contradiction is best understood as a kind of wrestling match between what the French psychoanalyst Jacques Lacan calls the "big Other" and "the unconscious." I'll look at each of these in turn before explaining how they relate and then conclude with some thoughts especially on how all of this relates to Louis C.K.'s jokes (with many nods to Lacan's hero-nemesis, Sigmund Freud).

Of Course, the Big Other

So, as I said, the one side of the contradiction is what Lacan call's the big Other, which is really society's unwritten rule book. It's the of-course part of the of-course-but-maybe contradiction. It's the thing that controls the way we act even while we're not completely aware of it. It's the puppet master that hides behind the scenes, yanking the strings of our lives so that we act in particular ways but not in others. It's evolution or karma or even a kind of false God (a God whom we can completely conceive of and whose rules are always alarmingly close to our own—you can tell that you've made God in your image, when she hates all the same people you do, right?).

We can become aware of this big Other to some extent—this of-course, in other words, can become apparent to us—but usually we just follow it blindly. For example, we stand in queues without even thinking about it. Now, naturally, this silly, innocuous act of standing right behind the person in front of you in a line can make a lot of sense. After all, without queues we'd find ourselves in a bloodbath every time we went to the supermarket to get supplies because we'd have to fistfight and knife our way to the cashier every single time we wanted to pay for something.

'What did those groceries cost you?' we might imagine a wife say to her husband when he returns from the store. 'Oh, these were pretty cheap,' he would reply. 'I only had to kill three people to get them.' So, of course, queues help to keep the peace. But maybe the fact that we stand in queues so automatically and without question goes to show that the big Other and its invisible rule book is always there. You could think of it as a useful fiction like a placebo that actually sometimes manages to keep the disease at bay. We do what we do primarily because, well, that's just the way things are done around here.

The big Other is, in a way, the bureaucracy of life—the checklist that you have in your head when you're trying to avoid making any social blunders. It certainly tells us what meanings are acceptable and what taboos we need to avoid committing—Taboo or not taboo? *That* is the question—but it would be a mistake to say that we're always aware of its influence over us.

The big Other is also the legitimating framework of existence. It's the way we get a feeling that what we're doing matters and has meaning. This is represented pretty well in a non-Louis-C.K. joke about a guy who gets stranded on a desert island with a world-famous supermodel. Since they can't think of anything else to do, the two of them end up having sex, which is fun for both of them for obvious reasons. Afterwards, though, the guy feels like something is out of place, so he sheepishly asks the supermodel to pretend for a little while that she's really his best friend, Pete. 'It's nothing kinky,' he tells her, 'but would you do it for me anyway?' The supermodel thinks it's a weird request but she doesn't really mind since she really has nothing better to do. So she goes away for a short while and then reappears, walking in as manly a fashion as she can and speaking with a fake deep voice. 'Hey, Pete,' the guy says to her excitedly, 'You are not going to believe who I just had sex with!'

The point is this: our actions are often just actions to us until we get someone else—some Other—to high-five us and tell us that we've done a good job or that we're on the right track or that we are acceptable and accepted. The big Other is the cause of our approval addiction. It's the audience to all of our 'You won't believe what just happened' pronouncements. We find ourselves validated through this big Other, even though it's all too likely that it's just a projection of our deepest longings and desires.

Louis is always somehow agreeing with this big Other even while he is constantly challenging it. He'll start one of his stand up gigs with all kinds of niceties, telling the audience how sweet and kind they are, and then soon he'll be talking about nearly everything that so-called ordinary society would find inappropriate. "I love to shit," he says, for example, almost a little too earnestly. "I don't know why they call it Number Two. I think it's easily the best one. In my book, it's Number One." Did he really say that out loud? Yes, he did. And in spite of the big Other, the audience loved it.

Sometimes, Louis just flirts with taboos, like when he tells his audience that if murder weren't outright against the law, he'd certainly be one to go around killing people (*Oh My God*). Wouldn't we all? If murder were, say, a mild felony, then occasionally people who irritated him or made him angry would end up dead. It'd make life so much simpler. But then, Louis doesn't always just flirt with taboos. Sometimes he grenade launches the taboo into the audience without them even knowing what just hit them, waiting for it to detonate.

Soon after telling the audience about the kid who should die from nut allergies, he says, "Of course, of course, slavery is the worst thing that ever happened." There's a sudden, awkward silence. Nobody in his audience laughs at this point because they all know what's coming. Slavery is a big taboo—way more offensive than that previous nut-allergy joke. After all, there are still thousands of slaves in the world today. Is Louis about to say that we actually believe slavery is something we're okay with? Louis picks up on this stunned silence and he calls the audience out on their hypocrisy: "Listen, listen. You all clapped for dead kids with the nuts, for kids dying from nuts. You applauded. So you're in this with me now. Do you understand? You don't get to cherry-pick. Those kids did nothing to you." The audience laughs at their own double-standard, and Louis is given permission to go on.

"Of course," he says, "of course slavery is the worst thing that ever happened. Of course it is, every time it's happened. Black people in America, Jews in Egypt. Every time a whole race of people has been enslaved, it's a terrible, horrible thing, of course, but *maybe* . . . maybe every incredible human achievement in history was done with slaves. Every single thing where you go, 'How did they build those pyramids?' They just threw human death and suffering at them until they were finished."

Of course, we don't like slavery, but maybe Louis has a point. How many of us aren't slaves in some sense? We get paid to work a specific number of hours per day, but the contract also includes an expectation that we will work as hard as we need to in order to get the job done, even if it means spending less time with our families, less time on our hobbies, and less time bettering ourselves in other ways. Of course, we all believe in justice and fair working conditions, but maybe we also, contradictorily, just really don't give a shit about what we believe. And it's irritating because we find ourselves forever split in two. It's not that the but-maybe is a different thing; instead it seems to be very much a part of the of-course of our experience. It seems like there is no of-course without the but-maybe. *This thing* is implicit in this thing.

But, of course, as Lacan says, "the big Other doesn't exist." We know that the rules we abide by are fictions made up by "someone out there beneath the pale moonlight," to quote some Disney song; we know things could be otherwise than what they are. So, we know this *of course*. We can name it and label it and identify it, because it's part of what Lacan calls the Symbolic order. It's symbolic because it's made up of words—of signifiers and signifieds, to use the technical terms. We can tell people what the law is, and we know that it has some kind of controlling function in our lives. But it's not the only thing that's going on, right? There's this thing and *this thing,* and, as it turns out, *this thing* is a little trickier to explain.

But Maybe, the Unconscious

Psychoanalyists call it the *unconscious* and the main reason it's called that is because we're not aware of it. The unconscious is made up of all the things that a person represses and can therefore not be expressed in any conscious way. But then, as we have already seen, other things happen that alert us to its presence: we dream weird things, repeat ourselves without realizing it, forget names or words, omit important details in stories we tell, bungle our actions, say the things we don't mean; sometimes we may even experience pathological symptoms because of the unconscious. These parapraxes—slips of the tongue, bungled actions, and so on—are what Lacan calls 'the discourse of the unconscious'; that is, they are the way that the unconscious speaks.

So, obviously, the unconscious is not something we know directly. We're forever looking at it using sideways glances. And, to make matters worse, it's also not something that's all that easy to spot or interpret. Lacan, like Freud before him, was fascinated by the unconscious for this very reason. He noticed that there are these expressions offered by people that seem to absolutely disconnect words from their meanings (or signifieds from their signifiers). And he figured that such parapraxes provide clues, first to the analyst and then to his analysand (which is what psychoanalysts call their patients), into why the analysand is even coming to therapy. Something is blocking the analysand's enjoyment, and that something is located in the unconscious.

Take, for example, a graduate student who has been suffering from terrible stomach pain and repeated vomiting. Medical doctors have done countless tests and have come to the conclusion that the pain must be psychosomatic. So the student goes to therapy and his analyst tells him that he's not going to cure the stomach pain and vomiting, but is going to instead listen to them with compassion and understanding. This may sound really crazy but the analyst is thinking of them as symptoms of the man's unconscious. Over time, it turns out, repressed anger from years of abuse during the childhood of the student are exposed as being directly related to the stomach pain and vomiting. This comes to the student as a complete epiphany. He recognizes a link between those childhood feelings and his current experience of working with a curmudgeonly supervisor. He puts all of this into words, which act as symbolic containers for things that are outside of his control, and the stomach pain and vomiting stop immediately. True story.

To be clear, though, the unconscious is not the man's stomach, nor is it something that is always completely clear. In fact, while the big Other belongs to Lacan's Symbolic order, the unconscious belongs to what Lacan calls the Real, which is a confusing title to give it because the Real isn't the same thing as what is real. Instead, it's that inexpressive, hidden part of our consciousnesses around which other aspects of ourselves warp and bend. It is a bit like a black hole: it's not at all easy to explain (or, in fact, it's not at all possible to explain), but it affects things nonetheless.

The Real, because it is really unimaginable, is also unsymbolizable. It is suggested by absolute states of pure terror and pure enjoyment, which are actually impossible to conceive of because life is never really that bad or that good. It appears when the glue between the signified and its signifier (the meaning and the word) disintegrates or dissolves. Our nice little believes can drop dead, as far as the Real unconscious is concerned. Still, the psychoanalytic aim—or at least one of them—is to try and help the analysand to have a sense that even the unconscious has its place. In fact, sometimes it's a good idea to give the unconscious room to breathe; to let it speak so that desire and enjoyment can flow again. This, it turns out, is one of the functions of humor, which Louis can teach us quite a lot about.

Jokes, the Release Valve of the Unconscious

In psychoanalysis, repression is always a bad idea. But this assertion is often criticized. GK Chesterton, for instance, said that Shakespeare's Macbeth and Lady Macbeth had all their problems, not because of what they repressed, but because of what they didn't. Psychoanalysts would say that there are healthy and unhealthy ways of dealing with repression, and, obviously, we should opt for what is healthy.

What is needed is certainly not something like what we have in Macbeth. Rather, what is needed most often is something called *sublimation,* which is when negative impulses from the unconscious are transformed into socially acceptable forms of behavior. The man who is thinking of murdering his neighbor's cat can go ahead, but he could also take his frustration out on a punching bag. His unconscious desire to kill something can be sublimated into some healthy exercise.

Sublimation is sometimes what Louis really excels at, although he does it through comedy rather than therapy. The comedy club or comedy channel then becomes a kind of space that allows the audience to sit back and unwind—to see their repression relieved, if only for a short while. Humor, at least as Freud and Lacan discuss it, admits that there is another conversation going on within a conversation. There is, in other words, a kind of latent communication in what we're saying that we're usually not aware of. We hear Louis speak and we find ourselves laughing in surprise, not at something purely imaginary or completely ridiculous, but at something that is really there in the very way we speak and live. What makes Louis particularly profound is that he's not telling lies at all. He's actually telling the truth, at least as he experiences it. So much of Louis's comedy comes from his brutal truth telling.

So, humor acts as a kind of release valve for the unconscious; jokes allow us to admit that there is this thing and then there's also *this thing.* And, if only for a moment, we're not entirely ashamed at the fact that we're so full of contradictions.

Maybe we can actually cope with the contradictions without necessarily always having to resolve them.

But there is a down side to this. The relief is temporary. Comedy of this sort is usually just confession without absolution. It'll give us a good laugh and it'll make us acutely aware of the wrestling match that's always going on between the big Other and the unconscious, but some of those things that we laugh at are genuine issues. Why is it that we teach ourselves to hate people? Why do we let ourselves be hypocrites? Why is it that if gun laws were removed we might actually go out and kill a few people? Louis doesn't have any answers and neither does psychoanalysis. Simply saying that the unconscious makes us do things we don't want to do feels too much like a copout.

In the end, comedy, like psychoanalysis, doesn't want to force us into any kind of overt self-awareness; that's not its job. That sort of thing can actually be a little too traumatic. Instead, it's a kind of therapeutic attempt to get us to reconcile ourselves, if only for a brief moment, to our own lack of self-mastery.

24
An Hour

JAMES BLISS

The first hour of Louis C.K.'s career lasted fifteen years. The bits from this period, filmed for his 1996 *HBO Comedy Half Hour* and 2001 *Comedy Central Presents*, were collected on his first album, *Live in Houston*. But beginning with his 2005 HBO *One Night Stand*, Louis began a new period of productivity, producing a new hour of stand-up on a yearly basis. His hour-a-year production, combined with his short-lived HBO sitcom, *Lucky Louie*, and his current FX series, *Louie*, has catapulted him to the forefront of American comedy.

What changed between that first hour and the next ten? Well, a lot. But I can't cover everything. Here's an example: In his first two specials, Louis does a bit about a case of mistaken identity. He's standing on a corner eating a peach and he sees his friend across the way waving at him. His hands are full so he waves the peach. Then he realizes it isn't his friend, and he's standing on a corner waving a peach in the air. So he shouts, "I HAVE A PEACH! LOOK AT MY PEACH!" The bit lasts a little under a minute and he moves on to a bit about the difference between being stupid and being crazy.

In *Shameless*, Louis does another bit about mistaken identity. Except this bit covers a lot more distance. Starting from a short riff on his "awesome possum" t-shirt (which has a cameo in Season Four of *Louie*), he moves from hipster coffee shops, to Boston's special form of human quality control (beating the shit out of people for no reason), to a banana-hammocked guy at Venice Beach, to picking people to hate in line at the bank, to lines at the post office ("like a silent movie of impatient people"), before finally bringing us back to the coffee shop. When his gesture towards a kid in an "awesome possum" shirt is rebuffed, Louis *explodes*. "And as I'm standing there in that anger I realize, I'm not wearing the shirt. I don't know why I thought I was." "Picking People to Hate" lasts some six and a half minutes. These digressive bits are the building blocks of all of Louis's later specials.

Early Louis was like an absurdist poet. His jokes were crystalline, precise deconstructions of language and meaning. A child named Fffffffffffffffffffffffffffffffff. "For me, growing up Chinese was really weird—you know—because nobody in my neighborhood was Chinese, and neither am I." Later Louis wanders across themes, ideas, and locations. He's no less precise, no less interested in language and how it works and how it doesn't. But his comic practice embraces digression in a new way. What is it about digression that is so powerful? As a form of storytelling, it relates to some of the twentieth century's most important developments in French philosophy. The free movement of digression is like the free play of the "signifier" in deconstruction, or like the practice of free association in psychoanalysis. ('Signifier' is the word deconstructionists use for the word, "word." More on this later, but a signifier is basically just a word.) There's something eerily similar between the close, obsessive attention to language in French post-structuralism and the wending paths of Louis's storytelling.

This era of Louis's career has illustrated a point made by the British psychoanalyst, Adam Phillips, that "digression is secular revelation," and "keeping to the subject is the best way we have of keeping off the subject." For Phillips, "digression may be the norm, the invisible norm, in conversation," and "what psychoanalysis shows is that one is digressive whether or not one wants to be. Indeed, the digressions one is unaware of are the most telling." From a philosophical perspective, psychoanalysis is all about how we say what we mean without meaning to. How the unconscious makes itself known through the cracks of our speech. How what we want, what we desire, is often completely unbearable, and how it undoes us while it defines us. Embracing digression, allowing his bits to wander far and wide, has let Louis produce some of the most probing stand-up of our era.

An Asshole

At the 2010 New York Public Library's Tribute to George
Carlin, Louis credits Carlin for giving him the courage to chuck
out his hour of shitty material and start from scratch. Louis
takes us down the path Carlin outlined for him: "When you're
done telling jokes about airplanes and dogs, and you throw
those away, what do you have left? You can only dig deeper.
Start talking about, you know, your feelings, and who you are.
And you do those jokes and they're *gone*. You gotta dig deeper.
So then you start thinking about your fears and your nightmares, and doing jokes about that. And then *they're* gone. And
you just start going into *weird* shit . . . And eventually you get
to your balls."

This is in the early 2000s, when Louis realizes he can't
afford to keep being shitty at his job. His directorial debut,
Pootie Tang, had failed. He's become a dad, and his daughters
need for him to, like, buy food and pay rent. And his daughters
enable the change in his comic practice in two ways. First,
they're the actual impetus for him to go to work, to work the-
aters and produce specials and make money from his craft. (Or
to give up the ghost and find a real job.) Second, they're the
source of the, let's call it "terror," that he first taps into on stage.

"What do I really want to say that I'm afraid to say?" The
first bit when Louis really knows he's onto something is when
he starts channeling his anxieties as a father onto the stage.
He recalls, "And I thought of the first thing—I said, 'I can't have
sex with my wife because we have a baby and the baby's a fucking *asshole*.' It's just what I was feeling and I said it. And the
audience went 'WHOA' and I thought, *Oh, I'm somewhere new
now*. And I said something like 'I never used to get babies in the
garbage but now I understand it.' And I thought, *I'd rather
have that"* (a stunned, uncomfortable audience) *"than the shit,
tepid laughter from my fifteen-year-old jokes."*

His daughters were both his reason to work and what
allowed him to begin tapping into what really was frightening
for him. Carlin himself had some pretty concrete reasons for
his own hour-a-year output. In the early 1980s Carlin changed
managers and discovered that he was massively in debt to the
IRS. That debt compelled him to put a new special together
every year, to tour the country, and to throw the material away

and start over once it was filmed. That debt wasn't fully repaid until 2003.

Sometimes it takes something traumatic to shake your words loose. Sometimes you need an external force to compel you to get down to the business of introspection.

A Trumpet

Psychoanalysis is about what can't be accounted for by self-consciousness. Beginning in the 1950s, the French psychoanalyst Jacques Lacan (1901–1981) led a "Return to Freud" that placed the emphasis of psychoanalytic practice squarely onto the spoken language of the analysand, or what a regular dumb person would call the "patient." The work of the analyst was simply to be attentive to the language of the analysand and to "punctuate" the analysand's speech. Punctuation, in speech as in writing, is a way of retroactively establishing meaning. It's the difference between "the building is on fire!" and "the building is on fire?"

An analyst, for Lacan, was someone who could help the analysand make better sense of their shitty life. And life *is* the problem. And we interact with life through language. We enter the world with no words of our own. We have to borrow a language that already exists before we're born. We're alienated in that language. It's our only way of expressing our thoughts, but it isn't our own. And when we enter into language, we're split between the ego, or conscious self, and the unconscious, a repository for all our repressed traumas, our desires and phobias and anxieties and passions.

In a great phrase, Lacan writes, "the essence of language has never been to serve the function of communication." And that's because the unconscious is never available to us. But we get glimpses of the unconscious in the form of symptoms: dreams, parapraxes (slips of the tongue), jokes, and so forth. Most of what makes you the person you are is completely inaccessible. Psychoanalysis is a way of learning to read your own symptoms.

In his 2010 appearance on the *WTF Podcast with Marc Maron*, Louis talks about buying a trumpet. He wandered into an instrument store and the salesman was showing him all these trumpets. And he doesn't know how to play the trumpet at all. But the salesman shows him this beautiful trumpet, slightly damaged and repaired on the bell. Louis goes to an ATM and takes out two thousand dollars to buy this trumpet. So now he has this beautiful trumpet in a beautiful black case. He's walking with the trumpet through Times Square and he stops in at a peep show. And he's sitting in a cubicle with the trumpet case crammed between his legs and he's masturbating to an unhappy Eastern European woman on the other side of the glass. After he comes he looks down at the trumpet case, and his come sitting there on it, and he thinks, "if I had gone here first, I wouldn't have had to buy the trumpet."

Louis tells Marc that he had been in therapy for a while, but he quit because he didn't see it going anywhere. So when he was telling his therapist he was quitting he asks if there's any advice he should take into the world with him. His therapist tells him that when he's in that moment, when he's buying a trumpet for no reason, to stop and to know that it's anxiety he's feeling. That's all it is, and if he knows it's anxiety, he can stop himself (sometimes) from doing something stupid.

Sometimes therapy can unearth *why* you do that—why your mom's face flashes before your eyes when you orgasm, or why you can't form a fist with your left hand even though you're physically fine. But sometimes it's enough that you just stop doing that.

An Optimist

We live in a culture that compulsively prohibits bad feelings. It's all coerced joy and compulsory happiness. Worse still, we live in a culture that says "Follow your dreams!" What a fucking awful thing to say to a person! Almost by definition, dreams are nonsensical, impossible, incoherent, unpleasant, disorienting, and disconcerting. And that's how I'm supposed to organize my life? Around *those*? It's no wonder everybody feels like shit. There's a cultural obligation to be happy about lives organized around selling off our time to assholes. Then having no resources to deal with how unbearable it is just to be a (mostly) living, (mostly) thinking person.

Desire is awful. Hope is just a thing that comes before failure and unhappiness. If there's one thing that links psychoanalysis and comedy, it's that they allow you to express bad feelings. And in both cases you find that there's pleasure in those bad feelings. It's pleasurable to say all the negative shit that you're not allowed to say in your day-to-day life. Or to hear someone else say all the things you think but can't say.

"You have to be stupid to be single," Louis observes in *Hilarious*, you have to ignore the fact that every human connection you have, even the good ones, will, at some point, dissolve into misery. "An optimist is someone who goes 'Hey, maybe something *nice* will happen'—why the fuck would anything nice *ever* happen?" The best of psychoanalysis begins from the premise that there isn't any "cure," just (some) relief from (some) symptoms. The disease, after all, is life itself. Which isn't an argument in favor of suicide, but more like a way of managing expectations. Like, the way to have the body you want is to want a shitty body.

And yet, we do indeed follow our dreams. At least in the sense that major parts of our lives—how we relate to others, how we develop our attachments, how we choose our objects of desire, how we pursue our desires—are products of unconscious processes that can't be explained just by thinking real hard about it. You follow your dreams in the sense that you move through the world in the wake of your unconscious.

When Louie, the character, follows Tarese (Adepero Oduye) home in the first season of *Louie*, he's not just stalking a stranger like an asshole (although he's definitely doing that), he's being led by a desire that he can't account for. And when he subsequently has sex with her neighbor, it just shows that a particular object of desire isn't as important as desire itself. By rejecting the demand for compulsory happiness, Louis, the comic, opens up a space for exploring the ambivalence characteristic of living. As he often says on stage, life is a pretty amazing thing, and it's also awful.

A Sign

In *Talking Funny*, Louis is in conversation with Ricky Gervais, Chris Rock, and Jerry Seinfeld on the ins and outs of stand-up comedy. Jerry asks what the very first bit was where Louis knew he really had something. It was a bit about street signs, and imagining different ways of punctuating them. Like, "drive *slow*, children!" or "No . . . *U* turn?"

From his earliest days in stand-up, Louis has been playing language games. The same has been said of post-structuralist thinkers, more generally: they're just playing language games. The writings of folks like Lacan or Jacques Derrida (1930–2004) are famous for their obscurity. Lacan's writing is said to mirror the logic of the unconscious as it unravels in the course of an analysis. Derrida's deconstructionist writings wriggle around inside of philosophical and literary works to pull them apart from within. Both writers, and the whole field of post-structuralist thought, rely on the insights of the Swiss linguist, Ferdinand de Saussure (1857–1913), who emphasized the arbitrariness of language.

At the turn of the twentieth century Saussure was exploring the nature of the "sign," the combination of a signifier and a signified. Okay, hang in there for a minute and I promise it'll be worth it. (I'm lying, but still just hold on.) A signifier is a word, and a signified is something that is represented by a word. Put together, they're called a sign. So, you have a buttplug, a molded piece of glass or plastic. That's a signified. And then you have the combination of letters or sounds that make "buttplug," a signifier. What Saussure discovered is that there's no essential relationship between signifiers and signifieds. There's nothing about a thing—an object, a concept, whatever—that requires the creation of a particular signifier.

This was revolutionary at the time because it disrupted a long tradition of insisting on foundations for meaning. As these ideas were taken up in different fields, meaning became less and less fixed. More thinkers were paying attention to how one might disrupt or distort meaning. Then there was an interest in how internally fragmented meaning always is, whether it's the meaning of a piece of writing, an artwork, or a road sign.

Derrida, especially, was interested in coming up with new types of writing that took seriously the arbitrariness of language. Like Louis, he was interested in the potential inherent in catachresis, which is a rhetorical term for the incorrect use of a word. The opening act in Louis's *Live at the Comedy Store*, Jay London, makes ready use of this particular rhetorical form. "This is my step ladder. I never knew my real ladder." Derrida described his writing as the search for "new forms of catachresis, another kind of writing, a violent writing which stakes out the faults and deviations of language." Louis's early stand-up operated much more along these lines, but it doesn't disappear in his later comedy.

A Bag of Dicks

It's hard to find a better example of the fundamental indeterminacy of the sign than the bag of dicks. What is the nature of the bag of dicks? Of course, this enigmatic figure is thrust upon Louis from outside. From the guy he just cut off in traffic whose anger is expressed through the demand that Louis "suck a bag of dicks."

And then we're all stuck there with Louis, pondering on the bag of dicks and what it means to suck such a bag. Is it a plastic bag with dicks smushed together like chicken parts? Or is it a paper bag with the dicks poking out of the top like baguettes? And do you suck the bag itself? Or do you suck all of the dicks individually? And do you have to make them all *come*?

We live inside of these gaps. We live in a world that we interact with through language, a language where meaning is never fixed, is always contingent and contextual. And then, furthermore, we are, ourselves, represented in the world by language. So we're also contingent and contextual. We aren't stable and coherent as beings in the world. In fact, any stable and coherent meaning requires that we disavow and deny all of the contradiction and contingency that are the conditions of any meaning.

And that scares some people. Some people think it means that nothing is real and nothing matters and there's no reason to live. Now, it is true that nothing matters and there's no reason to live—no good reason, at least—but it's not because meaning doesn't have stable or set foundations.

Consider another bit from *Shameless* that begins, "I was at a bar the other night, it doesn't matter where because I'm lying . . ." *And then he continues the story!* Louis reveals that the authenticity of the first-person perspective is basically irrelevant. He foregrounds the fact that he's an unreliable narrator. And then he tells his story. You could add parentheses and scarequotes all over that last sentence: (an unreliable) "he" (supposedly) "tells" (although it's made up and thus there's no proper owner to justify the possessive pronoun) "his" (fake) "story."

As a matter of fact, there have been many awful "deconstructionist" writings that do just that: expose in painful detail all of the contradictions and gaps internal to any seemingly straightforward sentence. But Louis shares with other great American deconstructionists like George Carlin, Steven Wright, and Richard Pryor their skill for pulling thoughts apart with a well-honed elegance.

A Digression

But anyway, like I was saying at first, the turn in Louis's comedy has harnessed the power of digression. Not exactly stream of consciousness—along the lines of his *Lucky Louie* co-star, Rick Shapiro—and not exactly the free association of psychoanalytic therapy. But a disciplined, honed, production of speech. Like, literally, producing speech. Words. On a stage. Out of the hole in the front of his head.

In his *WTF Podcast* interview, Louis says he stopped doing therapy because he didn't see it going anywhere. Plenty of comics describe being on stage as therapy. And what Louis does on stage is show exactly where talk therapy, at its best, is going. The stage becomes a venue for letting out all of those "of course . . . but *maybe* . . ." thoughts that you can't say in your everyday life. Louis is staging therapy; he's producing staged therapy. Which is why it's so cathartic to laugh at Louis's sets. He opens up a space to be in touch with all the good and bad, the pleasures you don't admit, the fears you don't face, that make up the subterranean part of your mind.

Now, he's *staging* all of this. His sets are refined over and over as he tours before filming the set and throwing it away. But it all begins from that open-mic energy. Starting a thought and not knowing where it will end or what will come next. And, with enough experience, you can find moments of profound inspiration in that space.

The idea behind psychoanalysis's "talking cure" is that the act of giving voice to the things you've repressed can open up new possibilities in your life. It isn't really a "cure," but you don't have to believe in such a thing as a cure for it to produce changes in your life. It can let you relate to your life, your desires, your anxieties, your traumas, your dreams, differently. Over the past several years, Louis has shown how digression can be secular revelation.

References

Adams, Robert Merrihew. 1985. Involuntary Sins. *The Philosophical Review* 94:1 (January).

Alexander, Samuel. 1920. *Space, Time, and Deity*. Peter Smith.

Alexander, Michelle. 2012. *The New Jim Crow: Mass Incarceration in the Age of Colorblindness*. The New Press.

Applebaum, Barbara. 2010. *Being White, Being Good: White Complicity, White Moral Responsibility, and Social Justice Pedagogy*. Lexington.

Arendt, Hannah. 1964. *Eichmann in Jerusalem: A Report on the Banality of Evil*. Penguin.

Aristotle. 1952. *Metaphysics*. University of Michigan Press.

———. 1999. *Nicomachean Ethics*. Hackett.

———. 2008. *Physics*. Oxford World's Classics.

Aurelius, Marcus. 2002. *Meditations: A New Translation*. Modern Library.

C.K., Louis (interviews). 2010. Marc Maron's WTF Podcast with Louis C.K. <www.youtube.com/watch?v=-Gw125AZtDU>.

———. 2011. Interview with Stephen M. Deusner. Pitchfork.

———. 2011. Interview with James Poniewozik. Part 1: Fatherhood and Fear. *Tuned In*, (June 22nd).

———. 2012. *The Daily Show with Jon Stewart*. <http://thedailyshow.cc.com/videos/4per11/louis-c-k->.

———. 2014. Interview with Charlie Rose, May 7th <www.hulu.com/watch/633527>.

———. 2014. Interview with Jonah Weiner. <medium.com/@jonahweiner>.

———. 2015. Louis C.K.'s Crabby, Epic Love Letter to NYC. *Hollywood Reporter*.

———. 2014. Interview with Terry Gross. Louis C.K. On His 'Louie' Hiatus: 'I Wanted the Show to Feel New Again'. *Fresh Air* (May 19th).

————. 2015. Interview with Terry Gross. <www.npr.org/templates/transcript/transcript.php?storyId=40256 0343>.

Card, Claudia. 1991. Rape as a Terrorist Institution. In R. Frey and C. Morris, eds., *Violence, Terrorism, and Justice*. Cambridge University Press.

Chamberlain, Timothy J., ed. 1992. *Eighteenth-Century German Criticism: Herder, Lenz, Lessing, and Others*. Continuum.

Corsello, Andrew. 2014. Louis C.K. Is America's Undisputed King of Comedy. *GQ* (May).

Dante Alighieri. 1984. *The Divine Comedy, Volume I: Inferno*. Penguin.

Davies, Madeleine. 2014. Louis C.K.'s Rant on Fat Girls Is Absolutely Magnificent. Jezebel. <http://jezebel.com/louis-c-k-s-rant-on-fat-girls-is-absolutely-magnificent-1575653738?utm_campaign=socialflow_jezebel_facebook&utm_source=jezebel_facebook&utm_medium=socialflow>.

Baltzly, Dirk. 2013. Stoicism. *Stanford Encyclopedia of Philosophy*. <http://plato.stanford.edu/entries/stoicism>.

Derrida, Jacques. 1980. *Writing and Difference*. University of Chicago Press.

René Descartes. 1996. *Meditations on First Philosophy*. Cambridge University Press.

————. 1999. *Discourse on Method and Meditations on First Philosophy*. Hackett.

Dobbin, Robert. 2008. Introduction. In *Epictetus: Discourses and Selected Writings*. Penguin.

Epictetus. 1983. *The Handbook (Encheiridion)*. Hackett.

Epicurus. 1964. *Epicurus: Letters, Principal Doctrines, and Vatican Sayings*. Pearson.

————. 1994. *The Epicurus Reader*. Hackett.

————. 2012. *The Art of Happiness*. Penguin.

Gendler, Tamar. 1998. Galileo and the Indispensability of Scientific Thought Experiment. *British Journal for the Philosophy of Science* 39:3 (September).

————. 2007. Philosophical Thought Experiments, Intuitions, and Cognitive Equilibrium. *Midwest Studies in Philosophy* 31.

Gibson, Kevin. 2014. *An Introduction to Ethics*. Pearson.

Goldstein, Ian. 2014. Burn It Down and Start Again: 4 Comics Who Threw Out Their Material and Reinvented Themselves. <http://splitsider.com/2014/07/burn-it-down-and-start-again-4-comics-who-threw-out-their-material-and-reinvented-themselves>.

Gooding, David. 1998. Thought Experiments. In *Routledge Encyclopedia of Philosophy*, Vol. 9. Taylor and Francis.

Griffiths, Trevor. 1976. *Comedians*. Faber and Faber.

Hadot, Pierre. 1995. *Philosophy as a Way of Life*. Blackwell.

Heidegger, Martin. 2008. *Being and Time*. Harper Perennial.

Hempel, C.G., and Paul Oppenheim. 1948. Studies in the Logic of Explanation. *Philosophy of Science* 15:2.

Hume, David. 1983. *An Enquiry concerning the Principles of Morals*. Hackett.

———. 1988. *An Enquiry concerning Human Understanding*. Open Court.

———. 1992. *Writings on Religion*. Open Court.

———. 2000. *A Treatise of Human Nature*. Oxford University Press.

Hurley, Matthew, Daniel Dennett, and Reginald Adams. 2011. *Inside Jokes: Using Humor to Reverse-Engineer the Mind*. MIT Press.

Jackson, Michael. 2013. The Myth of the Black-on-Black Crime Epidemic. *Demos*. <www.demos.org/blog/7/29/13/myth-black-black-crime-epidemic>.

Jones, Ward E. 2006. The Function and Content of Amusement. *South African Journal of Philosophy* 25:2.

Kant, Immanuel. 1996. *The Metaphysics of Morals*. Cambridge University Press.

Kierkegaard, Søren. 1986. *Fear and Trembling*. Penguin.

———. 1992. *Either/Or: A Fragment of Life*. Penguin.

Koziski, Stephanie. 1984. The Standup Comedian as Anthropologist: Intentional Culture Critic. *Journal of Popular Culture* 18:2 (Fall).

Lacan, Jacques. 2007. *Écrits: The First Complete Edition in English*. Norton.

Lovejoy, Arthur. 1936. *The Great Chain of Being*. Harvard University Press.

Mach, Ernst. 1972. *On Thought Experiments*. <www.tufts.edu/~skrimsky/PDF/On%20Thought%20Experiments.PDF>.

Lovell, Joel. 2011. That's Not Funny, That's C.K. *GQ* (August).

Morreall, John. 2009. *Comic Relief: A Comprehensive Philosophy of Humor*. Wiley-Blackwell.

Morris, Tom. 2004. *The Stoic Art of Living: Inner Resilience and Outer Results*. Open Court.

Friedrich Nietzsche. 1967. *The Will to Power*. Random House.

———. 1994. *The Birth of Tragedy*. Random House.

———. 2001. *The Gay Science*. Cambridge University Press.

———. 2006. *Thus Spoke Zarathustra*. Oxford University Press.

Nisbet, H.B., ed. 2005. *Lessing: Philosophical and Theological Writings*. Cambridge University Press.

Pager, Devah, Bruce Western, and Bart Bonikowski. 2009. Discrimination in a Low-Wage Labor Market: A Field Experiment. *American Sociological Review* 74.

Plato. 1997. *Plato: Complete Works*. Hackett.

Pogge, Thomas. 2008. *World Poverty and Human Rights*. Polity.

Rahula, Walpola. 1959. *What the Buddha Taught*. Grove Weidenfeld.

Rakesh, Kochhar, Richard Fry, and Paul Taylor. 2011. Wealth Gaps Rise to Record Highs Between Whites, Blacks, Hispanics. Pew Research Center. <www.pewsocialtrends.org/2011/07/26/wealth-gaps-rise-to-record-highs-between-whites-blacks-hispanics>.

Remski, Mathew. 2013. Louis C.K. Is Wrong about Boredom. <www.huffingtonpost.com/matthew-remski/boredom_b_4377366.html, 12.5.2013>.

Rowles, Dustin. 2012. Louis C.K.'s Guide to Parenting. Uproxx <http://uproxx.com/tv/2012/06/a-collection-quotes-on-louis-c-k-s-parenting-philosophies>.

Sartre, Jean-Paul. 1989 [1946]. Existentialism Is a Humanism. In Walter Kaufmann, ed., *Existentialism from Dostoyevsky to Sartre*. Meridian.

Saussure, Ferdinand de. 1986. *Course in General Linguistics*. Open Court.

Schopenhauer, Arthur. 1966. *The World as Will and Representation*. Two volumes. Dover.

———. 1974. *Parerga and Paralipomena*. Two volumes. Clarendon Press.

Siderits, Mark. 2007. *Buddhism as Philosophy: An Introduction*. Hackett.

Simplicius. 2014. *Commentary on Aristotle Physics* 1.3–4. Bristol Classical Press.

Singer, Peter. 1972. Famine, Affluence, and Morality. *Philosophy and Public Affairs* 1:3.

Sousa, Ronald de. 2011. Interview with Ronald de Sousa. *Pensées* <www.penseescanadiennes.com/archive/interview-entrevue/interview-2011>.

Spitznagel, Eric. 2009. Louis C.K.: "Starvation Can Be Character Building." *Vanity Fair* (March 2nd).

Taylor, Gabrielle. 1975. Justifying the Emotions. *Mind* 84:335 (July).

Wallace, David Foster. 2008. David Foster Wallace on Life and Work. Commencement speech given at Kenyon College in 2005. *Wall Street Journal* (September 19th).

World Bank. 2015. Poverty Overview. <www.worldbank.org/en/topic/poverty/overview>.

Some Dead People Who Haven't Died Yet

DANIEL ADDISON lives in New York. He teaches Ancient Philosophy, amongst other things, as a Visiting Assistant Professor at Hunter College/CUNY. His main focus, however, is on Kant and post-Kantian philosophy. He recently published his first book, *The Critique's Contradiction as the Key to Post-Kantianism: Longuenesse and the Collapse of Kant's Distinction between Sensibility and the Understanding* (2015). He also recently had a daughter, and looks forward to destroying her in monopoly.

JOEL AVERY, MA, is a graduate of Yale Divinity School and a father of two. He is fervently petitioning the Vatican for the beatification of Louis C.K. (St. Louie?) as the patron saint of sagging dads. In his spare time, Joel teaches high school physics.

JAMES BLISS has made a number of shitty decisions and also is a PhD student in Culture and Theory at the University of California, Irvine. James is in an impressive amount of debt and also has advanced degrees from Irvine and the University of Chicago. James lives in Irvine and also has a folder on his computer labeled, "Suicide Note—Drafts."

MYISHA CHERRY asks lots of "why" questions that may irritate many people. Her "why" questions are at the intersection of moral psychology and social and political philosophy. A former educator at the Fortune Society and Faculty Associate at John Jay College's Institute for Criminal Justice Ethics, she also asks questions about the relation between character, forgiveness, race, and the criminal justice system. Even if the philosophical answers she discovers are wrong, she's comforted by the fact that her wrongness is rooted in more knowledge because of her 'old' age. At least that's what Louis says. She hopes he's right. One would not know by her philosophical interests that, like Louis, she hates phones and likes to be alone. But she does take time out to serve as host and producer of the UnMute Podcast. Myisha has also taught philosophy at such schools as the City University of New York and St. Johns University.

MATT DESTEFANO is a PhD student at the University of Arizona. His own research takes to heart Louis's suggestion that the world is way too amazing to justify being bored. He works primarily in philosophy of mind and epistemology, but he takes every opportunity to talk about philosophy of religion. He loves comedy almost as much as he loves philosophy, and thinks they overlap more than one might think—especially for Louis.

JASON DOCKSTADER is a lecturer in the department of philosophy at University College Cork, Ireland. He is interested in the history of philosophy, meta-ethics, and moral psychology. He has a bunch of beliefs he does nothing about.

MAX ELDER is an Associate Fellow at the Oxford Centre for Animal Ethics, and works in philanthropy in New York City. He studied philosophy at both Kenyon College and Oxford University, and has published on topics ranging from fish ethics to the metaphysics of evil. Max tries to never be bored nor an asshole because life is too short to be either.

JOHN HEANEY is an adjunct lecturer at Queen's University, Belfast. While writing his doctoral thesis, his life was really bad, and then he completed it, which made it worse; but instead of resolving his problems, he started working as a teaching assistant, and so things went from worse to really bad, and things just keep happening to him and he keeps doing dumb things, so his life just gets worse and worse, and darker.

RYAN JAWETZ's "little believies" include the importance of self-sufficiency and making positive contributions to society, but instead he got a philosophy degree from Pomona College and spends his time rambling on the Internet about cultural minutiae.

JOSEPH R. KIRKLAND earned his Juris Doctorate from the University of Michigan Law School, where he also pursued graduate-level studies in philosophy. Joe is an adjunct professor of philosophy at the University of Michigan (Dearborn) and Wayne State University

(Detroit), an occasional attorney-at-law, an aging indie-rocker, a happy husband, and a very proud uncle. He is also the editor of two anthologies in philosophy: *From Wonder to Wisdom* and *On Wrong and Right* (Kendall Hunt Publishing). His second-favorite part of his day job is being allowed to wear the standard-issue Louis C.K. uniform of black T-shirt and jeans to work.

CHRIS A. KRAMER is an associate professor and academic chair of the philosophy department at Rock Valley College. He's also creator and advisor of the college philosophy club—"That club than which none greater can be conceived"—on rare occasions of self-reflection he admits that both he and the club are supercilious by definition. He has published on humor, laughter, and phenomenology, and recently completed his dissertation on "Subversive Humor."

DANIEL P. MALLOY is a lecturer in philosophy at Appalachian State University. In addition to researching various aspects of ethics and morality, he has published numerous chapters on the intersection of popular culture and philosophy, including contributions on *The Big Lebowski*, *Monk*, *Psych*, *Dexter*, and *Arrested Development*. After decades of practice, he has finally learned how to end a meal when he's full, rather than when he hates himself. The trick is to start hating yourself before the meal.

JENNIFER MARRA is a PhD student specializing in philosophy of culture and humor at Marquette University. She is an officer for the Lighthearted Philosophers' Society (a proud group of vaudevillian intellectuals with a penchant for the absurd) and has published on humor, German philosophy, and popular culture. Jennifer imagines she is a Greek myth every time she partakes in the miracle of human flight, and dedicates her chapter to Maury Bruhn, who can be a person without a smart phone or a driver's license.

ETHAN MILLS is an Assistant Professor of Philosophy at the University of Tennessee at Chattanooga. He specializes in the philosophical traditions of classical India and serves as the Book Review Editor for the *Indian Philosophy Blog* (indianphilosophyblog.org). His academic work has appeared in journals including *Philosophy East and West* and the *Journal of Buddhist Ethics,* and he has also contributed chapters to *Stephen Colbert and Philosophy* and *Philip K. Dick and Philosophy*. Aside from buying some shit that always breaks, he lives with his wife and two cats, pretends to be a beer and whiskey connoisseur, tells bad jokes to his students (a captive audience!), and maintains a blog, *Examined Worlds:*

Philosophy and Science Fiction (examinedworlds.blogspot.com). Other things will happen after he dies, none of which will include him. Doesn't matter.

SILAS MORGAN, PhD, teaches theology at Loyola University Chicago and publishes work in contemporary theology and philosophy. His research explores the relationship between religion and politics, and so you know he's very popular at cocktail parties.

BRANDON POLITE, much like Louie ("Louie, Louie, Louie . . .") and everybody else, is gonna die. Until he does, though, he'll keep teaching at Knox College, where he's currently an Assistant Professor of Philosophy; conducting research in Aesthetics and the Philosophy of Music; and generally trying to keep the "forever empty" at bay.

MARK RALKOWSKI is an assistant professor of philosophy and honors at George Washington University. He is the author of *Heidegger's Platonism* and the editor of *Time and Death: Heidegger's Analysis of Finitude* and *Curb Your Enthusiasm and Philosophy*. He is currently writing a book called *Don't Blame Socrates: Plato's Trial of Athens*. Ralkowski has many aspirations, but chief among them is the desire to be as happy as a three-legged dog.

DUNCAN REYBURN is very suspicious of categories and so spends a great deal of his time trying to escape definition. This is probably a side-effect of reading too much on metaphysics and philosophical hermeneutics. He is also perpetually being amazed by pretty much everything he encounters and has written about some of his perpetual astonishment in various contributions to books, blogs, and academic journals. He's also the author of a very attractive and provocative forthcoming book on the post-Victorian journalist G.K. Chesterton, which deals with the philosophical problem of trying to find meaning in a very messy world. He is a Senior Lecturer at the University of Pretoria, South Africa. He also lives in Pretoria, South Africa, because it's convenient. No animals were harmed in the process of writing this brief biography in the third person.

ROBERTO SIRVENT, PhD, is Associate Professor of Political and Social Ethics at Hope International University. He has written essays on many of his favorite movies and TV shows, including *The Social Network, Homeland, Justified*, and *House of Cards*. Roberto feels the same way about fortune cookies that Louis C.K. feels about capitalism: he just doesn't trust any of it.

ERIC SCHOLL is the associate chair of the Television Department at Columbia College Chicago and a documentary filmmaker. His documentaries address such depressing topics as police brutality and harsh prison sentences. He regularly teaches a course that examines *Louie* in excruciating detail. Every choice he makes is okay because he loves himself.

PHIL SMOLENSKI is a PhD Candidate at Queen's University in Canada whose research focuses on issues within liberal political theory, including Rawls, stability, and political community. He's contributed chapters to *The Philosophy of JJ Abrams* and *Sons of Anarchy and Philosophy*. When he's not shaking from his desire for candy, he takes a lot of pleasure in not being part of the food chain, because after you burn your toast, the last thing you want to deal with is cheetahs at the train station.

MARIE SNYDER teaches philosophy to high-school students without the benefit of a bouncer to eject the hecklers. She lives with three kids and many pets in Waterloo, Canada, which is home to the second largest Oktoberfest in the world *and* Research in Motion, the Perimeter Institute, and two renowned universities. Unlike Louis, they can drink and then *do* shit.

JOEL WALMSLEY is a lecturer in the philosophy department at University College Cork, in Ireland. He spends his professional time trying to answer why?-questions about philosophy of mind, philosophy of science, and artificial intelligence. He's also the father of an impertinent six-year-old daughter, so he spends the rest of his time trying to answer why?-questions about everything else, as well as writing sarcastic biographies of himself in the third-person.

JOSEPH WESTFALL is an Associate Professor of Philosophy at the University of Houston—Downtown. He is the editor of *Hannibal Lecter and Philosophy* (2015), and the author of *The Kierkegaardian Author* (2007) as well as numerous essays and articles on topics related to the arts, literature, authorship, film, and popular culture. He has three children who remain mercifully unaware of Pig Newtons, although they do arrogantly insist upon a slew of other misnomers, including his youngest daughter's penchant for calling all fruit "apples." He may be no gastronome, but he does know that those are *peaches*, motherfucker. ("*Apples.*") Apples? Really? How does she fuck with him on this? I mean, she's two and he's forty—what are the odds that she's right and he's wrong? Where is she getting her information?

BEKKA WILLIAMS has spent the past two years as a Visiting Assistant Professor in the Department of Philosophy at the University of Arkansas. When she's not teaching, Bekka does work in ethical theory and political philosophy. Like Louis, Bekka's thought process isn't always efficient. She has dumb thoughts, goes "What the fuck is wrong with you?!?" . . . and then figures it out. Bekka loves teaching philosophy because she and her students can work (and joke) through the first two steps together—and she likes academic writing because she can publish the figured-out part and pretend the rest never happened. While writing her contribution to this book, Bekka accepted a job as Assistant Professor of Philosophy at Minnesota State University, Mankato—and she can't wait to start doing the shit out of it.

Index

abyss (existential), 95, 146–47, 152

Adorno, Theodor, 168

agnosticism, 181–82, 186

Alexander, Samuel, 164

anger and hatred, 23–36

angst, 94, 97, 131, 136–37, 265

anxiety, 94–97, 104, 123, 129, 132, 135, 138, 143, 175, 262–63, 265, 281

Applebaum, Barbara, 252

Arendt, Hannah, 196–98

Aristotle, 23, 40, 83, 89, 97, 98–102, 104, 159, 162, 268

assholes:
children as, 81, 279, 108–09, 118, 279
the current generation as, 99
employers as, 281
how life is full of, 60–61
other kinds of, 35, 117, 122, 170, 281–82
privileged white, 225, 250–51
and self-knowledge, 234

atheism, 132, 167, 171–72, 174, 180, 182, 186

atomism, 76

St. Augustine, 108

Aurelius, Marcus, 39, 50–54, 56

authenticity, 48, 115, 136–142, 144–47, 149–151, 153

awesome possum, 28, 277, 278

bad faith, 40, 41, 56, 138–141, 145, 148–150, 152

Baker, Sarah, 240–41

Beauvoir, Simone de, 141

believies, 71, 189, 199, 201, 209, 211, 217, 269, 274

Big Other, 269–271, 273–74, 276

Blake (*Louie* character), 262–63

Bloom, Brooke, 260

boredom, xx, 10, 70, 71, 93–95, 97–99, 101, 103–05, 110–11, 113–14, 117, 137

Brooks, Mel, 84

Buddha, 69, 70–73, 75, 77–78

Buddhism:
the Four Noble Truths of, 71–73, 174
the Eightfold Path in, 73–75

Camus, Albert, 17

Card, Claudia, 243

Carlin, George, 279, 285

Cartesian, Never (*Louie* character), 257–266

causal determinism, 61

Cavanaugh, William, 173

cell phones:
  and authenticity, 137
  and being a person, 56
  and children, xv, 96
  and entitlement, 4, 29
  and sadness, 96–97, 113–15,
    131–32, 145
  and sweatshop labor, 139,
    197, 251
  and wasteful consumption,
    192
  and wonder, 71, 101, 105, 195
Chesterton, GK, 275
Chewed Up:
  on children, 81–82, 90,
    109–110
  on Cinnabon, 28
  on deer, 11
  on having a body, 71
  on the n-word, 26
  on underwear, 64
  on white privilege, 231–32,
    239, 247, 252
  on women, 243
children
  and anger, 29, 31–32, 34
  as assholes, 81–82, 108–09,
    161
  and boredom, 95, 97
  and cell phones, 113
  and comedy, 3, 175
  and death, 134
  and excuses, 137
  and famine relief, 189,
    191–93, 197
  and food, 114
  and God, 76, 167, 170, 185
  Louis's love for his, 21, 91
  and Louis's philosophy of
    parenting, 107–118, 203
  and the meaning of life, 21
  and morality, 203, 244
  and mortality, 49, 72, 134
  and nut allergies, 213, 216,
    268, 272
  and pedophilia, 27, 65, 216–17

  and philosophy, 81, 83, 157,
    161, 163
  and psychoanalysis, 267
  and the quality of one's life,
    18, 20, 82, 90, 107, 110–11,
    112, 126, 133
  and the sex drive, 13, 20, 21
  and video games, 113–14
  and white privilege, 249
Cinnabon, 28, 30, 21, 198
Clifford, William Kingdon,
  183–84
Columbus, Christopher, 231
comedy:
  and redemption, 8–9
  and truth, xvii–xx, 4, 65, 121,
    128–29, 149–152, 168, 275
  the therapeutic value of, 40,
    41, 56–57
Comedy Cellar, xv, 28, 89,
  190–91
Cook, Dane, 149
"Crabby, Epic Love Letter", 115

Dall, Jack (*Louie* character),
  150
The Daily Show, 238, 242
Dante Alighieri, 6, 99
Darwin, Charles, 14
death:
  and atheism, 180
  and comedy, 40, 56, 151
  Epicurus on, 180
  and famine relief, 17,
    189–192, 194–98
  the human awareness of, 134,
    135, 144
  and human finitude, 6, 39–57,
    69, 71–78, 146
  and Jesus, 9, 169, 185
  and medical research, 217
  morality and, 200, 217, 232
  and religion, 177
  suicide and, 128, 148
  and the unconscious, 268, 272

Deconstruction, 82, 161, 163, 278, 283–85
deer, 23–25, 29, 33
Derrida, Jacques, 283
Descartes, René, 258–261, 264–66
Dr. Bigelow (*Louie* character), 12, 41–48, 51–54, 69, 74
dreams, 62, 124, 248, 258, 260–66, 267, 273, 273, 280–82, 285
dukkha, 70–73

Eddie (*Louie* character), 15–16, 20–21, 128–29, 147–150, 152
Eichmann, Adolf, 196–97
Ellacuría, Ignacio, 175
environmentalism, 239
Epictetus, 40, 48–49, 52, 59–68
Epicurus, 41, 48, 52, 69, 75–76, 78, 180–81
ethics, 59–60, 91, 101, 114, 208–09, 211
"Everything is amazing and nobody is happy," 3, 10, 56, 98, 99, 101, 104, 105
explanatory regress, 158, 161–66

feminism
    and comedy as natural enemies, 237
    misconceptions of, 238
    and some of the values implicit in Louis's comedy, 239–245
Fig Newtons:
    mistaken for "Pig Newtons", 26, 29, 109, 116
Freud, Sigmund, 11, 14, 263, 267, 270, 273, 275, 280
FX, xi, xvii, 59, 116, 277

God:
    and the afterlife, 76
    and creation myths, 84
    and Descartes, 265
    and environmentalism, 139, 269
    and existential freedom, 132, 134
    in *Genesis*, 4
    and guilt, 258
    and happiness, 47
    and laughter, 8–9
    Louis's jokes about, 167–186
    and psychoanalysis, 270
    and thanking God for being White, 247–48
Gödel, Kurt, 166
Gendeller, Tamar, 227
Gervais, Ricky, xv, 55, 282
Global Poor, 190, 193–95, 197
Griffiths, Trevor, xiii, xvii–xx
Gross, Terry, 40

Hadot, Pierre, 48
Heaven, 75, 132, 167, 171, 177, 179–180, 183
hedonism, 54, 76, 180
Hegel, Georg Wilhelm Friedrich, 121–22, 129
Heidegger, Martin, 144, 148, 153
Hempel, Carl, 158–160
Hilarious (comedy special):
    on being single, 282
    on cell phones 4, 71
    on death, 69
    on entitlement, 135
    on how everything is amazing and nobody's happy, 98–99, 230
    on materialism, 193
    on parenting, 109–110, 114
    on "Pig Newtons," 29
    and the Sundance Film Festival, 39, 235

on "White people problems", 27

and writing a comedy special, xiv

Hitchens, Christopher, 165

Hume, David, 212, 214–17, 219–220

Huxley, Thomas Henry, 181

Identity privilege, 247–253

Ignatius of Loyola, 175

impermanence, 47, 53–54, 73–74

James, LeBron, 262

Jane (*Louie* character), 10, 20, 66, 69, 93–95, 97–98, 104–05, 148, 151, 261–62

Janet (*Louie* character), 18–19, 148–151, 259, 260, 262

Janice (*Louie* character), 17–18

Jesus, 9, 169, 185, 262,

Jizzanthapus (*Louie* character), 23, 29, 31–34, 118

Kant, Immanuel, 34

Kenyon College, 174

Kierkegaard, Søren, 121–25, 127–29

Lacan, Jacques, 269–270, 273–75, 280, 283

laughter, 4–5

Law of Excluded Middle, 162–63

Leno, Jay, 149, 249–250

Lessing, Gothold Ephraim, 47

Letterman, David, 42, 67–68, 102, 147–49, 152

Lilly (*Louie* character), 148, 151, 203

Live at the Beacon Theater, 205, 208;

on believies, 71, 208

on Clifford the Big Red Dog, 110

on doing your "favorite thing," 24

and environmentalism, 239

on Jizzanthapus, 23

and Native Americans, 231

on parenting, 30, 111, 116

on sexual deviance, 77, 205

Live at Carnegie Hall:

Jay London on, 183

on parenting, 110–13

on sex, 141

on slavery, 231

Live at the Comedy Store:

on American culture, 229

on children, 108

on death, 134

on the meaning of life, 133

on self-love, 234

on aging, 62

Live in Houston:

and Louis's first hour of comedy, 277

Live in Portland:

on being alone, 132

on technology, 139

Liz (*Louie* character), 263–64

London, Jay, 283

Louis C.K.:

on the content of his comedy, xix

on creative control at FX, xvi–xvii

on his development as a comedian, xiii–xiv, xix, 279

on laughter, 5

on making choices, 45

on manipulating his audience, xvi

on not trying to change the way people think, 41

on the relationship between himself and the character "Louie," xi
on the value of failure, xiv
on writing a standup comedy show, xiv–xvi
on writing *Louie*, xvi
love:
and the body, 63–64
and death, 72–74, 77
and existentialism, 140–41, 77
and God, 181
and loss, 43–56
and Jesus, 169, 185
and laughter, 4–5
of one's kids, 110–11, 113, 116, 190, 259
on self-love and self-knowledge, 234
and sex, 11, 13–14, 16, 18–20
Lovejoy, Alfred O., 86
Lucky Louie, 277, 285

Mach, Ernst, 227
Maron, Marc, xiv, 40, 67, 280
masturbation, 6, 67, 71, 140–42, 145, 152, 148, 152, 196, 217, 234, 245, 281
meta-ethics, 211
metaphysics, 14, 34, 84, 100, 102, 104, 162
mirth addiction, 232–234
Monti, Vittorio, 6
moral failure, 199, 200–03, 206, 209
moral motivation, 31, 185, 202–03, 207, 211–12, 214–220, 224;
internalism versus externalism, 212, 218–220, 224

Nietzsche, Friedrich, vi, 3–4, 5, 7–9, 54
NPR, xix, 91, 167, 171, 175

n-word, 26, 243

O'Brien, Conan, 10, 42, 96–97, 113–15, 129, 131, 143
Oduye, Adepero, 282
"Of course, but maybe," 56, 213, 268–270, 272–73, 283, 285
Oh My God:
on of course, but maybe, 194–95, 213, 268–69, 272
on doing the right thing, 205
on a new way to hurt someone's feelings, 35
on pedophilia, 34
on privilege, 251
and truth, 234–35
One Night Stand:
and Louis's evolution as a comedian, 277
on "Why?" questions, 82, 85–86, 157, 165
O'Neal, Patrice, 248
Opie and Anthony, 248, 250
Oppenheim, Paul, 158–160

Pamela (*Louie* character), 15, 20, 113, 124, 257
parenting, xx, 19–21, 32–33, 56, 86, 90–91, 93–94, 107–118, 123, 157, 163, 165, 168, 179, 184–85, 199, 203, 207, 213, 225, 230, 239, 279, 284
Parmenides, 85–90
Pascal, Blaise, 179–180
pets, 69
Phillips, Adam, 278
Pitchfork, 41, 54
Plato, 40, 81, 83–84, 88, 98, 102–04, 162, 226–27
pleasure, 13–14, 17, 31, 40, 54–56, 66, 67, 75–77, 100–01, 110–11, 124, 180, 232, 282, 285
Pogge, Thomas, 194–95, 197

Poniewozik, James, xi, xvi, 5
Pootie Tang, 279
Principle of Plenitude, 86–87, 89
Prior, Richard, 285
psychoanalysis, 168, 220, 268–69, 273–76, 278, 280–82, 285

race, xx, 108, 123, 229, 231, 239, 247–48, 250–53, 272
rape, 226, 238, 242–45, 276
rebirth, 72
religion, 7–9, 167, 168, 170, 173, 175, 176, 181
Reddit, 95–96, 98, 171
Remski, Matthew, 94–95, 97–98, 105
Rick (*Louie* character), 240
Rock, Chris, xv, 55, 282
Rose, Charlie, xiv, 41, 97

sadness, 40, 45–48, 53–54, 56, 73–74, 96–97, 129, 131–32, 135, 142–43, 145–46, 262
Sartre, Jean-Paul, 17, 131–32, 135–142, 144–46, 153
Saturday Night Live, 171, 177, 182, 189, 229
Saul, Jennifer Mather, 238
Saussure, Ferdinand de, 283
Schopenhauer, Arthur, 11–21
science, 100, 104, 158–160, 164, 166, 205, 217, 225, 227, 233, 248, 259
Seinfeld, Jerry, xv, 55, 62, 122, 149, 152, 282
September 11th, 147, 174
sex, xx, 11–21, 27, 33, 51, 65, 77, 88, 122, 134, 139–142, 146, 174, 229, 231, 233, 238, 240, 245, 247–249, 251, 258, 261–263, 265–266, 267, 271, 279, 282

Shameless:
   other mentions of, 28, 234, 277, 284
   on parenting, 81, 108–09, 112, 190
   on rape, 226
   on sucking a bag of dicks, 35
Shapiro, Rick, 285
Siddhartha Gautama, 70
Singer, Peter, 190–93
slavery, 56, 193, 213, 231, 250, 272
Socrates, 83, 91, 98, 102–104, 162
Sousa, Ronald de, 157
Springsteen, Bruce, 129, 131, 143
Stern, Howard, xvii, 93
Stewart, Jon, 237
"Suck a bag of dicks," 34–35, 195, 284
suffering, 9, 12, 16, 21, 43, 46–48, 52–54, 70–71, 75–76, 78, 123–124, 132, 139, 147, 169, 181, 185, 190, 194, 196–198, 207, 251, 272, 274
suicide, 65, 147–48, 241, 264, 282

Tardigan, Lars (*Louie* character), 62, 149, 152
Tarese (*Louie* character), 282
Talking Funny (HBO), xv–xvi, 40, 55, 282
Taylor, Gabrielle, 27
Thales, 84, 90
time machines, 226, 231, 239, 250
Tosh, Daniel, 242
thought experiments, 225–230, 235
Tillich, Paul, 173

the unconscious

in cognitive science, 233
in culture, 95
for David Foster Wallace, 174
for Lacan, 269, 273–76, 278,
280, 282–83
for Nietzsche, 3
for Schopenhauer, 13–15

Vanessa (*Louie* character),
240–42

Wallace, David Foster, 174

Watson, Susan Kelechi, 259
"White People Problems," 26, 27,
248
"Why?" (famous bit from *One
Night Stand*), xv, 81–83,
85–86, 90–91, 157–167
Wilde, Oscar, 9
wonder, xx, 74, 81–83, 90–91,
93–94, 98–101, 104–05
World War II, 226
Wright, Orville, 230
Wright, Steven, 285

Zeno, 89–90